Synology NAS Setup Guide for Home & Small Business

7.2

DSM 7.2 Version
Nicholas Rushton, BA Hons.
Callisto Technology And Consultancy Services
© CTACS 2023

DSM 7.2 Version. Updated August 2023
Copyright © Nicholas Rushton 2023

The right of Nicholas Rushton to be identified as the author of this work has been asserted by him in accordance with the Copyright, Designs and Patents Act 1988.

All rights reserved. No part of this publication may be reproduced, stored in or introduced into a retrieval system, or transmitted, in any form, or by any means (electronic, mechanical, photocopying, recording or otherwise) without the prior permission of the author. Any person who does any unauthorized act in relation to this publication may be left liable to criminal prosecution and civil claims for damages. An exception is granted in that up to 500 words in total may be quoted for the purpose of review. The information in this publication is provided without warranty or liability and it is up to the reader to determine its suitability and applicability to their own requirements. This book and its author are unconnected with Synology Inc. and this is an independently produced publication.

This book is sold subject to the condition that it shall not, by way of trade or otherwise, be lent, resold, hired out, or otherwise circulated without the author's prior consent in any form of binding or cover other than that in which it was published and without a similar condition including this condition being imposed on the subsequent purchaser.

All copyrighted terms and trademarks of the registered owners are respectfully acknowledged.

Table of Contents

1 GETTING STARTED 12

   1.1 OVERVIEW 13
   1.2 CHOOSING A DISKSTATION 16
   1.3 DISK DRIVES 20
   1.4 SWITCH AND WIRELESS ACCESS POINTS 22
   1.5 LOCATION AND ELECTRICAL CONSIDERATIONS 23

2 INSTALLING DSM 24

   2.1 OVERVIEW 25
   2.2 INSTALLATION USING SYNOLOGY ASSISTANT 27
   2.3 INSTALLATION USING DS FINDER 34
   2.4 FIVE MINUTE TOUR OF DISKSTATION MANAGER 37
   2.5 SETTING UP STORAGE 42
   2.6 CONFIGURING THE DISKSTATION 53
   2.7 QUICKCONNECT: THE KEY TO REMOTE CONNECTIVITY 64

3 SHARED FOLDERS 67

   3.1 OVERVIEW 68
   3.2 CREATING SHARED FOLDERS 70
   3.3 ENABLE ADDITIONAL SECURITY MEASURES 73
   3.4 CHANGING, DELETING OR CLONING A SHARED FOLDER 81
   3.5 LOADING EXISTING DATA INTO SHARED FOLDERS 83
   3.6 ENABLING HOME FOLDERS 84
   3.7 ACL (ACCESS CONTROL LISTS) 86

4 MANAGING USERS 88

   4.1 OVERVIEW 89
   4.2 CREATING USERS 90
   4.3 MODIFYING, COPYING, DEACTIVATING AND DELETING USERS 95
   4.4 IMPORTING A LIST OF USERS 97

4.5 GROUPS 99
4.6 DELEGATION 102
4.7 USER PERSONALIZATION SETTINGS 104
4.8 MANAGING USERS WITH DS FINDER 108

5 CONNECTING TO THE SERVER 110

5.1 OVERVIEW 111
5.2 USING A BROWSER AND FILE STATION 111
5.3 CONNECTING WINDOWS COMPUTERS 113
5.4 CONNECTING MACS 121
5.5 CONNECTING SMARTPHONES AND TABLETS 122
5.6 CONNECTING LINUX & UNIX COMPUTERS 124
5.7 CONNECTING CHROMEBOOKS 125

6 SECURITY 127

6.1 OVERVIEW 128
6.2 SECURITY ADVISOR 128
6.3 SECURITY ICON 131
6.4 ANTIVIRUS PROTECTION 139
6.5 PASSWORD SETTINGS 141
6.6 IMPROVING SIGN-IN SECURITY 144
6.7 ACCOUNT ACTIVITY 150
6.8 CHANGING THE ADMINISTRATOR ACCOUNT 151
6.9 CHANGE PORT NUMBERS & DISABLE UNNECESSARY SERVICES 153

7 BACKUPS 155

7.1 OVERVIEW 156
7.2 BACKING UP TO AN EXTERNAL DRIVE 158
7.3 RESTORING FILES FROM A BACKUP 166
7.4 QUICK & EASY BACKUPS USING USB COPY UTILITY 169
7.5 BACKUPS WITH SYNOLOGY C2 AND CLOUD SERVICES 173
7.6 SYNOLOGY TO SYNOLOGY BACKUPS 178
7.7 BACKING UP THE SERVER CONFIGURATION 183
7.8 BACKING UP COMPUTERS TO THE SERVER 185
7.9 SNAPSHOT REPLICATION 190

7.10 ACTIVE BACKUP 196

8 HOUSEKEEPING & MAINTENANCE 203

8.1 OVERVIEW 204
8.2 CHECKING FOR DSM UPDATES 205
8.3 INFO CENTER 210
8.4 WIDGETS 212
8.5 CHECKING DISK HEALTH 213
8.6 STORAGE ANALYZER 215
8.7 RESOURCE MONITOR 219
8.8 LOG CENTER 221
8.9 NOTIFICATIONS 223
8.10 CMS (CENTRAL MANAGEMENT SYSTEM) 231
8.11 ACTIVE INSIGHT 239

9 MULTIMEDIA & STREAMING 243

9.1 OVERVIEW 244
9.2 MEDIA SERVER (DLNA) 245
9.3 SYNOLOGY PHOTOS 249
9.4 AUDIO STATION 258
9.5 VIDEO STATION 263

10 SYNOLOGY DRIVE SERVER, OFFICE & APPS 270

10.1 OVERVIEW 271
10.2 INSTALLING AND CONFIGURING SYNOLOGY DRIVE SERVER AND OFFICE 273
10.3 ACCESSING DRIVE SERVER 278
10.4 SYNCING BETWEEN DISKSTATIONS 288
10.5 SYNOLOGY OFFICE 291
10.6 SYNOLOGY CHAT SERVER 293
10.7 SYNOLOGY CALENDAR 297
10.8 SYNOLOGY CONTACTS 300
10.9 NOTE STATION 302

11 OTHER REMOTE CONNECTIVITY OPTIONS 304

11.1 OVERVIEW 305
11.2 FILE STATION REMOTE CONNECTION 305
11.3 CLOUD SYNC 307
11.4 HYBRID SHARE SERVICE 311
11.5 DDNS, ROUTER CONFIGURATION & PORT FORWARDING 316
11.6 VIRTUAL PRIVATE NETWORKS (VPN) 320

12 STORAGE 330

12.1 OVERVIEW 331
12.2 REPLACING A FAULTY DRIVE 331
12.3 ADDING A HOT SPARE DRIVE 335
12.4 ADDING A DRIVE TO INCREASE STORAGE 338
12.5 DATA SCRUBBING 341
12.6 GLOBAL SETTINGS 343
12.7 SSD CACHING 345
12.8 SSD TRIM 350
12.9 SAN MANAGER AND ISCSI 351

13 SURVEILLANCE STATION 356

13.1 OVERVIEW 357
13.2 INSTALLATION 358
13.3 USAGE 363
13.4 C2 SURVEILLANCE 365
13.5 LIVECAM AND DS CAM 368
13.6 SYNOLOGY SURVEILLANCE STATION CLIENT 370
13.7 APPLICATION CENTER 370

14 VIRTUALIZATION & CONTAINER MANAGER 371

14.1 OVERVIEW 372
14.2 PREPARING FOR AND INSTALLING VIRTUAL MACHINE MANAGER 374
14.3 INSTALLING VIRTUAL DSM 375
14.4 INSTALLING MICROSOFT WINDOWS 382
14.5 CONTAINER MANAGER 386

15 MISCELLANEOUS TOPICS	389
15.1 OVERVIEW	390
15.2 PACKAGE CENTER	390
15.3 MANAGING YOUR SYNOLOGY ACCOUNT	395
15.4 SUPPORT CENTER	397
15.5 CUSTOMIZING THE LOGIN & APPLICATION PORTALS	398
15.6 PRINTING	401
15.7 UNIVERSAL SEARCH	405
15.8 TASK SCHEDULER	408
15.9 DOWNLOAD STATION/BITTORRENT	409
15.10 DOCUMENT VIEWER	411
15.11 PDF VIEWER	412
15.12 TEXT EDITOR	413
15.13 WEB STATION	414
15.14 DHCP SERVER	417
15.15 CONNECTING VIA A PROXY SERVER	419
15.16 LINK AGGREGATION	420
15.17 RESETTING THE ADMINISTRATOR PASSWORD IF LOST	422
15.18 REINSTALLING DSM WHILST RETAINING DATA	422
15.19 PREPARING THE DISKSTATION FOR DISPOSAL	423
INDEX	424

COMMENTS & REVIEWS FROM OTHER PURCHASERS

You are in good company - thousands of people have purchased guides from CTACS to help them setup their home and business networks. This is what purchasers of the *Synology NAS Setup Guide for Home & Small Business* have written in their reviews:

"…truly excellent insight and presents a fairly complex issue in an easy to follow and understand manner. You'll get all the important information you need to set up your NAS safely with DSM and maintain it properly. What I like best about the book/guide is that you can read a specific chapter on the topic you have an issue with or want more information on, and you don't have to read it from front to end cover to understand DSM. For me this guide is a must have and I quite regularly check up on a topic or two. - guyph7

"Excellent!!! I came looking for a book. This filled the need beyond my expectation. Well done with a great index to locate the exact topic of interest. Being familiar with Synology's NAS systems I was tempted to just skip over the early chapters. However, the book is so well written I found myself reading everything just to be sure I wasn't overlooking something I should have known. There aren't many books for the Synology NAS, but fortunately this author has done a great job." - SH

"Excellent step-by-step overview of setting up, running and maintaining Synology. Easy read and detailed instructions. Buy this book." - MM

"Should come with a new NAS! Invaluable for someone unfamiliar with a Synology NAS. Read before you setup your NAS!" - Irene H

"Excellent. I will finally be able to use my Synology that was sitting unused for 12+ months. Highly recommended book for someone with zero knowledge of networking" - AmGfADD

"If you purchase a Synology NAS, you should also purchase this manual. There is NO documentation included with the unit." - Ken

"Outstanding! Much more than sterile instructions from Synology Help. Author gives most likely examples and reasons for suggested settings. This book filled in the blanks left by the manufacturers. Highly recommend this as the companion you need while setting up the NAS and getting used to all of the features available." - JC

"I set up my Synology without the help of this book only to realize it was not doing what I wanted it to do. I bought the book, read through it page by page. Eventually, I realized I had to start over and reset my disk station to factory setting and then walk through the set up using this book. It made it simple and helped me understand the process better. Until I got this book my disk station was worthless to me because of my misunderstanding of how it all works together." – DK

"I have familiarity with most computers in general. But when I got my 1st NAS device, I decided it couldn't hurt to have some hands-on advice. Nick Rushton's book on setting up my Synology NAS has been the best spent money and has helped me get up and running in a small amount of time. No nonsense, easily understood step-by-step recommendations were what I needed. I highly recommend his guide." – G

"This is about as good as it gets for Synology NAS owners and tries to be a plain English guide to a very technical subject. Shame Synology couldn't include something similar with their NAS". – EB

"Oh man, wished I had this to start with" – MO

"Does everything it says on the tin. You really need one of these." – RT

"Simple, concise and no-nonsense guide to setting up NAS in the comfort of your home. Much better than Synology Help website." – AI

ABOUT THIS BOOK

With superb functionality and ease of use through the polished DSM operating system, Synology DiskStations are the NAS devices of choice for the discerning purchaser, providing shared storage, backups, cloud services, multimedia streaming, the ability to run applications and more. But this power and flexibility comes at a price and setting up a DiskStation for the very first time can seem a daunting prospect for someone who has not done so before, especially as it does not come with an instruction manual. This independent guide is based around the latest version of DSM, has easy-to-follow instructions, copious illustrations and is based on a decade of real-world experience with the product. It will take you through the whole process from start to finish and help ensure that your Synology NAS-based network is a success.

It has been written according to the Goldilocks Principle: Not too much information, not too little information, but just the right amount. Thousands of people have purchased this guide and it has been crafted to appeal to as wide an audience as possible so, regardless of your skill level (beginner, intermediate, advanced) and your planned usage (solo, home, small business, or other organization), you will find it useful.

The guide is organized into three main parts:

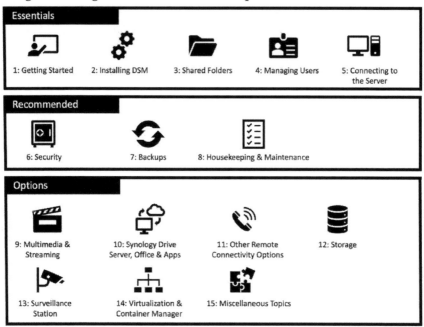

Figure 1: How this guide is organized

The first five chapters cover the *Essentials*, the things you absolutely must do, which consists of setting up the hardware, installing the DSM firmware, creating shared folders, creating the users, and then connecting your computers and mobile devices to the NAS. Chapters 6 to 8 comprise things which are strongly *Recommended*: setting up security; setting up backups for the server and the connected computers; learning about housekeeping and maintenance to keep the server in good health. Chapters 9 through 15 are other *Options* to explore and includes many ways to make your system more capable and useful, such as multimedia and setting up Synology Drive Server so you can securely access the DiskStation from outside the home or office.

Other subjects covered include productivity applications, surveillance, and virtualization.

In a hurry? The first five chapters will get you up and running ASAP. Then, return and explore at leisure.

About the Author

The author has worked in IT for over 40 years, on systems of all sizes and types throughout the world, with the largest companies to the smallest and including several of his own. He has authored more than 25 networking guides, published through CTACS as eBooks, paperbacks and hardbacks. Examples include *Synology Setup Guide; Little Book of Synology; Windows Server 2022; Windows Server 2019 Essentials; Little Book of macOS Server; QNAS Setup Guide; Using Windows 10 as a Server; Using Windows 11 as a Server.*

Declaration

No DiskStations were harmed during the writing of this book.

1 GETTING STARTED

1.1 Overview

If you are reading this, then chances are you already know what Network Attached Storage (NAS) is and may have purchased or are about to purchase a Synology NAS unit. But for those who are new to the subject, or by way of recap:

When two or more computing devices are connected, a network is created. The Internet is a worldwide, public network comprising billions of users, computers and servers. In contrast, a private, or local area network, is typically intended for the use of a household, business or educational establishment. Such networks are often built around one or more NAS devices. An alternative name for a NAS box is *server*, and we will use both terms interchangeably in this book.

The key word here is 'storage'. A NAS device consists of a large amount of disk storage contained in its own box. Unlike external disk drives, which typically connect to a single computer using a USB or Thunderbolt connection, a NAS links to a router or network switch using one or more Ethernet cables and this enables it to be accessed and shared by multiple computers and other devices on the local network.

The NAS can also be accessed remotely from anywhere via the Internet. It is protected by passwords, two-factor authentications, encryption and other security measures so that only authorized people can access it, not the public at large. To facilitate and make this easier, Synology provide a service called *QuickConnect*.

A NAS device runs its own operating system. This is not Windows or macOS, rather, it is a proprietary system and in the case of Synology it is called DSM or *DiskStation Manager*. Often, the term *firmware* rather than operating system, is used to refer to. Although specifically designed for sharing data, DSM can also run apps, known as *packages* in Synology terminology, that provide many additional capabilities.

A Synology NAS does not have a screen, keyboard and mouse. Rather, it is interacted with using a browser such as Chrome, Firefox, Safari or Edge, using any computer on the local network. At the simplest level it can be thought of as a 'black box' or computing appliance.

What can a NAS do? Many things, but popular uses include:

Storage - providing extra storage for computers

Backups - a backup system for computers and other devices

Shared Resources - shared, common areas where a business or family can store their documents and other files

Home Entertainment - comprising the heart of a home entertainment system, providing a central library for music, photos and videos, along with the ability to stream them to computers, tablets, smartphones and smart TVs

Private Cloud - running a private cloud system, providing controlled remote access to your data. Similar in principle to Google Drive or iCloud or OneDrive, but totally under your own control with no subscription charges and effectively unlimited capacity

Productivity Applications - running applications such as shared Calendar, Contacts and Notes, providing an in-house alternative to systems such as Microsoft 365, Google Workspace and iCloud

Surveillance – functioning as a professional level video surveillance system for the home, office or other premises

Software Development - a sophisticated development platform for software developers

A typical small network is depicted below. The key components are:

NAS (server) - this is the heart of the network, running DSM and upon which data is stored

Backup device – for example, an external USB drive connected to the server, or a cloud service

Internet connection - this may be a separate router or an all-in-one wi-fi router

Switch and Wireless Access Point(s) – to provide expansion in larger networks

Printer(s) – shareable printer(s), networked or plugged into the server with a USB cable

Desktops PCs – running Windows, macOS or Linux, connected using Ethernet or wirelessly

Laptops, Chromebooks, Tablets and Smartphones – connected wirelessly

Whilst it may not match your own setup exactly, it should be broadly similar. Further information about the components is given underneath the diagram and/or in later sections of the guide.

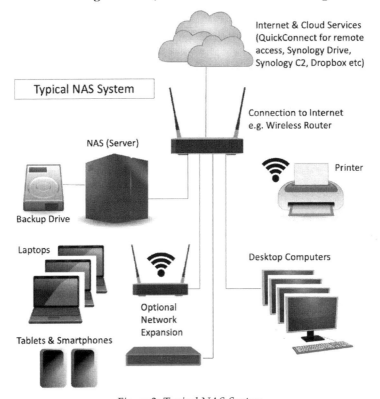

Figure 2: Typical NAS System

Just about any modern computer can be used with a DiskStation. The computers can be running any mixture of Windows 11 or Windows 10 and Home or Professional versions of Windows are equally suitable (older versions of Windows can be connected, but support is increasingly limited). Computers running macOS can be connected, as can Linux and Unix PCs. Devices running iOS/iPadOS (iPhone, iPad) or Android (tablets and Smartphones) can be connected, as can Chromebooks and most smart televisions and gaming boxes.

Suggestion: if you are at the research stage and yet to purchase or setup your DiskStation, you may want to try out the free Live Demo system, accessible from the *demo.synology.com* website. This allows you to test-drive some aspects of DSM and see what it is like in operation.

1.2 Choosing a DiskStation

Synology are one of the leading and most innovative suppliers of NAS and have sold millions of units. They offer a wide range of hardware, designed to cater for everyone from solo and home users, through to the largest of enterprises with thousands of users and high availability requirements. The models vary according to form factor, number of disk drives that can be used, performance, expandability and price.

Form Factor – DiskStations are standalone units designed to sit on top of a cupboard or desk, whereas RackStations are for mounting in standard 19 inch (48cm) wide computer cabinets ('racks'). Home and small business users will typically use DiskStations, although larger organizations may prefer RackStations. In this guide, the generic term 'DiskStation' is mostly used and this should be interpreted to mean any NAS unit from Synology, as they are the same thing other than in form factor.

Number of Disk Drives – Synology NAS units can hold between 1 and 60 drives, depending on the model. Having more drives allows more storage capacity and permits the use of RAID, which is a technique to improve resilience and throughput. Some models can be expanded using external cases to allow further drives. RackStations are the most expandable systems.

Performance - some DiskStations and RackStations have more powerful processors (Intel or AMD, rather than ARM), more memory (RAM), and are equipped with multiple network adaptors and/or higher Ethernet speeds. These are typically aimed at business users and power users with more demanding requirements. Some advanced features, particularly those of interest to enterprise rather than home or small business users, require DiskStations with Intel or AMD processors. However, ARM processors are highly optimized for multimedia usage, so can be a good choice for video streaming and are equally capable in most roles, plus use less energy. Lower-cost DiskStations are ARM-based.

Expandability – some models have slots for M.2 NVMe SSD's, which can be used for caching to improve performance, or high-speed storage on selected models only.

Some feature PCIe expansion slots, which can also be used to add M.2 NVMe SSD's or additional network adapters. The RAM on many x86-based DiskStations can be expanded, to boost capacity and performance. Synology only support the use of their own official branded memory; however, these parts are more expensive than identical modules from companies such as Crucial, Kingston, Corsair and others.

Synology have categorized their various models into several main groups:

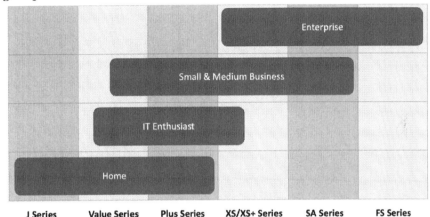

Figure 3: Synology range and typical usage

J Series - cost-effective models aimed at personal and home users, based around ARM processors.

Value Series - more capable systems aimed at demanding home users. Value Series models use ARM processors.

Plus Series – more powerful system for IT enthusiasts and small business.

XS/XS+, **SA** and **FS Series** – aimed at business and enterprise users. SA Series use higher performance SAS hard drives and the FS Series use flash (SSD) storage.

Synology have a naming convention for the DiskStations – they are generally labelled *DSdyy* where *d* is the number of drive bays and *yy* is the year that the model was released. Many of them have a suffix, to indicate J Series or Plus Series. Correspondingly, RackStations are named *RSdyy*.

Choosing the right model can seem confusing as there is sometimes overlap between them, but in general buy the most capable one you can afford. If you have or are planning to have large amounts of data, buy a model with multiple drive bays (it is not necessary to fill them with drives to start with, as more can easily be added later). With some of the J Series models, there may be restrictions on how many apps ('packages') you can run on them simultaneously, along with feature, performance and capacity limitations in DSM, although this is unlikely to be an issue in a small setup.

A previously used DiskStation might be an option for some people, provided it is in good condition and not so old than it cannot run the current version of DSM. It depends upon the model, but in general Synology support DSM on models up to seven years old. There are relatively few parts that can go wrong on a DiskStation; most commonly it is the fan or power supply that develops a fault, and these are usually easy to replace. If the unit is supplied with disk drives already installed, confirm that they are healthy; for instance, the drives in a DiskStation that has been used 24x7 for, say, 5 years may be becoming worn out and in need of replacement and you should budget accordingly. Synology also have their own online store, where they sell fully warranted refurbished models.

Typical Usage Scenarios

These are some examples of how some people are using Synology DiskStations and the equipment choices they made:

Individual – Sue has a Windows desktop PC as well as a MacBook. She wanted additional storage space and the ability to share files between them, along with the ability to backup the MacBook using Time Machine. Her choice was a 1-bay DS120j. The portable USB hard drive she was using previously was re-positioned as an external backup drive for the DiskStation.

Family – The Palmer family comprises two adults and three children. All have computers, plus tablets and smartphones. They are very keen on movies and music and want to store their large collections in a single location, then stream to any device in the household. For backing up the most important family data, they have connected it with Synology's C2 Cloud service. Their choice was the 2-bay DS223.

Enthusiast – Andy had previously owned a very basic NAS device from another manufacturer but had outgrown it and wanted something more capable. As a semi-professional photographer, he was concerned about data safety and wanted a unit with multiple drives, whilst being an IT enthusiast he also wanted the capability to run other operating systems such as Windows and Linux. His choice was a 4-bay DS923+.

Small Business – Helen Translation Services Inc. wanted a capable in-house network, but without the costs and complexity associated with traditional Windows or Unix-based file servers. As they have several offsite and home-based staff, they also wanted full remote access, but without the ongoing costs associated with commercial cloud services. They also felt more comfortable with the idea of their data being under their direct control, rather than with a third party. Their solution was an expandable, 8-bay DS1821+, backed up to a separate DS423 located elsewhere in the premises.

1.3 Disk Drives

DiskStations are not supplied by Synology with disk drives already installed in them. Instead, the customer buys the drives separately and installs them, which is easy to do and does not require any tools with many models. This approach is generally better, because it offers more choice and flexibility. However, ready-populated units are also available from resellers.

Synology NAS units are flexible in terms of the brand and type of disk drives that can be used in them, although it is recommended to use drives that have been specifically designed for use with NAS, as such drives are optimized for continuous 24x7 operation over several years and consider the heat and vibration characteristics of NAS enclosures, along with other technical requirements. Such drives are slightly more expensive than the regular disk drives as used by desktop PCs, but the investment can easily be justified given the importance of data integrity. The main NAS-specific drives are as follows:

Western Digital Red – these are available in three variants. WD Red are intended for use in NAS systems with 1 to 8 bays and are available in capacities of up to 6TB. WD Red Plus are similar, but better suited to more heavily utilized RAID systems, the technical difference is that they do not use Shingled Magnetic Recording or SMR. Also, they are available in capacities of up to 14TB. For systems with more drive bays, up to 24, WD Red Pro drives are recommended and these are available in capacities up to 22TB.

Seagate IronWolf – intended for NAS systems with 1 to 8 bays and available in capacities up to 12TB. For systems with more drive bays, Iron Wolf Pro drives are available in capacities of up to 22TB.

Toshiba N300 – designed for use in NAS systems with 1 to 8 bays, and available in capacities up to 18TB.

Synology HAT5300 – Synology's own brand hard drives. These are manufactured for them by other companies but use Synology developed firmware for tighter integration with DSM. They are available in capacities from 4TB to 18TB. Synology also offer the HAS5300 series, for enterprise-level servers that use SAS drives, along with the HAT3300 series, aimed at home and small business users.

Disk drives are manufactured in 3½ inch (8.9 cm) and 2½ inch (6.4 cm) form factors and most DiskStations can use either, although some models require adaptor brackets to use the 2½ inch ones and the DS Slim series is designed to use the smaller drives only. 3½ inch drives are mechanical with spinning platters and usually referred to as hard drives or HDDs, whereas 2½ inch drives mainly tend to be solid state drives or SSDs (although not exclusively so). For systems with more than one drive, it is preferable that all the drives are of the same model and capacity, although this not a prerequisite. In a DiskStation equipped with multiple drives, they can be configured for *RAID*, short for *Redundant Array of Independent (or Inexpensive) Disks*. There are various types of RAID, referred to using a numbering system i.e. RAID 1, RAID 5, RAID 6 and so on, plus Synology have their own variant, called SHR. RAID improves reliability and performance using multiple drives to provide redundancy and share the workload and a more comprehensive description can be found in section **2.5 Setting up Storage**.

Besides using SSDs for regular storage, DSM can also use them to boost performance through *caching*, where they act as a high-speed buffer to the slower, mechanical hard drives. Depending on the model, this can be done using 2½ inch SSD (SATA) drives or with M.2 NVMe drives in dedicated slots, the advantages of the latter bring that they are faster and do not use the regular drive bays. As drives used for caching take a lot of hits, it is essential to use high quality ones rather than low-cost consumer ones, and Western Digital, Seagate and Synology all offer NAS-optimized SSDs. This topic is discussed in section **12.7 SSD Caching**.

1.4 Switch and Wireless Access Points

The devices in a network are connected using Ethernet cabling and wireless access points (WAPs). In a home or very small business, everything might link back to an all-in-one router or wireless router, whereas in a larger setup there may be a separate router and possibly a separate firewall, with Ethernet switches and wireless access points being used to expand the network and provide greater capacity if required. The following guidelines are suggested:

- The NAS should be connected to the main network switch or combined wireless router using an Ethernet cable.
- Wired devices should be of Gigabit specification or better. Some DiskStations also support 10 Gigabit Ethernet (10GbE) and if so, it is worth connecting them to a 10GbE switch, even if most of the infrastructure still runs at Gigabit speeds.
- For wireless devices such as laptops and tablets, they should operate at 801.11n, 801.11ac or 801.11ax (Wi-Fi 6/6E) specification.
- Check the specification of the combined wireless router if you are using one. Many ISPs (Internet Service Providers) supply relatively low-cost models, often free of charge when signing-up with them. These may be of average specification, for instance the Ethernet ports may not be Gigabit or the latest wireless standards may not be supported. Spending money on professional or prosumer ("professional consumer") routers and switches will usually give better performance and reliability.

1.5 Location and Electrical Considerations

As with any electronic apparatus, some thought needs to be given to the location of the DiskStation(s). They should be placed away from direct sunlight and any source of heat, such as a radiator. Avoid locations that are wet or damp. As little physical access may be required the unit can be located out of sight and reach, for instance in a cupboard, a locked room, dedicated server room or otherwise out of reach. Smaller models generate very little noise and can usually be operated in an office or family room without too much disruption.

It is possible that data loss can occur if the mains electrical power supply fails unexpectedly whilst the DiskStation is running. The best way to mitigate against this is to use an intelligent UPS or *Uninterruptible Power Supply* with the DiskStation; in the event of power problems this will enable it to continue operating for short periods and to then shut down in an orderly manner if necessary. Most popular brands work with Synology (e.g. APC, CyberPower), and a full list of supported UPS units can be found on the Synology website. In a business environment, the use of an UPS should be considered mandatory.

If a UPS is not used, which is commonly the case in a domestic environment, then the DiskStation should be connected to a clean electrical power supply via a surge protector.

2 INSTALLING DSM

2.1 Overview

DiskStation Manager or DSM, the operating system or firmware, is what differentiates Synology from all the other brands of Network Attached Storage. It has such familiar features as a Desktop, Taskbar and a drag-and-drop interface, analogous to what people are accustomed to with Windows, Mac and Linux PCs. The current version is DSM 7.2 and this guide is based around it, although much of the material is also applicable to slightly earlier versions. Unlike a desktop computer or laptop, which usually comes with an operating system already installed, such as Windows or macOS, a NAS does not and hence the first thing to do is to install DSM.

The assumption in this chapter is that you are installing a brand-new DiskStation. If this is not the case, for instance, maybe you have obtained a previously-used model, you might find it helpful to first take a look at sections **15.17 Resetting the Administrator Password if Lost** and **15.19 Preparing the DiskStation for Disposal**, which will help you to re-initialize it.

Begin by physically installing the disk drive(s) into the unit; how to do this varies by model but is summarized in the getting started leaflet supplied with the DiskStation. Having done so, connect it to the network using an Ethernet cable; if the DiskStation has multiple network adaptors, only the first one should be connected for now (adding further connections later is covered in section **15.16 Link Aggregation**). You can then begin installing DSM and there are four possible ways of doing so:

Synology Assistant – this is a utility program that must first be downloaded and installed onto a computer. It can perform other tasks, in addition to installing DSM.

Web Assistant – this is a web-based installation method and only requires a device with a full-screen browser, such as a Windows, macOS or Linux computer.

DS Finder – this is an app for iOS and Android devices. You could use this if you have a smartphone or tablet rather than a computer, or simply prefer to work with a mobile device. In addition to being used for installing DSM, it provides a selection of the management features available in DSM and will be referenced where applicable throughout this guide for those who wish to use a mobile device.

Central Management System – This is a more specialized method. It uses Synology's *Central Management System* (CMS) and enables DSM to be remotely installed on other DiskStations. As it requires that a DiskStation running CMS is already in place, it is not applicable for a first-time installation and hence is described in section **8.10 CMS (Central Management System)** rather than here.

All these options might seem unnecessary – how do you choose between them, for instance? However, in practice the Synology Assistant method is the most flexible and reliable, and so will be used here. If you do not have a suitable computer or prefer to work with a mobile device, then the DS Finder method is available.

The overall installation process consists of loading the DSM firmware, configuring some essential settings, and setting up storage. Having done so, you will be able to create shared folders (**3 SHARED FOLDERS**), setup the users (**4 MANAGING USERS**), and connect computers and other devices (**5 CONNECTING TO THE SERVER**).

2.2 Installation Using Synology Assistant

The first step is to obtain a copy of the Synology Assistant utility. Go the Synology website – www.synology.com – and click **Support > Download Center**. Click the *Select product type* dropdown and choose **NAS**, then find your DiskStation model using the *Select your Synology Product* dropdown which will appear to the right of it. Click the **Desktop Utilities** tab, locate Synology Assistant and click the blue **Download** button. It is available for Windows, macOS, and for 32- and 64-bit versions of Ubuntu Linux – choose the version appropriate for your computer.

Figure 4: Download Center

Having downloaded Synology Assistant, install and run it on your computer. If you receive a message during installation from the computer's firewall, allow access for Synology Assistant. After a few seconds it should find the DiskStation; if it does not, click the **Search** button to try again as it might be a timing issue. If it still cannot find it, check for possible network and cabling problems. Make a note of the IP address displayed on the main panel; in this example it is 192.168.2.52 but it depends on your network and will be different on your system.

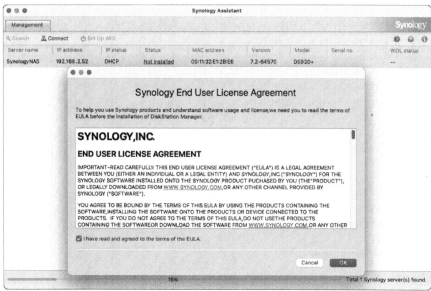

Figure 5: Synology Assistant

Once the DiskStation is located, the Synology End User License Agreement is displayed. Tick the **I have read and agreed to the terms of the EULA** box and click **OK**. The internet browser on the computer will launch and display a screen along the following lines, with a picture of your DiskStation model. Click the blue **Install** button:

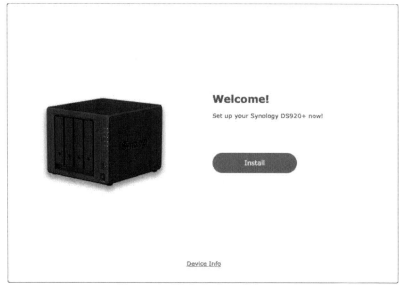

Figure 6: Click the Install button

On the resultant screen, most commonly you would choose **Automatically download the latest DSM from Synology website** and click **Next**. Alternatively, you could manually upload a *pat* file (a copy of DSM) which had previously been downloaded to your computer, which you might do if you needed to use a specific version of DSM rather than the current one. DSM pat files are obtained from the Download Center, same as downloading Synology Assistant as described above, but from the Operating System tab.

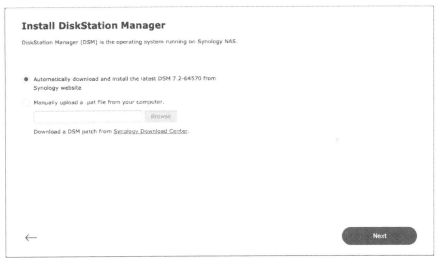

Figure 7: Download options for DSM firmware

A warning message is shown, advising that any data on the disk drive(s) will be destroyed. Acknowledge this warning by ticking the box and clicking **Continue**. There may be an additional warning message, asking you to type in the product model e.g. DS120j, DS923+, DS2422+ etc. Click **Delete**. The installation will now proceed, during which time a status screen is displayed. Do not click the screen or close the browser whilst the installation is running. After installation is completed, which typically takes around 10 minutes, there is a *Welcome* Screen – click the blue **Start** button to begin. The following panel is displayed, for you to name the server and create the administrator account. It is not necessary to tick the box which reads 'Allow this Synology NAS to be displayed in Web Assistant'.

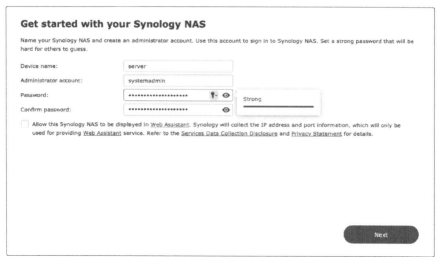

Figure 8: Name device and create administrator account

For the *Device name*, you could simply call it *server*, although if you have or envisage having further DiskStations you may want to adopt a naming scheme e.g. *server1, server2*, or something meaningful to your organization such as location, business function, classroom etc.

The *Administrator account* is the main account, used for administering and managing the server. Traditionally, this has tended to be *admin* on Synology but can largely be whatever you want and in our example we have chosen the name *systemadmin*. Enter and confirm a password; use something non-obvious and a mixture of upper- and lower-case letters, numbers and symbols, which does not include the username, and is at least 8 characters in length. DSM will provide feedback on the strength of the password and it should be something 'strong'. If you click the small eye icon you can view the password you are entering, to help ensure that mistakes are not made. Click **Next**.

The following screen is for specifying updates and there are three options. Synology recommend the first one, which will automatically install updates that fix security problems and critical bugs. The second option will automatically install all the latest versions of DSM and packages. The third option provides notification of updates, but they must be installed manually. Which to choose? Most people, particularly in a domestic environment or if they lack access to technical support, will be best served with the first option.

However, some business users will prefer control over updates, for instance if they have multiple servers which need to be kept 'in step' or to avoid the risk of an unplanned update causing problems or compatibility issues. Make a choice and click **Next**.

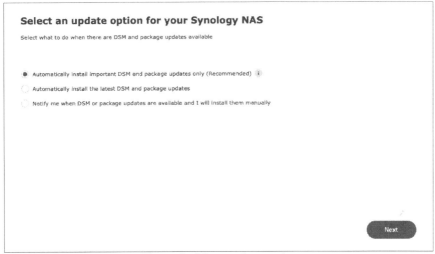

Figure 9: Select update option

You will then be prompted to create a *Synology Account*. This is a totally separate account from the one you have just created: its purpose is to establish your relationship with Synology and is used for setting up remote access, monitoring and other purposes. It is required for full use of the DiskStation, but for now click **Skip** as we will return to it later (also click **Skip Anyway** on the reminder that pops up). However, if you have an existing Synology Account, for instance this is not your first Synology NAS, you can sign in using that.

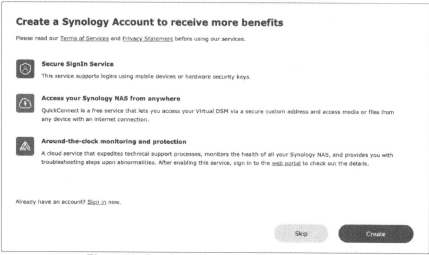

Figure 10: Synology Account - click Skip for now

A screen about *Device Analytics* is displayed, which controls whether anonymous usage information (which is not personally identifiable data), is sent back to Synology for product improvement purposes. This is optional and does not affect the working of the DiskStation; decide, then click **Submit**.

There may be a panel to enabling the installation of *Synology Drive Server*, *Synology Office* and *Synology Photos*. These are popular packages ('apps') and are discussed comprehensively in this guide, but to save time for now you may wish to click the **No thanks** or **Remind me later** option at the bottom of the screen.

The next two panels are for enhancing security. The first is for enabling *2-Factor Authentication (2FA)*. This adds an extra layer of security by requiring a second identify verification step when signing into your account (you may have encountered something similar if you use internet banking). This topic is discussed subsequently in section **6.6 Improving Sign-In Security**, but for now click **No thanks**. The second panel is for configuring *Adaptive Multi-Factor Authentication (Adaptive MFA)*. If the system detects suspicious login attempts, you will be asked to verify your identify by email. This topic is also discussed in section **6.6 Improving Sign-In Security**, but for now click **I don't want to secure my account**. On the reminder message about not enabling additional security, click **OK**.

Figure 11: Enhanced security messages

Having completed this section, please go to **2.4 Five Minute Tour of DiskStation Manager**.

2.3 Installation Using DS Finder

Download DS Finder from the respective App store for iOS or Android and install on your smartphone or tablet device (you may find that your DiskStation comes with a leaflet or packaging containing a QR code, which can be scanned to find the App). The mobile device needs to be connected to the same local network as the DiskStation. From the Welcome screen, tap **Set up new NAS**. The next screen is a prompt to insert one or more drives into the NAS and we will assume that this has already been done, so tap **Skip**. On the subsequent screen tap **Search** to locate the NAS, although in some instances DS Finder will do this automatically. On the result screen, tap where it reads 'Not installed' and a more detailed screen is shown. Before you proceed, make a note of the IP address, which is 192.168.2.31 in this example, but which will be different on your system:

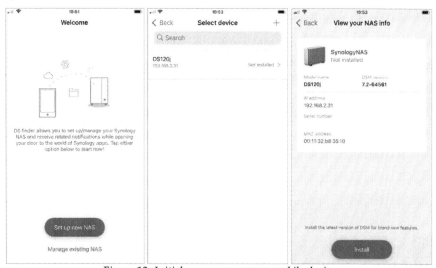

Figure 12: Initial screens as seen on mobile device

Tap **Install** to begin the process. Acknowledge the subsequent warning message about the disk drives being formatted by tapping **OK**. The next screen covers the licence agreement, terms of service and privacy statements – tap **Agree** (having read them all carefully, naturally). A message about notifications is displayed: tap **OK**, followed by **Allow** if so prompted. Whilst DSM is installing, which typically takes about 10-15 minutes, a status screen is displayed.

After installation is completed, you will need to specify the server name plus a name for the main administrative account, along with a password. It is suggested you simply call the NAS *server*, although if you have or envisage having further DiskStations you may want to adopt a naming scheme e.g. *server1*, *server2*, or something meaningful to your organization e.g. location, business function, classroom.

Specify the account name. This is for the main account, used for administering and managing the server. Traditionally, this has tended to be *admin* on Synology but can largely be whatever you choose. As hackers tend to look for obvious names, an alternative is preferable and in our example we have chosen the name *systemadmin*. Enter and confirm a password; use something non-obvious and a mixture of upper- and lower-case letters, numbers and symbols, which does not include the username, and is at least 8 characters in length. DS Finder will provide feedback on the strength of the password and it should be something 'strong'. Tap **Create**.

Figure 13: Setup main DSM account, as seen on a phone

The subsequent screen is for creating a new or logging in to an existing Synology Account. This is a totally separate account from the one you have just created, which establishes your relationship with Synology and is used for setting up remote access and monitoring.

It is important, but for now click **Skip** and we will return to it later. It is followed by one about sending anonymous statistical information to Synology; decide whether you want to do this or not and tap **Submit**. You will then be taken into the *General* screen:

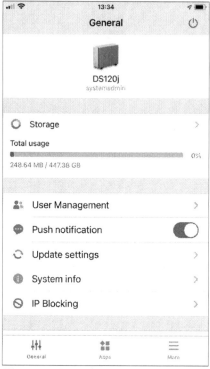

Figure 14: General screen as seen on phone

It is possible to manage many although not all aspects of the DiskStation using DS Finder. Because of this you may wish to acquaint yourself with the regular web interface, as introduced in **2.4 Five Minute Tour of DiskStation Manager**.

Note: one downside of using DS Finder is that sometimes it does not find the latest version of DSM from Synology, or have the ability to download specific versions of DSM. For instance, at the time of writing DSM 7.2 has been available for several weeks, yet DS Finder does not 'see' it and downloads a version of DSM 7.1.1. This behavior may be specific to certain DiskStation models.

2.4 Five Minute Tour of DiskStation Manager

Having completed the installation, you will be signed in ('logged in') to DSM. To sign in on subsequent occasions, enter *http://server* in the address bar of the browser (assuming you called your DiskStation *'server'*, otherwise enter the name you specified). If it cannot be found, enter the IP address of the server instead e.g. *http://192.168.1.2* - you may recall the suggestion earlier on to make a note of it, or you can use the Synology Assistant utility to locate it. Enter the administrative user name - *systemadmin* in our example - along with the password you defined earlier. Once signed in, there may be an advertisement to register for an extended warranty on the DiskStation, plus an invitation to take an optional tour.

You will then be presented with the Desktop, which will look familiar to anyone who has used a Windows, macOS or Linux computer. There are several icons on the Desktop, which is customizable, and the top line of the screen acts as the Taskbar. The background wallpaper can be changed if desired and how to do so is described in section **4.7 User Personalization Settings**).

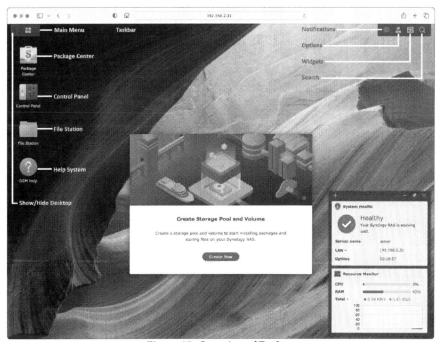

Figure 15: Overview of Desktop

On a newly installed system, a message to *Create Storage Pool and Volume* is displayed; close it for now by clicking the Show/Hide Desktop button in the very top left-hand corner of the screen. It is important and you cannot do anything useful with the NAS until storage has been configured, but we will return to it shortly after a quick familiarization tour.

The *Main Menu* provides access to important system programs and features, similar to the Start button in Windows or Launchpad in macOS. When clicked it expands, displaying icons which can be clicked to run the underlying programs or features. The icons can also be dragged onto the Desktop for convenience and this has already been done for a number of them i.e. *Package Center, Control Panel, File Station* and *DSM Help*. When a program is running, its icon appears at the top of the screen or *Taskbar*, and you can right-click to pin it there permanently. To close the Main Menu, click anywhere within it or click its icon in the top left-hand corner of the screen.

Figure 16: Main Menu

Depending on the DiskStation model, you may have a slightly different initial selection of icons to those shown above, for example *USB Copy* will not be present if the feature is not available on the DiskStation. When further packages (apps) are installed, they are added to the Main Menu and will initially be highlighted so you can identify them; if many are added it can become cluttered, in which case the search facility at the top of the screen can be useful.

The arrangement of the icons can be changed, by holding down the mouse and dragging an icon to the desired location.

The *Package Center* is DSM's equivalent to Apple's App Store and Google's Play Store, used for downloading and maintaining applications from Synology that provide additional capabilities, such as security and multimedia. It is discussed in detail in **15.2 Package Center** and because of its importance you may want to read that section at any early opportunity.

The *Control Panel* provides icons to setup and customize the DiskStation, grouped into four main categories of *File Sharing, Connectivity, System* and *Services*. As with the Main Menu, icons can be dragged onto the Desktop for convenience. The Control Panel and most other windows can be resized, minimized or closed using the small icons in the top-right hand corner of the window. Windows can also be moved around and resized using a mouse.

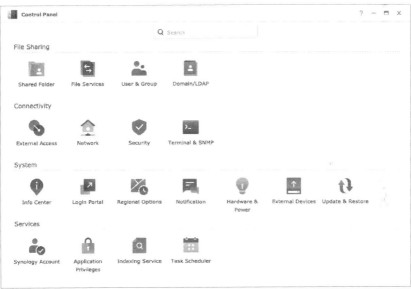

Figure 17: Control Panel

File Station displays the contents of the disk volumes and folders and can be used for manipulating files, similar to File Explorer on a Windows PC or Finder on macOS. The first time you launch it there will be a message advising that '*There is no shared folder available*' and it will offer to assist you in creating one. You can defer for now by clicking **Cancel** as we will return to the topic shortly.

The *DSM Help* icon provides searchable help and includes links to online tutorials, frequently asked questions, and video tutorials. In addition, many screens in DSM have a context-sensitive link to the online help system, accessed by clicking the small question mark icon in the top right-hand corner.

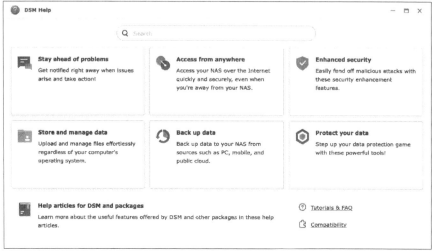

Figure 18: DSM Help system

Notifications provide status information about events that have occurred e.g. backup successfully completed, system error etc. A new notification is indicated by the presence of a red dot on the icon.

Widgets are small panels that provide status information, most of which relate to the health of the system. These can also be dragged onto the Desktop to further customize it, and by default some widgets for monitoring system status are already present in the bottom right-hand corner of the screen. Widgets can be pinned, removed, moved about and so on.

Search, as the name suggests, enables you to search files and file contents. The first time it is run, you will need to click **Create Now** to initiate indexing.

The *Options* icon provides some configuration choices and is used for signing out, restarting and shutting down the system. NAS devices are commonly left running 24x7 and only administrative users can shutdown the system.

When you have finished working with DSM, you should sign out of the system. If you are working with DSM but there has been no activity for a while, you will automatically be signed out of the system after 15 minutes. If this period is too short, it can be increased and how to do so is described in section **6.3 Security Icon**.

Although DSM is usually navigated using a mouse or other pointing device, it is also possible to use keyboard shortcuts. For instance, pressing **Alt A** will display the Main Menu. A full list of shortcuts can be displayed by pressing **Shift ?** (question mark). If desired, desktop keyboard shortcuts can be disabled by removing the tick from the **Enable desktop keyboard shortcuts** box.

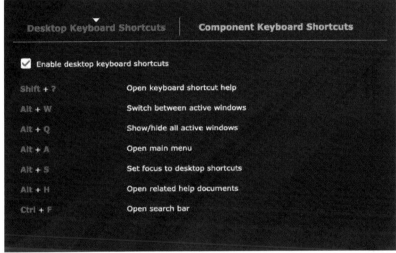

Figure 19: Keyboard shortcuts

2.5 Setting up Storage

Overview

Storage management is flexible and sophisticated in DSM, as it must cater for a wide variety of scenarios, ranging from home users with a single DiskStation with one hard drive, through to mission-critical enterprise setups with hundreds of DiskStations, thousands of drives and Petabytes of data. DSM must cater for these disparate requirements in a consistent and understandable manner and it has succeeded, although some of the methods may seem over-complicated for people who just want to 'get on with it'. During the installation of DSM, the disk drives in the DiskStation will have been initialized, but they will still need to be configured before they are ready for use. This contrasts with setting up a typical Windows PC or Mac, where the operating system takes care of this and without generally involving the user too much.

First, some basic concepts. DiskStations use disk drives, which might be traditional mechanical hard disk drives (HDD), solid-state drives (SSD) or a mixture of the two (subject to some constraints). If SSDs, they can be used for conventional storage, but on some models can also be used for *caching*, which provides high speed access to frequently used data as described in **12.7 SSD Caching**.

The basic storage unit is the *volume* and all data – shared folders, documents, applications - are held on volumes. Before you can store anything, it is necessary to create at least one volume. If a DiskStation has a single drive, it would become the single volume (it is not possible to split a single drive into multiple volumes, as can be done on Windows or macOS).

Multiple drives can be combined to create a *storage pool*. When this is done, volumes can be created on the storage pool and as these volumes can encompass multiple drives, they can be significantly larger in size. The drives making up the storage pool are usually configured for *RAID - Redundant Array of Independent (or Inexpensive) Disks* - to improve performance, provide redundancy (protection against drive failure), plus share the workload. There are various types of RAID and they referred to using a numbering system i.e. RAID 0, RAID 1, RAID 5 and so on.

Synology support multiple RAID levels and depending on the model and the physical drives installed, the following RAID levels might be available: RAID 0; RAID 1; RAID 5; RAID 6; RAID 10; JBOD. In addition, Synology have their own, unique system called Synology Hybrid RAID (SHR) and this offers several advantages over conventional RAID for many users. On a system with a single drive, RAID is not applicable and Synology refer to the storage as 'basic'.

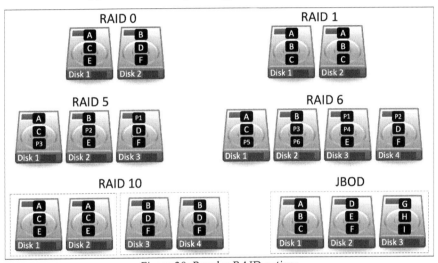

Figure 20: Popular RAID options

RAID 0 consists of two identical drives. When data is written, some goes on one drive and some goes on the other. As both drives are being written to or read simultaneously, throughput is maximized. However, as sections of files are scattered across the two drives, if one drive fails then everything can be lost. Also, the speed of the disk drives may not be a bottleneck in some NAS systems. For these reasons, RAID 0 on its own is not commonly used. In a RAID 0 system, the total usable storage amount is equal to that of the total drive capacity installed. For example, if a DiskStation has two 4TB drives installed then the total amount of usable storage capacity is 8TB.

RAID 1 consists of two identical drives that mirror each other. When a file is saved there are physically two separate but identical copies, one on each drive, though you can only see one as the mirroring process itself is invisible. If a drive fails, the other one automatically takes over and the system carries on without interruption.

At the earliest opportunity the faulty drive should be replaced with a new one; the system is then synced so it becomes a true copy of the remaining healthy drive in a process known as *rebuilding the array*. In a RAID 1 system, the total usable storage capacity is half that of the total drive capacity installed. For example, if a DiskStation has two 4TB drives installed, then the total amount of usable storage capacity is 4TB rather than 8TB.

RAID 5 requires three or more four drives. Data is written across all the drives, along with *parity information* - in simple terms, 'clues' that enable lost data to be reconstructed. The benefit of this is that the system can cope with the failure of any one single drive. RAID 5 is considered to offer a good combination of price, performance and resilience. Whereas a RAID 1 system loses half of the total drive capacity to provide resilience, RAID 5 loses only a third on a 3-drive system and a quarter on a 4-drive system. For instance, if a DiskStation has three 4TB drives installed then the total amount of usable storage capacity is 8TB rather than 12TB; if the DiskStation had four 4TB drives installed, the total amount of usable storage capacity would be 12TB rather than 16TB.

RAID 6 needs four or more drives. It is like RAID 5 but uses two sets of parity information written across the drives instead of one. The benefit of this approach is that the system can cope with the simultaneous failure of two of the drives, thereby making it more resilient than RAID 5, but it loses more capacity to provide that resilience. There may also be a performance hit compared with RAID 5 due to the additional parity processing, but overall RAID 6 is considered superior. If a server has five 4TB drives installed in a RAID configuration, then the total amount of usable storage capacity is 12TB rather than 20TB.

RAID 10 (also known as RAID 1+0) combines RAID 1 and RAID 0 techniques. Requiring an even number and a minimum of four drives, it comprises a pair of RAID 1 mirrored drives, with data being striped across the pair in the way that RAID 0 operates. It thus combines both performance (RAID 0) and redundancy (RAID 1), making it beneficial where high throughput in needed, for instance in demanding applications such as 4K/8K video editing. The amount of available storage is half that of the total drive capacity e.g. a system with four 4TB drives would give 8TB of usable space rather than 16TB.

SHR and SHR-2 (Synology Hybrid Raid), developed by Synology and proprietary to them, offers a more flexible approach to RAID. For maximum efficiency, a conventional RAID system requires multiple drives of identical capacity, otherwise it is limited by the size of the smallest drive. For instance, in a RAID 5 system with four x 4TB drives, there would be 16TB of physical storage, with 12TB of usable space and 4TB of protection. But, if it comprised three x 4TB drives and a single 2TB drive, there would be 14TB of physical storage but only 6TB of usable space and 2TB of protection, with the remaining 6TB unused/wasted. The reason for this is that everything reverts to the lowest common denominator and hence the system only 'sees' 2TB volumes.

However, SHR can work with drives of differing capacities. It creates a mixture of usable space plus puts some aside for redundant storage, described as 'protection' by Synology. Besides this benefit, it is much easier to expand by adding further drives later, plus it avoids the need for any detailed technical knowledge of what is going on behind the scenes as 'it just works'. SHR is Synology's recommended system for home and small business users, however, it is not suitable for large servers and hence is not supported on enterprise-level DiskStations and RackStations.

SHR can cope with the loss of a single disk, whereas SHR-2 can cope with the loss of two (in simple terms, they can be considered as similar to RAID 5 and RAID 6 respectively, although it is not an exact analogy). By way of example, if you had the three x 4TB drives and single 2TB drive as described above, SHR would provide 10TB of usable space, 4TB of protection and no wasted space, representing a significant increase over RAID 5.

One potential disadvantage of SHR is that there is a small performance hit when compared to regular RAID. This is unlikely to be an issue in many deployments, but if absolute maximum disk performance is required then standard RAID should be used.

JBOD stands for *Just a Bunch of Disks* and is not actually a RAID system at all. Rather, it aggregates all the drives together to create one large volume that provides the maximum amount of storage space, but without any protection. This differs from RAID 0, as the drives do not have to be of identical capacity, plus you can use as many drives as are in the NAS.

For example, with the same drives as in the previous example (3 x 4TB plus 1 x 2TB) you would get the full 14 TB storage with JBOD rather than 10 TB storage as with SHR.

What to do? If you have a DiskStation with a single drive, then the question of RAID does not arise. If you have a DiskStation with two drive bays, then you can use SHR or RAID 1 if data protection is most important to you or use JBOD if you need the maximum amount of space. If you have a DiskStation with four drive bays, it can be configured as SHR or RAID 5 if protection is most important, or JBOD if you need the maximum amount of space. If you have a DiskStation with five or more drives, it can be configured as SHR-2 or RAID 6 if protection is most important, or JBOD if you need the maximum amount of space. And if you are using any DiskStation with a variety of differing drive capacities, then you should use SHR.

Synology have a useful web page for calculating the amount of available storage for different RAID configurations on their website (go to www.synology.com and search for 'RAID calculator').

It is important to note is that a RAID system is **not** a backup system. Whilst it can help prevent data loss in the event of problems, it is still necessary to make separate provision for backup. For instance, if the server was stolen or the premises went up in flames then the data would be lost regardless of whether and whatever RAID system was used.

Before they can be used, volumes must be formatted. You may be familiar with the disk formats used by Windows and macOS, such as NTFS, FAT-32, ex-FAT and APFS. With DSM, there are two different disk filing systems, *ext4* and *Btrfs* (sometimes pronounced 'butter-F-S'). Ext4 is a universal format, available to all DiskStation users. Btrfs is a more sophisticated file system with advanced features, available on x86-based DiskStations but not necessarily on all ARM-based models. One of these advanced features is *snapshots*, which can be thought of as a built-in backup mechanism whereby the system makes a note of what has been altered when a file or folder has changed, then writes away those details to a different part of the disk or to a different disk altogether. Information on snapshots is in section **7.9 Snapshot Replication**.

Creating Storage Pools and Volumes

Most aspects of storage in DSM are managed using the *Storage Manager* utility, which is launched by clicking its icon in the Main Menu. The first time it is used the *Storage Creation Wizard* will run – click **Start** to begin:

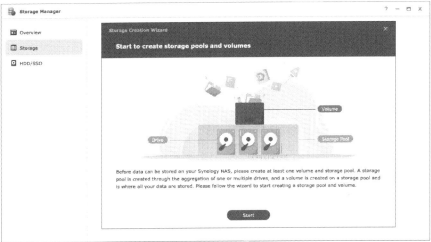

Figure 21: Storage Creation Wizard

On the next panel, specify the *RAID type* using the dropdown. Only the options applicable to your DiskStation are listed, and the wizard will default to what Synology considers to be the most suitable RAID type. In this example we have a four-drive system and the wizard suggests SHR (Synology Hybrid RAID), which is the best choice if you consider yourself a non-technical person or just want things working as simply and quickly as possible. On a one-drive system, RAID is not possible so the type can only be 'Basic' i.e. a normal, regular drive. Optionally, enter a *Storage pool description*. Click **Next**.

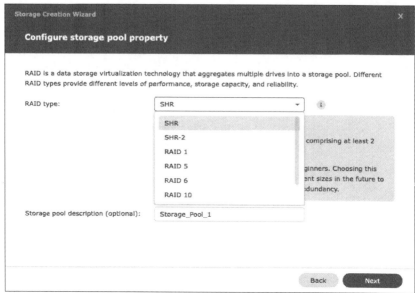

Figure 22: Configure storage pool property

On the subsequent panel, select the drive(s) to be used, with the simplest option being to select all of them unless you have specific requirements.

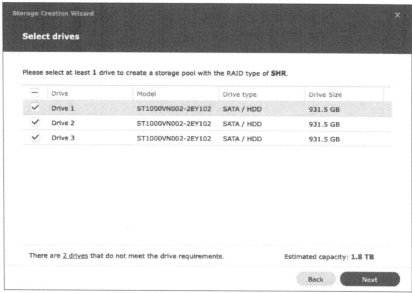

Figure 23: Select drives

The drives used in a storage pool must all be of the same type i.e. all HDD or all SSD or all SAS, as it is not possible to mix them at this level (if you tried to do this, a message will appear on the panel advising that some drives 'do not meet the drive requirements'). Depending on the RAID type, the maximum number of drives can be 6, 12, 16, 20 or 24. The estimated capacity of the storage panel will be displayed in the bottom right-hand corner of the panel.

Having clicked **Next**, you may receive a message advising that the drives are not on the *Synology Products Compatibility List* – this does not mean that they are unsuitable, but simply that Synology have not formally evaluated them. Acknowledge the message by clicking **Continue**. You will then receive a message asking whether to perform an optional 'Drive check'; this is recommended but will slow down the storage creation process. Make a choice and click **Next**.

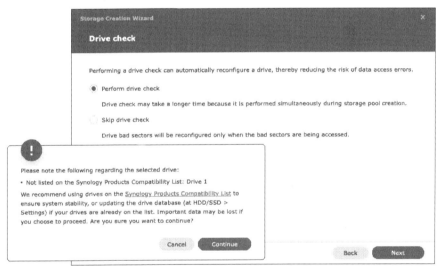

Figure 24: Drive compatibility and Drive check messages

The subsequent screen is for allocating volume capacity, meaning how much of the storage pool will be assigned to the volume. The easiest thing is to allocate all of it, which can be done by clicking the **Max** button, and this is suggested for most people. However, you could choose to allocate only part of the storage pool and then subsequently use the rest of it to create an additional volume or volumes (multiple volumes may be of interest to advanced users and for larger networks). Optionally, a *Volume description* can be specified.

Click **Next**. In the case of a single disk system, the volume capacity cannot be specified and will always be the entire capacity of the drive.

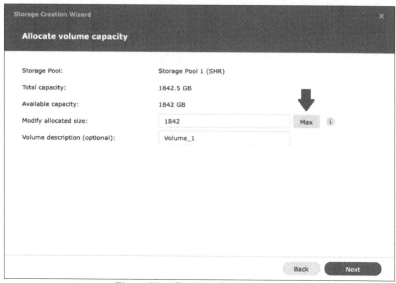

Figure 25: Allocate volume capacity

Depending on your DiskStation model, you may receive a screen about selecting a file system.

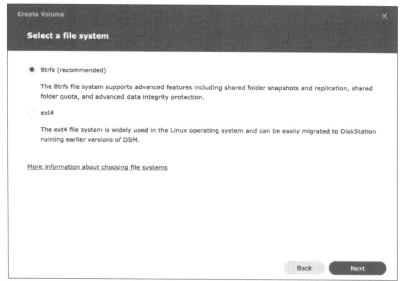

Figure 26: Select a file system

There is a choice of two: *ext4* is a universal one, available to all DiskStation users, whereas *Btrfs* (sometimes pronounced 'butter-F-S') is a more advanced one with additional features, available on x86-based DiskStations but not on all ARM-based models. If you have the option of Btrfs you should choose it. Click **Next**.

The next panel gives the option of encrypting the volume, which helps protect your data should the DiskStation be lost or stolen. If you do not require encryption, leave the **Encrypt this volume** box unticked and click **Next**. If you do want encryption e.g. because the volume will hold confidential information, tick the **Encrypt this volume** box, click **Next**, then enter and confirm a *Vault password* on the pop-up panel, followed by **Enable**.

Note: encryption is not supported on all DiskStation models. On unsupported models, this panel does not appear and you will be taken to a *Volume information* panel, where you enter an optional Volume description and click **Next**.

Figure 27: Configuring optional encryption

A *Confirm Settings* panel is displayed. Assuming you are happy with your choices, click **Apply**. If you chose to encrypt the volume, a copy of the password will be downloaded, which you should store in a safe location in case it is ever needed e.g. on a USB memory stick. Note that the same password will apply to any further encrypted volumes which are created.

You will receive a message about existing data on the drive(s) being erased - click **OK**. The Storage Pool is then created. The time taken for this depends upon the type, number, capacity of the drives and the RAID option selected. There will be a message advising that the system is *'Optimizing in the background'*, although it is usable in the meantime. Optimization may potentially take several hours; when complete, Storage Manager will be updated upon the following lines, the specifics of which depend upon your system. On a single-drive system, options which do not apply will not be available.

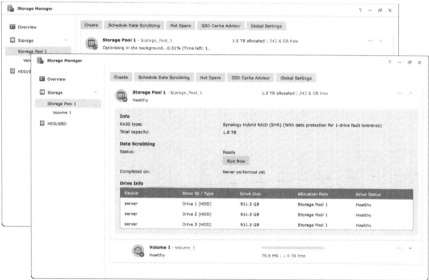

Figure 28: Storage Pool details within Storage Manager

There is a separate chapter in this guide dedicated to the topic of storage (**12 STORAGE**), in which some more advanced topics are discussed.

2.6 Configuring the DiskStation

Setting the IP Address

Note: if you are familiar with IP addresses, you can skip the first four paragraphs and jump to the one that begins 'Click Control Panel followed by Network...'.

Every device within a network is represented by a unique number, known as the *IP address*. This consists of four sets of three digits, separated by periods, ranging from 000.000.000.000 through to 255.255.255.255. Most of these IP addresses are reserved for websites and other internet applications, although they are not generally used in a direct manner, thanks to the internet's Domain Naming System or DNS, which translates an IP address such as 142.250.200.46 into the more understandable name of *google.com*. These addresses are known as *public IP addresses*. However, a limited set of numbers are not routable over the internet, making them 'invisible' to it, and these private IP addresses are used within local area networks. The sequences which must be used are 10.0.0.0 to 10.255.255.255, 172.16.0.0 to 172.31.255.255 and 192.168.0.0 to 192.168.255.255. As these addresses are isolated, they can safely be used by anyone without risk of duplication and the same numbers are used worldwide in millions of separate networks.

Much of the equipment intended for use in small businesses and homes assumes a *192.168.nnn.nnn* numbering scheme; for instance, internet routers commonly have addresses such as *192.168.1.1*, *192.168.2.1* or *192.168.0.254* or similar pre-defined, depending on the brand. However, devices such as computers, printers and NAS boxes do not come with IP addresses already allocated; instead, they must be configured with a suitable address and there are two ways of doing so - you can use *static IP addresses* or *dynamic IP addresses*.

With static IP addresses, it is necessary to visit each device and individually configure it. For instance, you might set the first computer to *192.168.1.101*, the second to *192.168.1.102*, the third to *192.168.1.103* and so on. You must be careful to keep track of everything and above all make sure there are no duplicates. If this sounds like hard work then that's because it is – you might get away with it if there are only a handful of devices, but beyond that it rapidly becomes unmanageable.

With dynamic IP addresses, the numbers are assigned automatically by a DHCP (*Dynamic Host Configuration Protocol*) server and it keeps track of everything. This is not usually a separate device or physical server, although it could be in a large network, and most all-in-one routers of the sort used in small businesses and homes have DHCP server software built-in. During the installation of DSM, the DiskStation will have received a dynamic IP address from the router's DHCP server. Although dynamic IP is more practical for devices such as computers and tablets and smartphones, NAS boxes work better with fixed or static addresses so we do need to assign one to the DiskStation.

Click **Control Panel** followed by **Network** and the **Network Interface** tab. There will be several entries, such as *LAN* and *PPPoE*; if the DiskStation has multiple network adapters they will be labelled *LAN 1*, *LAN 2* and so on. The first or only *LAN* entry will have a status of 'Connected' – click to highlight it, then click the **Edit** button:

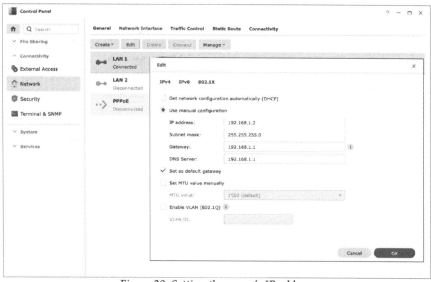

Figure 29: Setting the server's IP address

On the *Ipv4* tab, click **Use manual configuration** and specify an IP address that is adjacent to that of the router, which is shown on the panel under the alternative name of *Gateway*. It is the fourth and final set of digits that is significant in small networks, defined here as those with less than 255 devices, and the first three sets of digits should not normally be altered.

In this example, the gateway is 192.168.1.1, so a suitable address for the server would be something like 192.168.1.2. The *Subnet mask* should be set to 255.255.255.0. Confirm that the **Set as default gateway box** is ticked and click **OK**. The settings will be applied and the screen will refresh; you may possibly lose connectivity to the DiskStation and have to refresh the browser and/or have to sign in again.

In most cases that is all the networking configuration required; however, there are several exceptions. One of these is where the router does not supply IP addresses through DHCP, which might be the case in a larger organization. A second is where internet access is via a *proxy server*, which is uncommon but might be the case when the business is in, say, managed or serviced offices, or in an educational setting. Thirdly, if you are in a larger setting, defined here as one with more than 255 network devices (i.e. not a typical home or small business), then you will need to use multiple subnet masks. This is outside the scope of this guide and a more detailed explanation can be found online at *https://en.wikipedia.org/wiki/Subnetwork*. Finally, some DiskStations have multiple network adapters in them to improve reliability and throughput. All these scenarios are considered in Chapter **15 MISCELLANEOUS TOPICS**.

Note 1: if you have multiple servers, you could use sequential IP addresses. For instance, the first server might be 192.168.1.2, the second 192.168.1.3, the third 192.168.1.4 and so on.

Note 2: there are two 'flavors' of IP: TCP/IPv4 and TCP/IPv6. In this guide we are using the more common IPv4, as most people find it easier to deal with addresses such as 192.168.1.254 rather than something like, say, 3ffe:1900:4545:3:200:f8ff:fe21:67cf.

File Services

File Services refers to the *protocols* by which DSM provides access to files and folders for different types of client computers, which can be running Windows, macOS, Linux and other Unix variants. Other devices, such as tablets and smartphones, may be able to access files on the DiskStation if they support the underlying protocols associated with these computer types or are equipped with suitable apps. Further protocols – *FTP* and *rsync* – allow the connection of other DiskStations and servers.

By default, DSM assumes that you will be using Windows PCs and Macs and it is not usually necessary to adjust any settings in File Services, so most people reading this can simply skip to the next section. However, if any of the following conditions apply, then you may need to make changes: the Windows workgroup is not actually called *Workgroup*; you want to backup Macs to the server using Time Machine; you need to make a shared printer available to Mac clients; you are using very old versions of macOS; you wish to use Linux or other Unix-based computers in a manner which uses features specific to those operating systems.

Windows

To review and change settings, go to **Control Panel,** click the **File Services** icon and then click the **SMB** tab. If your workgroup is not called *Workgroup*, in the *SMB* section change the name of the **Workgroup** to match that of your computers. Having to do this would be unusual, as *WORKGROUP* is the default name on Windows computers. There are additional options and advanced settings relating to the SMB protocol and which may be of interest to experienced Windows Server administrators. If you are using Windows XP computers, network media players, smart TVs, network printers or IP cameras, you may potentially need to enable NTLMv1 authentication, which is turned off by default in DSM due to its weak security (click the **Advanced Settings** button and on the **Others** tab tick the **Enable NTLMv1 authentication** box, followed by **Save**).

Figure 30: File Services (SMB)

macOS

Macs and Windows computers both use the SMB network protocol, although historically Apple computers used their own protocol called AFP (*Apple Filing Protocol*). Support for AFP was removed in macOS 11 ('Big Sur'), meaning it is no longer required. An exception to this would be if you are using versions of macOS prior to 10.9 ('Mavericks'), it which case it can be checked/enabled by ticking the **Enable AFP service** box on the **AFP** tab.

If you are planning to use Time Machine, which is covered in detail in section **7.8 Backing up Computers to the Server**, or print from Macs, click the **Advanced** tab within **File Services**. In the Bonjour section, tick the first three boxes, followed by **Apply**. You may receive a warning message that SMB3 will also be enabled, in which case click **Yes**.

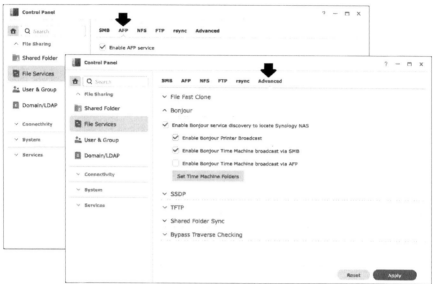

Figure 31: File Services (AFP) and Bonjour support

Linux/Unix

Linux/Unix distributions include the ability to connect to SMB-based systems such as DSM. Unless you have specific requirements, you may find it easier to use SMB, in which case you do not need to do anything additional. However, if you use Linux or other Unix-type variant computers in an 'advanced' manner – defined here as use of the NFS protocol – you will need to enable NFS on the DiskStation. Within **Control Panel,** click the **File Services** icon and on it click the **NFS** tab. Under the **NFS File Service** section, click the **Enable NFS** service tick-box and specify the **Maximum NFS protocol**. There are further options accessible by clicking the **Advanced Settings** button.

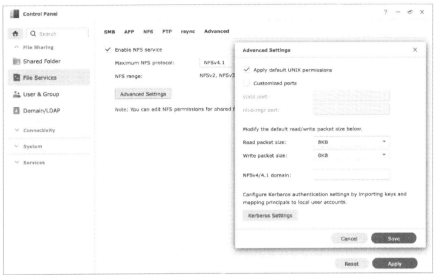

Figure 32: File Services (NFS)

Other Services

Additional tabs within File Services enable other protocols to be managed:

FTP – used for configuring File Transfer Protocol, including Secure FTP (SFTP)

Rsync – used if the DiskStation is to be backed up to other DiskStations This topic is detailed in section **7.6 Synology to Synology Backups**.

Advanced – used for configuring Trivial File Transfer Protocol (TFTP) and enabling SSDP, in addition to configuring Bonjour as described above.

Power Management & Hardware Settings

DiskStations have various power management options, some of which are concerned with energy saving and can be used to reduce power consumption and potentially save energy costs. To configure them, go into **Control Panel** and click **Hardware & Power** to display the following panel. As the options available depend on the DiskStation model, there can be minor variations in this screen:

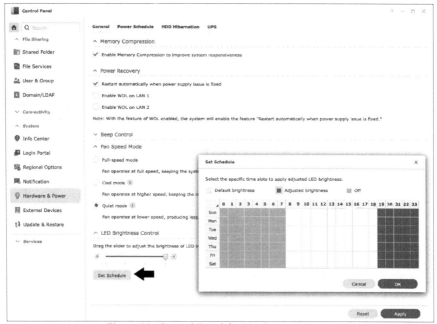

Figure 33: Control Panel for Hardware & Power

On the **General** tab, tick **Restart automatically when power supply issue is fixed**. If electrical power is lost, this will cause the server to automatically restart upon resumption of power.

If the *Memory Compression* option is listed (selected models only), tick the **Enable Memory Compression to improve system responsiveness** box.

The *Beep Control* section defines the error conditions which will cause the DiskStation to make a beeping noise, such as a drive or fan problem.

Set the *Fan Speed Mode* to **Quiet Mode** if the DiskStation is located in a quiet area e.g. at home, or to **Cool Mode** if a small amount of noise is acceptable e.g. typical office environment.

If the DiskStation is in a warm place or climate, or where noise is unimportant, you may want to set it to **Full-speed Mode** for maximum cooling.

On some DiskStations, it is possible to set the brightness of the LED indicators on the unit using the slider in the *LED Brightness Control* section. This can lower power consumption, plus reduce visual distractions if the DiskStation is in, say, a bedroom or next to a television set. A schedule can be defined to dim the LEDs at particular times e.g. overnight, by clicking the **Set Schedule** button and then clicking and dragging to select days and times in the resultant matrix.

In a similar manner, from the **Power Schedule** tab, the DiskStation can be scheduled to power on and off automatically. Doing this can save on energy costs and enhance security. However, if this is done then check that the DiskStation will not be powered down when an activity such as backup or an anti-virus scan is scheduled to take place.

To create a schedule, click the **Create** button on the **Power Schedule** tab.

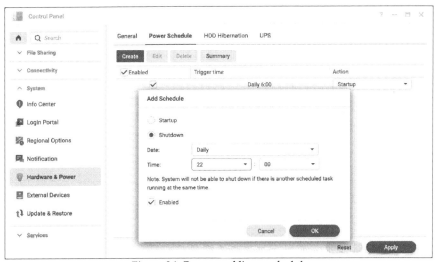

Figure 34: Power – adding a schedule

Specify whether the event is to Startup or Shutdown the server and whether it is to run daily, weekly or at weekends (it is also possible to specify particular days of the week). Click **OK** followed by the **Save** button.

Make sure the task is **Enabled**, which it should be if it has just been created. In this example, the server will startup every day at 0600 (6:00am) and shutdown at 2200 (10:00pm). Click **Apply**:

From the **HDD Hibernation** tab, disk drives can be programmed to hibernate after a set period. This saves energy and reduces overall noise but may result in a short delay when the DiskStation is subsequently accessed if mechanical (hard) disks spin up, typically in the order of 15-30 seconds. The default hibernation time of 20 minutes is suitable in most cases; any external USB hard drives (e.g. backup drives) can also be made to hibernate. Suggestion: if you are using applications where maximum responsiveness is required (e.g. video editing) you might not want to enable hibernation.

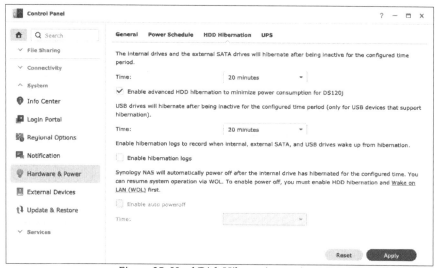

Figure 35: Hard Disk Hibernation settings

The final tab is for managing an Uninterruptible Power Supply (UPS). A UPS can be connected with a USB cable, or over the network. If a network UPS is used which supports SNMP, then other DiskStations can also be controlled from this screen. On the **UPS** tab, tick the box to **Enable UPS support**. The default values can be left as is. Click **Apply**. Note: the contents of this panel will vary, depending on the UPS type.

Figure 36: Enabling UPS Support

2.7 QuickConnect: The Key to Remote Connectivity

Remote access has two aspects. The first is about the actual capabilities of cloud storage, syncing, backup and other features that DSM and the optional packages provide, and the second is how to connect the DiskStation to the internet and be able to access it in a simple, secure and safe manner. This is what *QuickConnect* does: it provides an easy, straightforward mechanism for remote access, suitable for most home and small business users. It works as a relay service, passing data to and from computers and the DiskStation over the internet via Synology. No data is stored at Synology itself and it remains your data on your computers. Because the service uses standard web protocols, it avoids the need for techniques such as port forwarding, router configuration and paid domain services. This also means remote access can be made available in many places where there may be no option to make technical changes to the underlying environment, such as in schools, colleges, managed premises and corporate workplaces.

To use QuickConnect, you need an account with Synology, which you can obtain instantly and freely by going to **Control Panel > Synology Account** and clicking the **Sign in to or sign up for a Synology Account** link. If you already have a Synology account and QuickConnect ID - for instance, this is not your first Synology - you can re-use those credentials rather than register for new ones.

Having registered, go into **Control Panel > External Access**, tick the **Enable QuickConnect** box and enter a *QuickConnect ID* of your choosing. The QuickConnect ID must begin with a letter and can contain a mixture of letters, numbers and dashes e.g. *acme-1234*. Click **Apply**. Assuming all is well, after a few seconds the QuickConnect screen will update and give you an external internet address (domain) - known as the *hostname* - for the DiskStation. This takes the form of:

http://QuickConnect.to/nnnnnn e.g. *http://QuickConnect.to/acme-1234*.

This domain name is handled by an external company called *Let's Encrypt*.

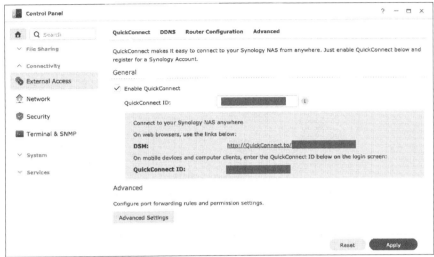

Figure 37: Setting up QuickConnect

Assuming no problems, you can now test the system. From a computer on the network, launch an internet browser and enter the hostname that you were assigned e.g. *http://QuickConnect.to/acme-1234* or whatever it is. Alternatively, go to the *http://QuickConnect.to* website and enter your QuickConnect ID. After a few seconds, you should be greeted with the standard DSM logon screen.

Note: a QuickConnect ID will expire after 60 days of non-use. A few days before this is due to happen, Synology will send out a warning email.

Enabling QuickConnect Within DS Finder

To access your Synology Account using DS Finder, tap **General** at the bottom of the screen, followed by **QuickConnect**. Slide the **Enable QuickConnect** switch to the 'On' position. Tap the **QuickConnect ID** section and enter a QuickConnect ID. This can be an existing QuickConnect ID or you can create one. Tap **Save**.

Figure 38: Enabling QuickConnect using DS Finder

3 SHARED FOLDERS

3.1 Overview

The main purpose of most networks is to provide an environment for users to safely store and share information. This is done by creating folders on the server, some shared and some private, then defining access rights to control who sees what. The structure and names of these folders will depend upon the requirements of the household or organization, but a typical scenario might be: one or more shared folders that everyone has access to; folders for different departments and functions within a business or classes within a school; folders for music, photos and videos in a home system; individual private or 'home' folders for each user, analogous to the Documents folder on a PC or Mac; optionally, a central location to store master copies of programs, drivers, utilities and so on. These folders are referred to as *shared folders* and they reside on the storage volume(s) created in section **2.5 Setting up Storage**. Some applications e.g. Media Server, create their own shared folders.

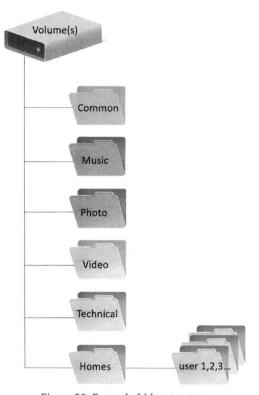

Figure 39: Example folder structure

In this example we have one volume, upon which all the shared folders are created. In a larger system, there may be multiple volumes with the shared folders allocated across them; this technique can be used to enhance security, for instance an organization might keep confidential information on a separate volume away from the main company data, or simply for purposes of tidiness e.g. a separate volume for each class in a school.

3.2 Creating Shared Folders

To create a shared folder, go to **Control Panel > Shared Folder** and click **Create > Create Shared Folder**, which will run the *Shared Folder Creation Wizard*. Our first folder will be for everyone to use and to help make this apparent we will name it *'common'* (or you could call it *family* or *company* or whatever is appropriate for your situation. All the names in this guide are for example only). Optionally, specify a *Description*. If you have multiple volumes on the system, you can use the *Location* drop-down to define which volume the folder will be on. Tick the **Hide sub-folders and files from users without permissions** box. If you want to be able to recover files that have been deleted, tick the **Enable Recycle Bin** and optionally **Restrict access to administrators only** boxes. Click **Next**:

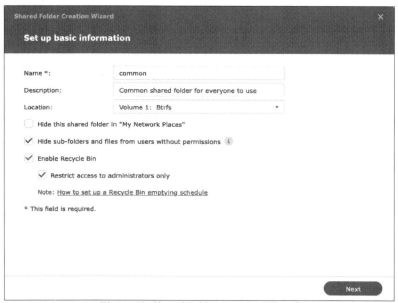

Figure 40: Shared Folder Creation Wizard

On the next panel there are options to *Enable additional security measures*. Because this is optional and further considerations apply, this topic is covered separately in **3.3 Enable Additional Security Measures**. For now we will assume we are using regular folders, so use the **Skip** option and click **Next**:

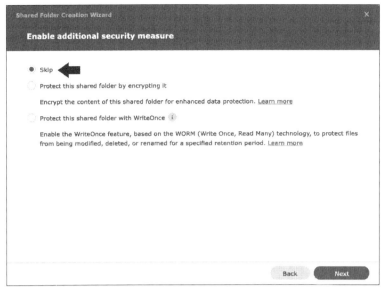

Figure 41: Choose the Skip option

The next panel is to *Configure advanced settings*; however, this is only available if the folder is being created on a volume that has been formatted with *Btrfs* and is grayed out if the volume is formatted as *Ext4*.

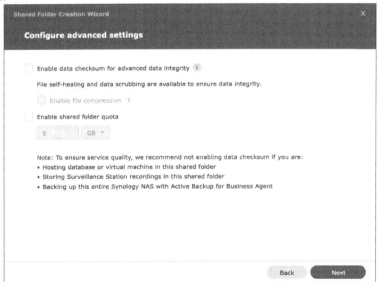

Figure 42: Configure advanced settings

It is recommended that the **Enable data checksum for advanced data integrity** box is ticked, but not the one for file compression.

As there is a performance overhead with data integrity, Synology advise against it if the shared folder is being used to store databases, virtual machines, video recordings from Surveillance Station or Active Backup for Business Agent. Optionally, the maximum size (quota) of the folder can be specified. Click **Next**.

A *Confirm settings* screen is displayed – click **Next** to create the folder. Having done so, you will be taken to a screen for configuring user permissions, meaning who has access to the folder and the nature of that access. There are three basic options: *Read/Write* (do anything); *Read only* (access it, but no changes allowed); *No access*; along with a fourth *Custom* option. This can be a chicken-and-egg situation, as you may not yet have created any users, a topic which is covered in section **4.2 Creating Users**. For now, give the administrators **Read/Write** access (i.e. *systemadmin* in our example, in addition to the built-in *admin* user). By default, the user *guest* does not receive access to shared folders. Click **Apply**. If you need to return to this screen on a subsequent occasion, go into **Shared Folder**, highlight the folder, click **Edit** then click the **Permissions** tab.

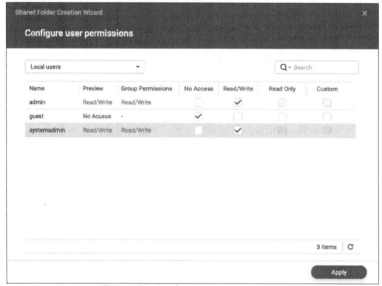

Figure 43: Configure user permissions

Optionally, create a further folder called *technical*, this time with the **Hide this shared folder in My Network Places** box ticked in addition to the **Hide folders and files from users without permissions** box. As the folders are created, they will be listed in the Shared Folder section of the Control Panel.

3.3 Enable Additional Security Measures

When creating a shared folder, there is a panel to *Enable additional security measure*. Some users may not need this and hence skip it, as we did when creating shared folders in section **3.2 Creating Shared Folders**. However, the available options provide higher levels of security for storing confidential information and, in the case of businesses, may also help in compliance with local legislation regarding data protection and privacy.

Create a new shared folder by clicking **Control Panel > Shared Folder > Create > Create Shared Folder**. Specify the *Name*, *Description* and *Location*, click **Next**, and the second panel is displayed. If the shared folder is being created on a volume formatted as Btrfs, there will be two, mutually exclusive, security options: *Encryption*, and *WriteOnce*. If the volume is formatted as ext4, WriteOnce will not be available.

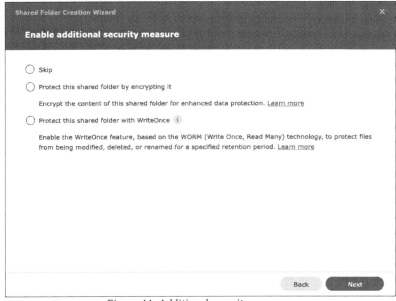

Figure 44: Additional security measures

Encryption

An encrypted shared folder cannot be accessed without a copy of the encryption key that is generated during its creation, thereby protecting it. Individual shared folders can be encrypted, regardless of whether the underlying volume is encrypted or not and can be on Btrfs or Ext4 volumes. Encryption can also be applied retrospectively to an existing shared folder.

The following considerations apply with encrypted folders:
- The encryption key needs to be at least 8 characters in length.
- There is no way to recover the data if the encryption key is lost.
- Folders can be mounted and unmounted as required.
- Access to encrypted folders can be slower than to standard (unencrypted) ones, which may be a consideration on less powerful systems.
- Encrypted folders cannot be accessed by Linux/Unix computers.
- The name of any file or folder within an encrypted folder must be less than 143 English alphabet characters or 43 Asian characters in length.
- Optionally, an additional feature called *Key Manager* needs to be enabled.

It is only necessary to enter and confirm an encryption key. Click the **Protect this shared folder by encrypting it** option, followed by **Next**. On the resultant panel, enter and confirm the encryption key; the key needs to be at least 8 characters in length and you should use something non-obvious, such as a mixture of random letters and numerals. Click **Next** and continue working through the steps to create the shared folder. On the *Confirm settings* screen, there will be a message that the encryption key will be downloaded automatically to your computer, but that you might wish to save a copy elsewhere. Click **OK** to acknowledge the message.

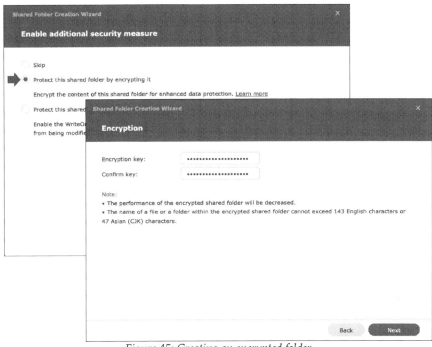

Figure 45: Creating an encrypted folder

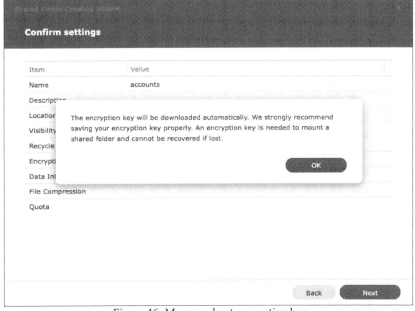

Figure 46: Message about encryption key

On the next panel, specify the user permissions for the folder, which will then be created and listed in the *Shared Folder* Control Panel screen. It has a small padlock on the folder icon to indicate its status, which will be open if mounted or locked if unmounted:

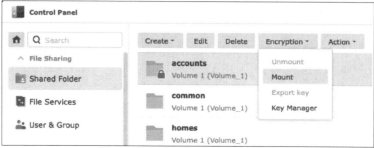

Figure 47: Mount an encrypted folder

When an encrypted shared folder is created, it will initially be unlocked and mounted. However, each time the DiskStation restarts it will be unmounted. To mount and make it available for users, highlight and click **Encryption > Mount**. Clearly this need for manual intervention may be inconvenient or impractical and hence there is a way to automate the process. Within **Control Panel > Shared Folder**, highlight the encrypted folder and click **Encryption > Key Manager** to display the following panel:

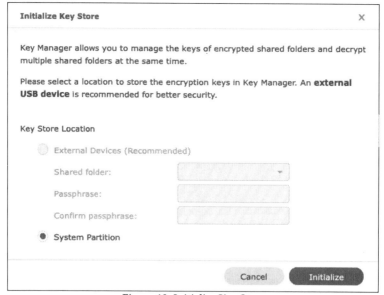

Figure 48: Initialize Key Store

The location of the Key Store can be specified. Many users will find it more convenient to keep it on the System Partition (meaning the DiskStation itself), although it could be kept on an external USB memory device, which would greatly enhance security as if the memory stick was not present then the folder would not be available. Click **Initialize**. Note that this is a one-off screen and you will not see it subsequently, so if you intend to use a USB memory stick it should be inserted and selected before proceeding. The memory stick should be formatted as *Ext4*.

On the next screen, click **Add**. Check that the Shared Folder is selected (*accounts*, in our example), that the Cypher is set to **Machine key**, enter the Encryption key or import it from the download generated previously, then click **OK**. Upon returning to the previous screen, make sure the **Automount** box is ticked for the folder. To confirm everything is working, restart the server and make sure that the folder mounts correctly.

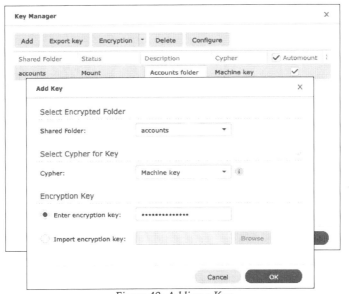

Figure 49: Adding a Key

Encrypting an Existing Folder

Encryption can be added to existing shared folders. Go into **Control Panel > Shared Folder**. Highlight the folder and click the **Edit** button. Click the **Encryption** tab. Tick the **Encrypt this shared folder** box, specify and confirm the Encryption key and follow the instructions given previously in this section.

WriteOnce

The WriteOnce security feature is based on WORM (Write Once Read Many) technology. Files stored in WriteOnce folders cannot subsequently be modified, deleted or renamed for a specified retention period, or ever. There are many scenarios where this is useful or required: legal records which cannot be amended need to be stored; unalterable accounting records must be retained for a specified period; a school or college requires a 'drop zone' where students can post their assignments. WriteOnce is only available on volumes which have been formatted with Btrfs.

When creating a new shared folder, tick the **Protect this shared folder with WriteOnce** option and click **Next**. Acknowledge the message about the Recycle Bin being automatically disabled by clicking **Yes**.

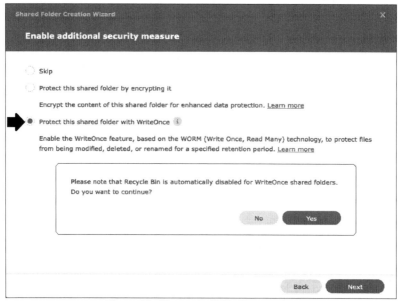

Figure 50: Choose the WriteOnce option

On the subsequent screen, there is a choice of *Enterprise mode* or *Compliance mode*, using a dropdown. With the former, the folder can only be deleted by administrators; with the latter, nobody can delete it i.e. it is truly permanent. Various options can be set; with *Auto Lock*, a file can be modified for a fixed period, after which it is locked. A *Retention* period can be chosen, or the file can be set to remain locked forever. Finally, the *Lock state* can be specified, whereby information can be appended to a file, or it can be set as immutable.

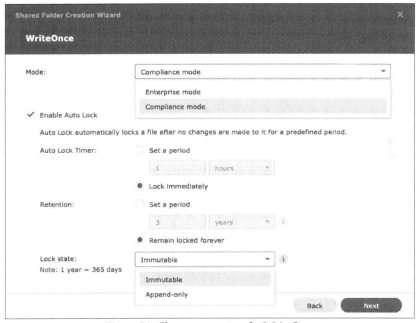

Figure 51: Choose parameters for WriteOnce

Click **Next** to proceed to the *Configure advance settings* panel. Specify any required options and click **Next**. Note that the **Enable data checksum for advanced data integrity** option is pre-ticked and cannot be changed if you are using Compliance mode. Click **Next** on the *Confirm settings* panel. If you are using Compliance mode, a message will be shown, advising that the folder cannot be subsequently deleted – tick the box and click **Continue**.

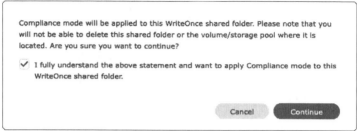

Figure 52: Message about Compliance mode

On the next panel, configure user permissions and click **Apply** to create the folder. It will appear in the list of shared folders, with a small 'WriteOnce' indicator against it to show its status:

Figure 53: Indicator for WriteOnce folder

3.4 Changing, Deleting or Cloning a Shared Folder

Changing
If there is a subsequent need to change the settings of a shared folder, for instance to rename it or change the user permissions, this must be done from the **Shared Folder** option in **Control Panel** (it cannot be done using *File Station*). Highlight the folder and click the **Edit** button.

Deleting
To delete a shared folder, highlight it and click **Delete**. There will be a warning message that has to be acknowledged, plus it is necessary to enter the administrator password as an additional safety check.

Shared folders which have been created automatically by certain applications and services should not be changed in any way. Examples include: *ActiveBackupforBusiness*, *NetBackup* (created when rsync is enabled), *surveillance* (created by Surveillance Station), and *web* (created by Web Station).

Figure 54: Deleting a shared folders

Cloning
When creating a shared folder, you may have noticed that there is an option to clone an existing folder as well as create a new one, although this option will only be available if you are using a Btrfs volume.

The advantages of cloned folders are that they are created instantaneously and use only a fraction of the storage space at the time of their creation. To clone an existing shared folder, highlight the folder, click **Create** and chose **Clone** from the dropdown:

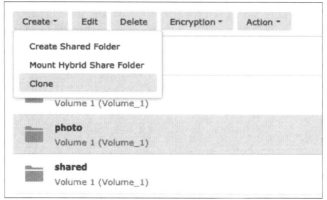

Figure 55: Clone option

On the resultant panel there are two tabs, *General* and *Advanced*. On the **General** tab, specify the *Name*, optional *Description* and other parameters, as when creating a new shared folder. On the **Advanced** tab, a quota (maximum size) for the folder can be specified (the other options will not be available). Click **Save**. Specify the user Permissions as per usual and click **Save**. The cloned folder will be created.

3.5 Loading Existing Data into Shared Folders

There may be a requirement to load data from existing computers or systems onto the NAS and into the new shared folders that have been created. There are a couple of ways to do so:

Method One: Wait until the network is up and running i.e. shared folders have been created, users have been defined, computers are connected and able to access the server. Then, login from each computer and copy data from the user's folders to the appropriate folders on the server.

Method Two: Visit each individual computer and copy data from the user's folders to an external plug-in USB drive. Then, connect the USB drive to the server and copy it to the appropriate folders on the server. The advantage of this method is that it can be done before or in parallel with setting up the server, thus saving time.

An anti-virus/malware check should be run on the computers *before* copying any data. It is also a good idea to first review the data on the computers and prune (delete) any unrequired and duplicate data, rather than carry it forward to the new environment.

3.6 Enabling Home Folders

The folders that have just been created are shared folders, potentially for the use of everyone on the network. It is also possible to create individual *home folders* for users, where they can store their own personal data that only they need access to, analogous to the Documents folder on personal computers. Also, some apps and features assume home folders and will not function unless they are used. To enable home folders, click **Control Panel > User & Group**, then click the **Advanced** tab. In the *User Home* section, which is towards the bottom of the screen, tick the **Enable user home service** box. If you have multiple volumes in the system, you can optionally specify a *Location*. Click **Apply**, which will result in home folders being created automatically when users login for the first time. From the user's perspective, their home folder is simply called *home*. Behind the scenes, the individual home folders correspond to the names of the individual users, contained within a shared folder called *homes*.

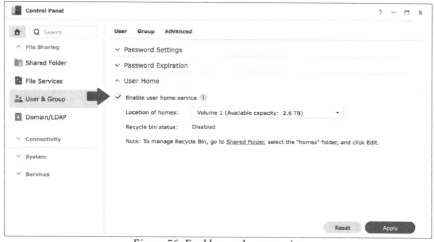

Figure 56: Enable user home service

Having enabled the User home service, go back to **Control Panel** and click on **Shared Folder**. Highlight the entry for the *homes* folder and click **Edit**. Tick the **Hide this shared folder in 'My Network Places'** and **Hide sub-folders and files from users without permissions** boxes.

If you wish users to recover items that they have deleted, tick the **Enable Recycle Bin box** (if you want only Administrators to be able to undelete files, tick the **Restrict access to administrators only** box). Click **Save**. The Shared Folder section in the Control Panel should now appear something like this:

Figure 57: List of shared folders

3.7 ACL (Access Control Lists)

When a shared folder is created on the DiskStation, the access permissions are specified as *Read/Write*, *Read only* or *No access* and in most home and small business environments, that choice of options will be sufficient. However, in some scenarios it will not provide the necessary granularity for precise control over folders and individual files. If you work in information technology and have used Windows Server, then you may be familiar with ACL or *Access Control Lists*, which are designed to do this, and DSM supports the ACL mechanism. The purpose of this section is not to explain ACL, but to illustrate how it is implemented in DSM for the benefit of those who understand what it is and wish to use it.

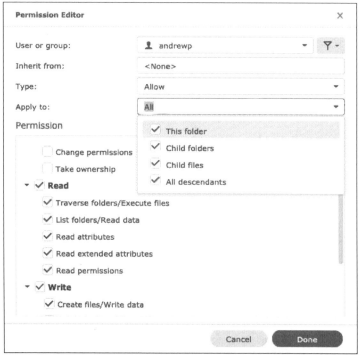

Figure 58: Permission Editor and ACL attributes

Go into **Control Panel > Shared Folder**. Highlight the folder you wish to exercise greater control over and click the **Edit** button. Click the **Permissions** tab. A list of users – or you can choose to display groups instead – is displayed, along with four columns that show the current access permissions.

Click a user/group name to highlight it, then click the **Custom** column, which will launch the *Permission Editor*. From here you can control the access attributes supported by ACL, plus whether those rights are inherited and what folders and files they apply to. Having made changes, click **Done**, followed by **Save** on the previous screen.

4 MANAGING USERS

4.1 Overview

To access the DiskStation, it is necessary to have a *user account* for it. During the installation of DSM an initial administrator account had to be created; if you are the only person who will ever use the DiskStation, you can work with that user account for everything and skip this chapter altogether. However, if other people will also be using it, as is typically the case in a home, business or educational environment, then you will need to create user accounts for them.

You should consider a naming convention and a different approach can be taken depending on whether it is a home or business or educational network. In the case of a home or small network, the user names can be anything you want, although there is merit in following a scheme. For instance, you could use the first names of the family or household members. In a business or educational environment, a more formal approach may be more appropriate and the greater consistency there is, the better. Two popular conventions are to use the first name plus the initial of the surname, alternatively the initial of the first name plus the surname, although in some parts of the world other conventions might be more appropriate. In the case of particularly long names and double-barrelled names, one option is to abbreviate them. For example:

Name of Person	User Name	or	User Name
Nick Rushton	nickr		nrushton
Daniela Petrova	danielap		dpetrova
Mary O'Hara	maryoh		mohara
Ian Smith	ians		ismith
Amber Williams	amberw		awilliams
James Hanson-Smith	jameshs		jhansmith

4.2 Creating Users

To create a user, go into **Control Panel** and click the **User & Group** icon. On the **User** tab, click the **Create** button. This button is a dropdown with three entries: the first is to create a single user; the second is to import a list of names to be turned into users which is useful in, say, a larger organization or educational institution; the third is to copy an existing user. However, if the main section of the button is clicked quickly then DSM will assume you want to create a single user.

As a household or small business will typically have a relatively small number of users, we will create them one at a time (for creating users in bulk, see **4.4 Importing a List of Users**). Enter the user's account name, an optional description for them e.g. their full name, a password plus its confirmation. The best passwords are non-obvious and comprise a mixture of upper- and lower-case letters, mixed with numbers and symbols; DSM can also generate a random password if required, by clicking the **Generate Random Password** button. By default, DSM requires a password of at least eight characters (to modify this requirement see section **6.5 Password Settings**) and will rate its strength as it is created.

Optionally, click the **Disallow the user to change account password** box - this can be useful in schools with young children, or where shared accounts are used. It is not necessary to specify the email address or send a notification mail to the newly created user, although this may be helpful in the case of remote users. Click **Next**.

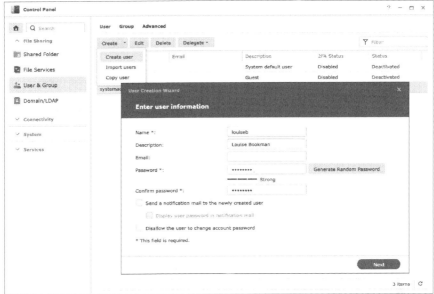

Figure 59: Creating a new User

The following screen is for defining which *groups* the user will be a member of; by default they will become a member of the built-in *users* group. Do not make them a member of the *administrators* group, as access to this should be restricted to the main administrator user(s) only. Click **Next**:

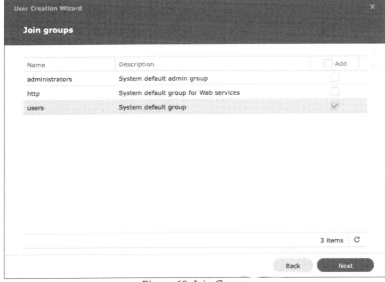

Figure 60: Join Groups

The subsequent screen defines which folders the user has access to. The three choices are: *No access*, meaning they have no access at all to the folder; *Read/Write*, meaning they can do anything with the folder; *Read Only*, meaning that the user can use the files in the folder but cannot update them or add to the folder. Assign the appropriate permissions as follows: **Read/Write** to *common*; **No access** to *technical*; leave *homes* blank. If you have created additional folders, you may wish to set permissions for them. Click **Next**.

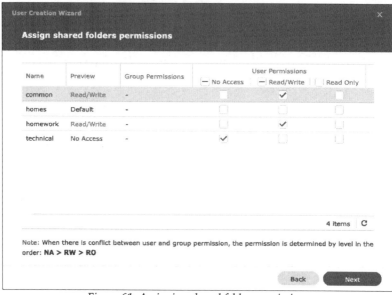

Figure 61: Assigning shared folder permissions

The follow-on screen is for setting a storage quota, meaning how much disk space in Gigabytes (GB), Megabytes (MB) or Terabytes (TB) the user is permitted, specifiable on a per-folder basis. As disk space is cheap and plentiful this is not commonly done in a home or small business setting, so you may wish to ignore this step by clicking **Next**. However, it may be useful in, for example, an educational setting, or in a commercial operation where users are charged for how much storage they have.

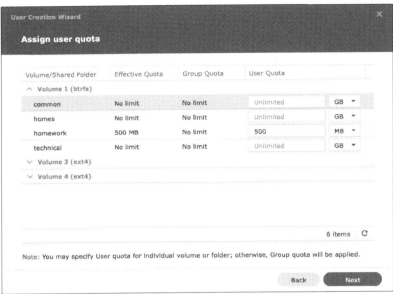

Figure 62: User quota setting

The subsequent screen controls which applications the user can access. At a minimum, everyone should have access to *DSM, File Station* and *SMB*, but the other applications would only be if needed. Click **Next**. Note that if applications are subsequently installed from the *Package Center* then this list of applications may gain additional entries and it may be necessary to revisit the user's settings. The list of default application privileges for users can be edited using **Control Panel > Application Privileges**.

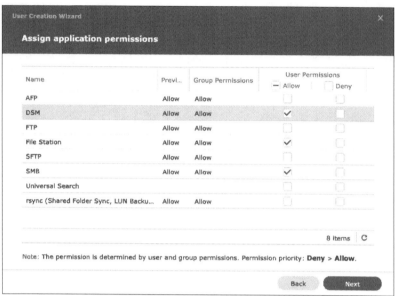

Figure 63: Assigning application permissions

The following screen is for controlling the speed of access to certain applications. This is not something that would commonly be used is most settings, so just click **Next** to ignore it. Finally, a *Confirm Settings* screen is displayed - click **Done** to proceed and the user will be created, with their details subsequently listed on the main User panel.

This process should be repeated until all the users have been created. If you have multiple users to create, you may find it helpful to first create a checklist of their names and to make a note of the passwords.

4.3 Modifying, Copying, Deactivating and Deleting Users

To modify an existing user, go to **Control Panel > User & Group**. Highlight the user's name and click the **Edit** button. This provides access to the information that was specified when the user was created and which can now be modified e.g. group membership, permissions, applications. The user's password can be changed on the **Info** panel. Having made any changes, click **Save**.

A new user can be created more quickly by copying an existing one. Go to **Control Panel > User & Group**, highlight an existing user, click the **Create** dropdown and choose **Copy user** to invoke the first panel of the *User Creation Wizard*. It is only necessary to enter the new user's name, password and password confirmation, click **Next** and then **Done** on the Confirm settings screen. The new user will have the same permissions and characteristics as the original user.

When a user leaves an organization, their account should in the first instance be deactivated to prevent it being used. It is preferable to do this rather than immediately delete the account, as there may subsequently be a need to access it or the user may return at a later date e.g. if they are on parental or long-term sick leave. To deactivate an account, highlight the user's name, click **Edit**, place a tick in the **Deactivate this account** box and click **Save**. There is a choice between deactivating the account immediately, or after a certain date. Another use for this feature is in educational settings, where student accounts can be set deactivate when the student is scheduled to leave the institution.

To permanently delete a user, go to **Control Panel > User & Group**. Highlight the user's name then click the **Delete** button. A warning message is displayed, advising that the user's data will be deleted. Acknowledge it and click **Delete**. Then, enter your administrative password and click **Submit**.

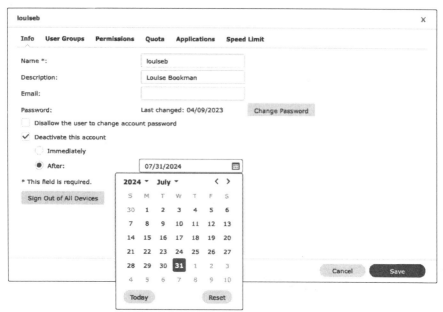

Figure 64: Deactivating an account on a specific date

4.4 Importing a List of Users

In a domestic or small business setting, creating users one at a time is unproblematic. But when many need to be created, such as in a larger business or an educational setting, it can be time consuming. To speed up matters, DSM can create users from a list in spreadsheet format; this list can be produced manually using a program such as Excel, or it might be possible to generate it from another computer system, such as a school registration system or human resources application.

The file needs to be in CSV format with UTF-8 encoding. It should be structured as follows:

Column A – Username

Column B – Password

Column C – Description

Column D – Email address (optional)

Column E – User Group. Should be defaulted to *users*. To specify multiple groups, separate them using commas and put quotation marks around the list e.g. "sales, marketing, accounts"

Column F – Storage quota in MB – optional, otherwise leave blank for no quota (quotas are for ext4 volumes only and are not supported on Btrfs volumes). This column is for *volume1*, if there are multiple volumes then column G would be *volume2*, H would be *volume3* and so on.

	A	B	C	D	E
1	danielap	Bulgaria1234	Daniela Petrova		users
2	stevew	France5678	Steve White		users
3	ians	Canada9012	Ian Smith		users
4	jasveenk	India3456	Jasveen Kumar		users
5	gustavh	Germany7890	Gustav Horst		users
6	maryo	Ireland1234	Mary Ohara		users
7	andrewp	America5678	Andrew Palmer		users

Figure 65: Example spreadsheet for creating users

To import the list, go to **Control Panel > User & Group** and click **Create > Import users**. On the resultant panel, change the *Delimiter* to **Comma** then click **Browse** to locate the file containing the list of users. The *Status* column should be blank; if it is not, correct the underlying problem in the spreadsheet and retry. Optionally, tick any required boxes e.g. 'Force password change for imported users upon initial login'. Click **OK** and the usernames will be created:

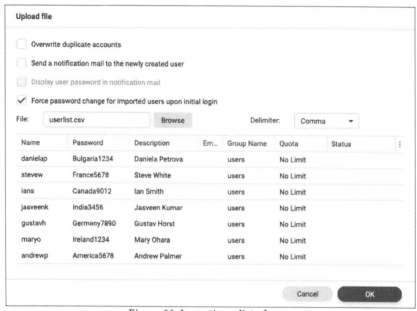

Figure 66: Importing a list of users

Note that having created the users in this time-saving manner, it may still be necessary to edit them on an individual basis to assign permissions and applications. This process can be expedited using groups, as described in the next section.

4.5 Groups

In an organization with a relatively small number of users, specifying who has rights to shared folders and applications is easy to manage. But as the number of users increases it clearly becomes more time consuming, for instance consider having to define the access rights for, say, 30 people. Such organizations are usually large enough that they contain departments or teams to carry out the different functions, for example there might be several people working in accounts, several in sales, several in marketing and so on. A further example would be an educational institution, where students need to be organized into classes or cohorts.

To support these typical structures, DSM features the concept of *groups*. A group consists of multiple users who have something in common within the organization, such as they are all members of the same team. Access rights can be specified for the group, which means they then apply to all members of that group. If a new person joins the team they can be defined as a member of the group, at which point they inherit all the relevant access rights. There is a built-in group in DSM called *users* which all users are automatically members of, but you can create additional ones to reflect the specific needs of the organization.

In this example, we will create a group called *sales* whose members alone have access to a corresponding folder of the same name (although it does not need to have the same name and we only doing this for convenience). Begin by creating a shared folder called *sales*. The method for creating shared folders is described in **3.2 Creating Shared Folders**, but in summary: **Control Panel > Shared Folder > Create > Create Shared Folder**. Name the folder *sales* and tick the **Hide this shared folder in My Network Places** and **Hide sub-folders and files from users without permissions** boxes. Give **Read/Write** access to the administrator user only.

Launch **Control Panel**, click **User & Group**, and on the **Group** tab click the **Create** button. Name the group *sales*, enter an optional description and click **Next**. On the subsequent screen, select the users who will be members of the new group, then click **Next**:

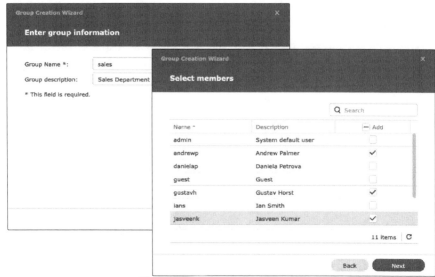

Figure 67: Group Creation Wizard

On the subsequent screen give **Read/Write** permissions to the *sales* and other required folders, **No access** to *technical*, and leave *homes* blank (this is just for example, your organization may have different requirements). Click **Next**.

Figure 68: Assign shared folder permissions

Skip the next three screens of *Assign group quota*, *Assign application permissions* and *Set group speed limit* unless you have specific requirements, then click **Done** on the *Confirm settings* panel. After a few seconds the new group will be created and you will be taken back to the Group section within Control Panel, where it will be listed.

To make changes to an existing group e.g. add or remove members, highlight it within **Control Panel > User & Group > Group** and click **Edit**. Click the **Members** tab, place or remove ticks against the users and click **Save**.

The benefit of groups is that the creation of additional users or changes to existing users becomes easier. For instance, when a new user is created they just have to be specified as being a member of a particular group to automatically inherit all the rights associated with that group. The larger and more structured the organization, the more benefits accrue from this approach.

You may have noticed that there were already some groups in existence: *administrators*, *http* and *users*. These are special built-in groups created by DSM and should not be modified.

4.6 Delegation

When users are created in DSM, they are automatically assigned as a member of the built-in *users* group; optionally, they also may be assigned to other groups that have been created, as described in **4.5 Groups**. They should not normally be assigned as *administrators*, due to the capabilities that admin users have and which are not needed by ordinary users and, as a general principle, there should only be one administrator on the system. However, whilst this is fine in a typical home or small business system, in a larger organization it can lead to bottlenecks if a single person is responsible for all aspects of managing the system. To help reduce this management workload, certain pre-defined roles can be delegated to selected regular users. For example, in a large business with many departments it might be appropriate for each to have a 'point person' who could create local users and shared folders, likewise in an educational institution with multiple classrooms and year groups.

The following parameters apply to delegated users:

The maximum number of users who can be given delegated roles is 32.

The maximum number of groups who can be given delegated roles is 32.

A delegated user is unable to manage settings that belong to admin users or the *administrators* group.

A delegated user cannot change their own settings in Control Panel.

Delegated users cannot assign higher privilege settings than they possess to other users. For example, if they have only read only access to a particular shared folder, then they cannot assign read and write permissions to it for another user.

To delegate roles to a user, in **Control Panel > User & Group**, highlight the user's name on the **User** tab and click **Delegate > Delegated Administration**. There are initially six roles which can be delegated: *Local user and group management; Directory account and group management; Shared folder management; Access control and management; System monitoring; System service management.* Some packages may add additional roles when installed e.g. Hyper Backup. Place ticks in the required boxes, click **OK** and enter the administrator's password to authorize the change when prompted.

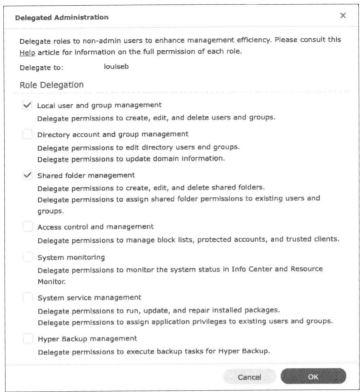

Figure 69: Delegation options

Roles can be delegated not just on a user level, but also on a group level. For instance, you could create a new group called, say, *localadmin* and then delegate roles to that group rather than to named individuals.

4.7 User Personalization Settings

Each user can personalize their individual desktop and the behavior of DSM. This includes wallpaper, choice of desktop icons and their size, Main Menu style and language. A user can also reset their password. To change items, the user should click the **Options** icon in the top right-hand corner of the screen – it looks like the head and shoulders of a person - and choose **Personal** from the drop-down menu. The Personal screen contains six tabs: *Account*, *Security*, *Display Preferences*, *Email Delivery*, *Quota* and *Others*.

Account

Click the **Account** tab to display the following panel:

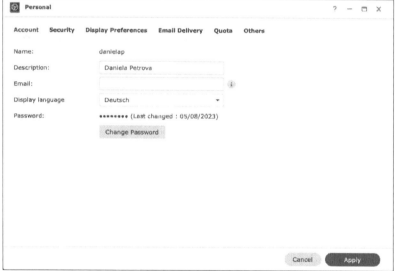

Figure 70: Account information

Although the user's *Name* cannot be changed, the user *Description* can be changed at any point, which may be useful if a person subsequently changes their given name. The user can also add, or change an existing email address, which can be used to contact them if they forget their password.

A user can work with DSM in the language of their choice, regardless of which language the server is configured in, with more than 20 are supported. This can be useful in environments where multiple languages are used, such as English and Spanish in parts of the United States, or French and English in Canada.

To switch language from the default System setting, use the *Display language* drop-down.

A user can change their password by clicking **Change Password**. They should enter the current password, their new password, confirm the new password and click **Apply**.

Having made changes, click **Save**.

Security

Click the **Security** tab to display the following panel:

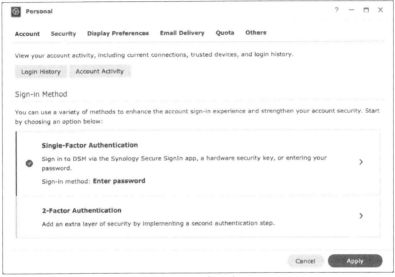

Figure 71: Security

By clicking the **Login History** and **Account Activity** buttons, the user can check when they have previously used the NAS. To improve security, they can opt to use Passwordless Sign-In or 2-Factor Authentication if these have been activated on the DiskStation (see **6.6 Improving Sign-In Security**). Having made changes, click **Apply**.

Display Preferences

Clicking the **Display Preferences** tab enables the user to customize their view of DSM.

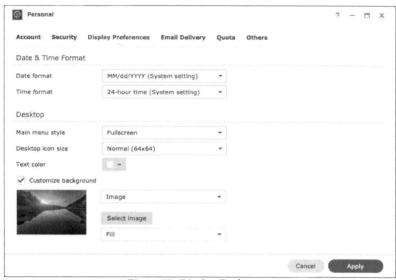

Figure 72: Display Preferences

The date format can be changed using the dropdowns. There is a choice of nine, e.g. YYYY/MM/dd, dd-MM-YYYY, MM/dd/YYYY and so on. The time format can be switched between the 12- and 24-hour formats.

The Main Menu can be viewed full-screen or as a drop-down in the top left-hand corner of the screen. Click on the *Main menu style* dropdown and choose.

Using the dropdown, the *Desktop icon size* can be switched between two sizes. The color of the text for the icons can be changed, using the *Text color* dropdown. When viewing the Main Menu or the Control Panel, drag an icon from it towards the left-hand side of the screen and a copy will be placed on the Desktop. To remove an icon from the Desktop, right-click it and click **Remove Shortcut**.

The Desktop background ('wallpaper') can be customized. Tick the **Customize background** box and use the dropdown to choose between an image or a solid color. To specify a particular image, click the **Select image** button. There is a choice between several built-in wallpapers, or a picture on the NAS can be selected, or a file can be uploaded from the local computer (**My Images > Upload**). If uploading an image, it should be JPEG/JPG or PNG format and preferably no larger than a couple of Mbytes.

Having made any changes, click **Save**.

Email Delivery

If an email account is added, it becomes possible to send files from File Station as attachments, share files with others via Synology Drive, and send invitations via Synology Calendar. To set this up, go to the **Email Delivery** tab and click **Add**. Choose an email service provider, click **Next** and enter details of the email account, with a choice of Google, Outlook or a customized SMTP service.

Quota

If storage quotas for shared folders have been set, they can be viewed from the **Quota** tab.

Other

Having signed into DSM, the user is presented with a clear desktop. However, it might be desired that DSM remembers the applications and windows that were open when the system was last used. To enable this, tick the **Resume DSM to my previous logout status when signed in** box.

Desktop keyboard shortcuts can be enabled by ticking the appropriate box. These shortcuts can be used to navigate DSM without having to use the mouse. To see a list of keyboard shortcuts, press **Shift ?** (question mark).

Having made any changes to any settings in Personal, click the **Save** button, which will also close the screen.

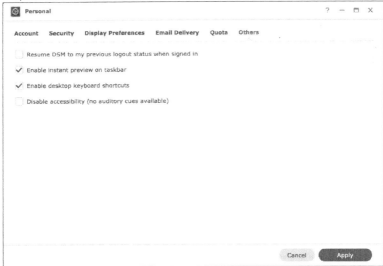

Figure 73: 'Others' tab

4.8 Managing Users with DS Finder

The most comprehensive options for managing users are available by logging in to DSM using a browser, as described in the previous sections of this chapter. However, users can also be created using the DS Finder app on an Android or iOS tablet or smartphone.

To create a user, launch and login to DS Finder. From the General screen, tap **User Management**. A list of existing users is displayed; to create a new one, tap the + ('plus') sign in the top right-hand corner of the screen.

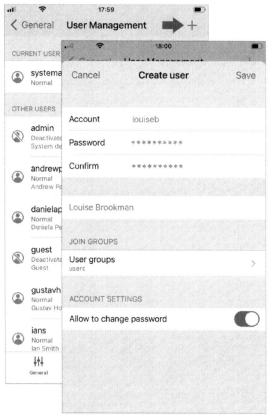

Figure 74: Creating a new user with DS Finder

Enter the user's login name, a password and its confirmation (the best passwords are non-obvious and comprise a mixture of upper- and lower-case letters, mixed with numbers and symbols), an optional description for them e.g. their full name.

Optionally, slide the **Allow to change password** switch if you want users to be able to do this. If they need to be specified as members of a group, this can also be done by tapping the User groups section. Tap **Save**. There will be a message about sending a notification to the newly created user.

The newly created user will then be listed on the previous screen, from where they can subsequently be edited if required. User accounts can be disabled, immediately or after a specific date, on this screen.

5 CONNECTING TO THE SERVER

5.1 Overview

There are multiple methods for accessing the DiskStation, some of which are specific to Windows only, some to macOS, whereas others work for most platforms. There are also apps available for connecting smartphones and tablets.

5.2 Using a Browser and File Station

This is a universal method for accessing the DiskStation and works for Windows PCs, Macs, Linux computers and Chromebooks. Using any computer on the local network, launch a browser such as Firefox, Edge, Chrome or Safari, and type in the name or IP address of the server e.g. *server*, *192.168.1.2* etc. The standard DSM sign-in screen is displayed; the user should enter their name and password and they will be presented with a minimalist Desktop. By default, all they can access is File Station (unless additional options have been granted to them) and which can be launched by clicking its icon, which appears on the Desktop and in the Main Menu. Within File Station they can see the folders and files that belong to them or to which they have been granted access, such as their home folder and any shared folders.

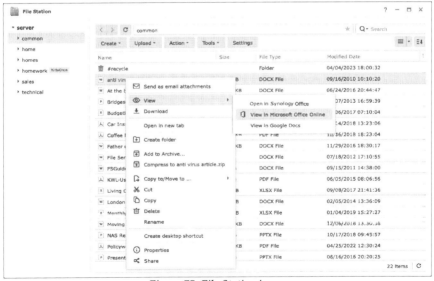

Figure 75: File Station in use

To work with a file or folder, right-click it and a pop-up menu will appear with the various available options. Alternatively, highlight it and click the **Action** button.

There are options to view and edit documents, spreadsheets and presentations using *Google Docs* or *Microsoft Office Online*, or *Synology Office* if it has been installed (see **10 SYNOLOGY DRIVE SERVER, OFFICE & APPS**). To edit a file, choose the **Download** option to first download it to the local computer. Make the changes to the document using Word, Excel or other preferred application, then use the **Upload** button in File Station to upload the new version back to the server. An alternative, but for viewing files only and on x86 DiskStations, is described in **15.10 Document Viewer**. Most graphic files and photographs can be viewed by double-clicking them, and from there they can be zoomed and manipulated. MP3 music files and MP4 video files can be played. There are also common file manipulation commands for copying, renaming, deleting files and so on.

If QuickConnect has been configured (see section **2.7 QuickConnect: The Key to Remote Connectivity**), then the DiskStation can also be accessed remotely using a browser in the same way. Instead of entering the internal IP address, when away from the premises you enter the hostname that you assigned e.g. *http://QuickConnect.to/acme1234* or whatever it is. Alternatively, go to the *http://QuickConnect.to* website and enter your QuickConnect ID. After a few seconds, you should be greeted with the standard DSM sign-on screen.

When the user has finished, they should click the **Options** icon in the top right-corner of the screen depicting a human head and shoulders and choose **Sign Out**.

5.3 Connecting Windows Computers
File Explorer/Windows Explorer
A simple way to access the server directly is by going into File Explorer (called Windows Explorer in early versions of Windows). Expand the left-hand panel to view the Network and down the left-hand side the server should be visible. Click on it and the list of shared folders will be displayed:

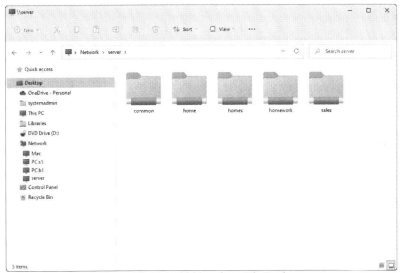

Figure 76: List of folders from File Explorer

To access a shared folder, double-click it – you will be prompted to enter a user name and password as defined previously on the server. If you wish, tick the option box to remember the login details, although you should only do this if you are the sole user of the computer. Although many shared folders may be visible, you can only access the ones to which you have privileges.

Accessing Shared Folders Using the Run Command
To access a shared folder from a Windows computer, right-click the **Start** button and choose **Run** if using Windows 11, 10 or 8.1, else click **Start** and **Run** if using Windows 7. Alternatively, hold down the **Windows key** and press the letter **R**. In the small dialog box that appears, type in the name of the shared folder using the format *server**name_of_folder* e.g. *server**shared* and click **OK**.

The contents of the folder will be displayed in File Explorer/Windows Explorer, from where the files can be used in the standard way. Note that you may be prompted to enter a user name and password as defined previously on the server.

Mapping Drives Manually

Some techniques provide access to shared folders by referring to them using what are called UNC or *Universal Naming Convention* names, which take the form of *server**shared*. However, many Windows users are accustomed to and prefer to use drive letters, such as C, D, E and so on. The process by which a UNC name can be turned into a drive letter is known as *mapping* and there are several ways to do this, discussed in the following sections. You can use whatever drive letters you wish, provided they are not already in use, but using corresponding letters makes things easier. For example, map the *home* drive to H. In our system, we are using a shared folder called *common* – this cannot be mapped to C as that is always in use on a Windows computer, so you could consider using Z as an alternative.

The first method for mapping uses File Explorer, and the process varies slightly between different versions of Windows.

Windows 11

Open File Explorer, which appears on the Taskbar by default. Expand the left-hand panel to view the Network and click the server to display the list of shared folders. You may be prompted to enter a valid user name and password as previously defined on the server; if you wish, tick the option box to remember the login details, although you should only do this if you are the sole user of the computer. Right-click the shared folder and choose **Show more options** or press **Shift F10**, followed by **Map network drive**. On the resultant panel, specify the Drive letter using the dropdown and click **Finish**. Upon a successful connection, the contents of the newly mapped drive will be displayed. The process should now be repeated for each shared folder that is needed.

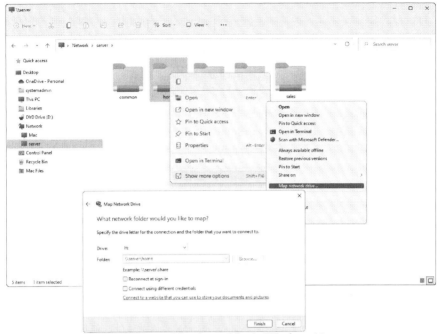

Figure 77: Mapping a drive in Windows 11

Windows 10

Open File Explorer, which appears on the Taskbar by default. Expand the left-hand panel to view the Network and click the server to display the list of shared folders. You may be prompted to enter a valid user name and password as previously defined on the server; if you wish, tick the option box to remember the login details, although you should only do this if you are the sole user of the computer. Right-click the shared folder and on the pop-up menu click **Map network drive**.

On the resultant panel, specify the Drive letter using the dropdown and click **Finish**. Upon a successful connection, the contents of the newly mapped drive will be displayed. The process should now be repeated for each shared folder that is needed.

Windows 7

Open Windows Explorer, which usually appears on the Taskbar by default, else click **My Computer** on the Start menu. If the menu bar is not displayed, click **Organize > Layout > Menu bar** to display it. Expand the left-hand panel to view the Network and click the server to display the list of shared folders. You may be prompted to enter a valid user name and password as previously defined on the server; if you wish, tick the option box to remember the login details, although you should only do this if you are the sole user of the computer. Right-click the shared folder and choose **Map network drive**. On the resultant panel, specify the Drive letter using the dropdown and click **Finish**. Upon a successful connection, the contents of the newly mapped drive will be displayed. The process should now be repeated for each shared folder that is needed.

Using Synology Assistant

Synology Assistant is a flexible utility that can do multiple things, one of which is mapping drives. One benefit of using it is consistency in a Windows environment: when drives are mapped manually as described above, there are small variations in the procedure depending on which version of Windows is being used, but with Synology Assistant it is the same process regardless of the version. Mac and Linux versions of Synology Assistant are also available but do not map drives, which is a Windows concept, and so are not applicable here.

Download and install Synology Assistant on each Windows computer. If you receive a message from the computer's firewall, grant the Synology Assistant access. An icon will be placed on the computer's desktop – double-click it to run it and the following window is displayed.

The server should be listed after a few seconds. If it does not appear click the **Search** button; if it still does not appear then there is a problem of some sort, such as the computer is not connected to network, the DiskStation not powered on, or the firewall needs configuring on the computer. Highlight the server entry and the **Map Drive** button will be enabled – clicking it will cause the *Synology Assistant Setup Wizard* to run. Click **Next** and you will be prompted to enter logon details for the user, then click **Next** on the following screen.

Figure 78: Finding the server using Synology Assistant

The subsequent screen shows the folders to which the user has access. Choose a folder and click **Next**. On the next screen choose a drive letter for the folder from the drop-down; the default is Z but you can use any free letter. If the computer is only ever used by one person you can optionally tick the **Reconnect at logon** box, then click **Next**.

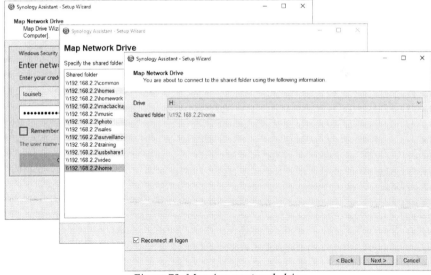

Figure 79: Mapping a network drive

You may receive an additional logon prompt from Windows, in which case enter the login details, optionally tick the **Remember my credentials** box if only one person uses the computer, followed by **OK**. If you are already logged in, a confirmatory message will be received. The drive will then be mapped – click **Finish** on the confirmation screen. Repeat the process for as many times as necessary to provide access to all the desired folders. When complete, close the Synology Assistant (in fact, it will continue to run on the Taskbar unless explicitly shutdown) and open File Explorer to verify that the folders have been mapped to drives. The drive mappings are permanent, assuming the **Reconnect at logon** and **Remember my credentials** boxes were ticked, and hence will survive reboots of the computer. It is not necessary to run Synology Assistant again unless it is required to make changes to the mappings.

As stated, you can use whatever drive letters you wish, provided they are not already in use (for instance you cannot use C as that is always allocated on a Windows computer). However, using corresponding letters makes things easier, for example, you could map *home* to H.

Using a Command/Batch File

Setting up a batch file is a more advanced technique for Windows PCs but can be useful when a computer is used by more than one person, for example, in a school or college. Start off by creating a plain text file called *ConnectNAS.cmd* using a tool such as Windows WordPad or Notepad. The contents of the file will need to be adjusted depending on the names of the shared folders to be mapped or if the NAS is not called 'server'. In this example, users have personal home folders and there are four shared folders called *music, photo, video* and *sales*:

@echo off
ping server -n 1 > nul
if errorlevel 1 goto offline
:online
: remove drive mappings if already present
net use * /delete /y > nul
: map the drives
net use h: \\server\home /persistent:no
net use m: \\server\music /persistent:no

```
net use p: \\server\photo /persistent:no
net use s: \\server\sales /persistent:no
net use v: \\server\video /persistent:no
goto end

:offline
cls
echo You are not connected to the network.
echo If you are outside the office then this is expected.
echo If you are inside the office then it means there is a problem.
echo Data stored on the network is not currently available.
pause
:end
```

The file should be placed on the Desktop of the computer. After the computer starts up, the user should run it by double-clicking its icon. A window is displayed prompting for the user name, followed by a prompt for the password. After the user has successfully entered their details, the mapped drives will be available until the computer is shutdown or they logoff using the Start menu. The drive mappings can be verified by launching File Explorer.

If the DiskStation is not available, the drives cannot be mapped and an appropriate warning message is displayed. It is to be expected that this message will appear if using, say, a laptop computer outside of an office, but if it appears inside then it indicates a problem. This could be a connectivity issue on the computer e.g. network cable unplugged or wireless disabled. If everyone in the office is receiving it then it would suggest that the DiskStation may be powered off or otherwise out of action.

When a user has finished with a computer, they should logoff or restart the computer.

Preferably, computers should be setup with only one Windows user defined on them. If this is not the case, then the *Connect-to-NAS.cmd* file needs to be placed in *C:\Users\Public\Public Desktop*, which will cause it to appear on the Desktop for all users. The Public Desktop folder is a hidden folder and will therefore first need to be made visible before it can be used. To do this, go to **Control Panel** on the computer and choose **Folder Options** or **File Explorer Options** depending on your version of Windows.

Click on the **View** tab, enable **Show hidden files, folders and drives** and click **OK**. Copy the *Connect-to-NAS.cmd* file to the Public Desktop folder, then make the Public Desktop folder hidden again.

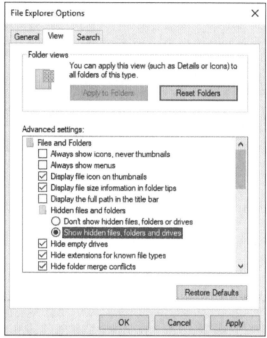

Figure 80: Folder Options to view hidden files

Unfortunately, *ConnectNAS.cmd* is not very forgiving of errors. If the user enters the wrong logon details, there will be a brief error message and the drives will fail to map. The user will need to run the file and try again.

5.4 Connecting Macs

On the Menu bar of the Mac, click **Go** followed by **Connect to Server**; alternatively, press **Command K.** A dialog box is displayed. Enter the name or IP address of the server, prefixed with *smb://* e.g. *smb://192.168.1.2* or *smb://server*. To add the server to your list of Favorites for future reference click the **+** button. Click **Connect**. Enter the user name ('Registered User') and password as previously defined on the NAS and click **Connect**. You can also tick the **Remember this password in my keychain** box if you are the only person who uses the computer:

Figure 81: Specify server and user logon details.

A list of available shared folders (*volumes*) is displayed. Choose the volume to mount and click **OK**. To mount multiple volumes at once, hold down the **Command key** and click on the required folders in turn. Icon(s) for the folder(s) will appear on the Desktop, assuming you have set Preferences in Finder to show Connected Servers. Click an icon to display the contents - they behave the same as standard Mac folders.

Alternatively, click Finder and navigate to the server in Locations, click the **Connect As** button and then login and mount one or more volumes/shared folders.

*Note: if you are using older versions of macOS (before 10.9 Mavericks), you should check that the Mac File Service (AFP) is enabled on the NAS, as described in section **2.6 Configuring the DiskStation**. You will need to prefix the server's name with 'AFP' rather than 'SMB'.*

5.5 Connecting Smartphones and Tablets

Smartphones and tablets can be connected to DiskStations using apps, but they meet different needs and are complementary rather than exclusive. As such, you may need to download and become familiar with several different ones. The first type comprises apps that provide direct access to the files on the server and is the focus of this section. The second method involves Synology Drive, which enables files to be synchronized between devices and the server using the internet and is discussed in chapter **10 SYNOLOGY DRIVE SERVER, OFFICE & APPS**. The third method uses apps which are optimized for specific purposes, such as playing back music or videos, and these are referenced in chapter **9 MULTIMEDIA & STREAMING**.

DS File (Android, iOS/iPadOS)

The simplest method to connect to a DiskStation is with *DS File*, which is a free download from Synology and is available for iOS/iPadOS and Android from the respective App stores. Download, install and launch DS File on the portable device; enter the QuickConnect ID or IP address of the server, along with the user name and password. It can be used to navigate the filing system and open documents using the built-in file viewers. Files can be downloaded to and from the device, and printed if you have a compatible printer. There are also basic commands for manipulating files.

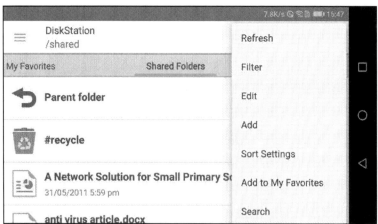

Figure 82: Viewing a folder using DS File on Android phone

Files App (iOS/iPadOS)

The Files App is an integral part of iOS and iPadOS. There are some minor variations, depending on the version of iOS or iPadOS. Having launched it, tap the three-dot menu at the top of the screen and tap **Connect to Server**:

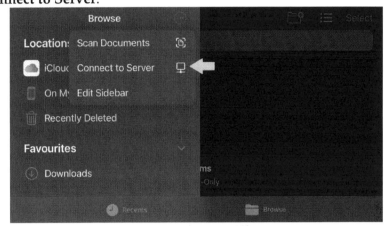

Figure 83: File App on iPhone

On the subsequent panels enter the name of the server or its IP address and click **Connect**; choose the **Registered User** option; enter the name and password of a user that has previously been defined on the server and click **Next**. After a few seconds, you should be connected to the server, from where you can navigate through the file system to locate specific folders and files:

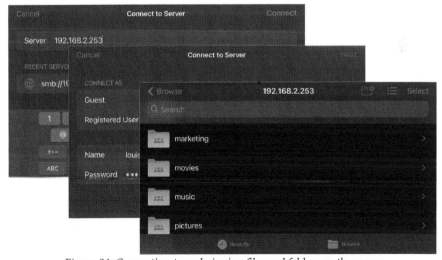

Figure 84: Connecting to and viewing files and folders on the server

5.6 Connecting Linux & Unix Computers

Although DSM includes comprehensive support for the NFS filing system used by Linux and Unix computers (see **2.6 Configuring the DiskStation**), Linux and Unix distributions can connect to SMB-based filing systems, such as that used by DSM. Unless you have specific reasons for using NFS, you might want to consider just using SMB for connecting to the server. In this example, we are using a popular Ubuntu Linux distribution.

On the Linux computer, click on the **Files** icon, followed by **Other Locations**. The NAS should be listed under the Networks section; click on it and on the resultant panel, enter the user's name and password as defined on the server and click **Connect** (the *Domain* field can be ignored). The shared folders on the server will be listed. To access a folder, double-click it. You may be prompted to provide the username and password again, in which case do so. The folder will then open and you can use the files in the standard manner.

Figure 85: Enter the address of the server

5.7 Connecting Chromebooks

Chromebooks are a popular computing choice, particularly in education. In essence a Chromebook is a laptop that primarily runs Google's Chrome browser, and the underlying operating system is minimalist compared to Windows or macOS. However, Chromebooks work well with NAS and can be used in the following ways:

Browser

Access the server using the Chrome browser, as described in section **5.2 Using a Browser and File Station**. Anything which can be accomplished within a browser such as administering the server, accessing File Station, playback of music using Audio Station and so on, can be done.

Files

To access the folders and files on the NAS, use the Chromebook *Files* utility. Click the three-dot 'snowman' icon in the top right-hand corner of the screen, followed by **Services > SMB file share**. On the resultant panel, enter the *File share URL* e.g. *server**public*, an optional *Display name*, plus the *Username* and *Password*. Optionally, tick the **Remember sign-in info** box. Click **Add**. The shared folder will now be added to the Chromebook's filing system.

Figure 86: Adding a file share

Android Apps

As most Chromebooks can run Android Apps from the Play Store, this means that many of Synology's mobile apps can be used, including DS Finder, DS Note, Synology Chat, DS audio, DS video and Synology Photos. Most of these apps are covered in chapters **9 MULTIMEDIA & STREAMING** and **10 SYNOLOGY DRIVE SERVER, OFFICE & APPS**.

6 SECURITY

6.1 Overview

The DSM software at the heart of the DiskStation is considered to be a very secure platform, but is not and cannot be totally immune to the numerous and continuously evolving security threats which exist. To help protect it, Synology provide a variety of tools and mechanisms and it is recommended that you familiarize yourself with and make use of them, plus supplement them with a regular set of procedures and checks.

6.2 Security Advisor

Security Advisor is the starting point for DSM security and provides an 'at a glance' assessment of the areas in which the DiskStation may potentially be vulnerable. Run it by clicking its icon in the **Main Menu**. It is good practice to run it on a regular basis e.g. once a week, once a month.

The first time Security Advisor is run it asks whether the DiskStation is being run in a home and personal or work and business environment, as the security requirements and recommendations between them are different (in simple terms, the business option provides tighter security). Make the appropriate choice and click **Start**:

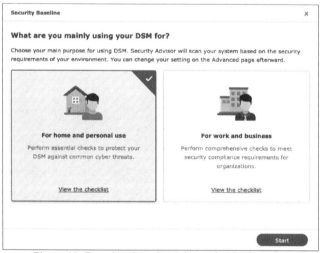

Figure 87: Running Security Advisor for the first time

It runs for a short while and then displays a screen of its findings, along with any recommendations:

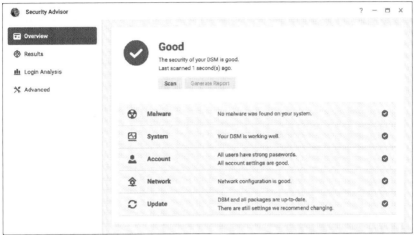

Figure 88: Results and recommendations from Security Advisor

There are five categories assessed - *Malware*, *System*, *Account*, *Network* and *Update* – and they are helpfully traffic-lighted as *Red* (a problem needs to be addressed), *Amber* (warning – something needs looking at) or *Green* (everything is okay). One or more messages may be listed against a topic and clicking them will display additional information, such as a suggested course of action, which should then be followed through.

Clicking on **Results** on the left-hand side of the screen will display a more comprehensive list of items that were tested during the security scan. The entries on the results screen are clickable to provide more information.

If you have used online services such as Amazon, iCloud and eBay, you may have received an email when accessing them from a new or unfamiliar location or computer. *Login Analysis* on DSM does something similar, analyzing each login with its public IP address and geographic location, and using AI techniques so it can spot patterns and anomalies. Clicking **Login Analysis** will cause it to enter learning mode, which ideally should be left running for 14 days, although it will not begin analysis until an attempt to login from an external IP address is made.

If an anomalous login is subsequently detected, then the following steps should be considered: change the password; use secure sign-in and two factor authentication (see **6.6 Improving Sign-In Security**); restrict the range of IP addresses that can be used to access the DiskStation (see **Security > Account** in the following section). Also see section **6.7 Account Activity** for another method of analysing logins.

Security Advisor can be customized in several ways, controlled by clicking on the **Advanced** option listed on the left-hand side of the screen. From here you can change the security level between home and personal and work and business, or define your own custom level. To see which security rules are being employed and optionally customize them, click **Customize checklist**. To setup a regular scheduled security scan, tick the **Enable regular scan schedule** box. You can specify a location where security reports will be stored, plus arrange for reports to be received by email if email notifications have been enabled in Control Panel.

Figure 89: Advanced options in Security Advisor

6.3 Security Icon

In the **Control Panel** is an icon for **Security** settings, used to improve security on the DiskStation and help protect it against malicious attacks by hackers and other miscreants. Whilst it is impossible to create computer systems that are 100% secure, there are several simple techniques that can be used to reduce the risk of problems. There are seven tabs within the Security system, described below.

Security

The first tab is called *Security*. In the first section, *General*, it is suggested that you tick all the boxes except *Enhance browser compatibility by skipping IP checking*. The second section controls *Login Settings*. Being logged in to DSM for a long time is not a good idea from a security perspective, and to prevent this users are logged out automatically after a period of inactivity. The amount of time for automatic logout can be adjusted from this tab; the default value is 15 minutes, but it can be changed if desired and set to any amount from 1 minute to 65535 minutes (which corresponds to roughly 45 days). The third and final section enables *Trusted Proxies* to be defined (not a common requirement in home and small business networks). Click **Apply** to effect the changes.

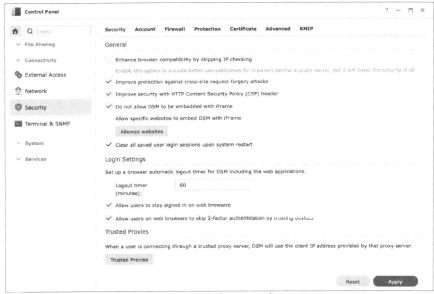

Figure 90: Security tab

Account

This tab comprises three sections:

2-Factor Authentication

The process of setting up two-factor authentication or 2FA is described in section **6.6 Improving Sign-In Security**. However, this tab is used to control whether it is then enforced and the choices are for administrators, all users, or specific users or groups. It is recommended that 2FA is enforced for administrators.

Figure 91: Account tab

Adaptive MFA

If 2FA has not been enabled, *Adaptive Multi-Factor Authentication* (AMFA) can be used. This will demand confirmation when DSM admin accounts are accessed from untrusted external connections, which might indicate attempts at hacking.

If AMFA has been enabled, it will be triggered for unrecognized devices, external connections, and password-only admin accounts. It will then require the login to be confirmed through the Secure SignIn client, DS Finder, or through Email.

Account Protection

In the *Account Protection* section, click the **Enable Account Protection** box. If too many unsuccessful attempts are made to login within a prescribed time, the account will temporarily be blocked. The default values are suitable in most circumstances.

Firewall

Firewalls allow the creation of rules that define which applications may or may not access the NAS. It is almost certainly the case that your internet connection already has a firewall of some sort, either within the router itself, or in the form of a separate appliance if you are a larger business user. DSM has an optional, built-in second level firewall program, controlled from this tab, which can be used to further enhance security.

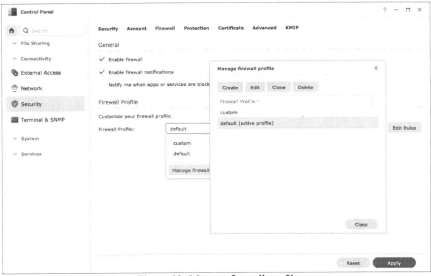

Figure 92: Manage firewall profile

In this example, systematic attempts are being made by a remote hacker to try and access the server using port 1783, so we are going to create a firewall rule to block this port.

Tick the **Enable firewall** and **Enable firewall notifications** boxes in the *General section*. A set of rules constitute a *profile* and the firewall supports multiple profiles; only one profile can be active at any time, but they can be switched between according to requirements. Click the **Firewall Profile** dropdown and select **Manage firewall profile**.

Click **Create**. On the resultant panel, give the new profile a meaningful name and click the **Create** button to display the *Create Firewall Rules* panel. There are three sections, to control the *Ports*, the *Source IP* and the resultant *Action*. How you use these depends upon what you are trying to achieve, but in this example we want to block a specific port, so click **Custom**. From the dropdowns, set the *Type* to **Source port**, the *Protocol* to **All**, and the *Port* to 1783. Click **OK**. Returning to the previous panel, the *Source IP* is set to **All**. For the *Action*, we want **Deny**. Make sure that the **Enabled** box is ticked and click **OK**.

Figure 93: Creating a rule

The newly created rule will now be listed on the Create Firewall Profile panel – click **OK**, followed by **Close** on the subsequent one. You will now be back to the original Firewall tab within the Security section. Change the **Firewall Profile** dropdown to choose your new profile, which will have been added to the list, and click **Apply** to make it active.

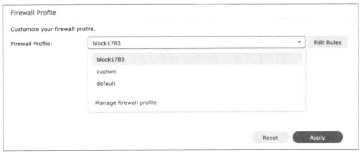

Figure 94: Set the profile

Protection

This tab has two sections, *Auto Block* and *Denial-of-Service (DoS) Protection*. The first is used to block IP addresses that are repeatedly trying to access the DiskStation but are failing to do so because the login credentials are incorrect. Most computer systems have accounts called *admin* or *administrator* and hackers try to login to them using commonly used passwords, which is why you should never use ones such as 'password', 'secret', 'admin', '123456' and so on. The auto-block facility can provide some protection against this. It is suggested that **Enable auto block** is ticked and the number of failed login attempts is set at the default value of 10 within a 5-minute period. Also, that the **Enable block expiration** option is ticked and set to at least 1 day. If you are aware of suspicious activity from specific IP addresses, you can block them by clicking the **Allow/Block List** button and entering the details on the resultant panel.

Figure 95: Protection tab

A *Denial-of-Service* or *DoS* attack is a common technique of hackers and miscreants to make a computer system unusable by trying to overload it with bogus access attempts. DSM has some protection against this, and the **Enable DoS protection** option should be ticked for the appropriate *Network Interface*; if there is more than one, it can be selected using the dropdown. Click **Apply** to effect the change.

Certificate

This option is used for managing SSL (Secure Socket Layer) certificates. SSL certificates provide higher levels of security when servers provide encrypted web-based services and which are indicated by website addresses that begin with *https* rather than *http*. The basic principle is that certificates are provided by recognised issuing authorities – known as *CAs* or *Certificate Authorities* – and constitute a form of guarantee that a site is what it purports to be. Certificates may be provided on a commercial basis but are also available freely from some sources.

If you are a home or small business user or just starting out, you may not want to worry too much about this section. By default, Synology have already provided you with a working certificate and, when you setup QuickConnect, a further certificate is provided. If you are an experienced IT professional and you wish to maximize security, then you will want to pursue this topic further. This section does not discuss the detailed use of certificates, just how to get started.

Clicking on the **Certificate** tab will display the following panel. Notice that the default Synology certificate is already listed. To add a new certificate, click the **Add** button. On the resultant screen you can choose to *Add a new certificate* or *Replace an existing one* but regardless of choice, the subsequent screen will be the same. There are two choices plus the option to set the default certificate:

Figure 96: Certificate section within Security

Import certificate – import an existing certificate that has previously been obtained.

Get a certificate from Let's Encrypt – Let's Encrypt is an organization that provides certificates free of charge (although they accept donations).

Your certificate needs to be given a Description. You can also set it as the default certificate from this screen.

The subsequent screens depend on what type of certificate you choose to work with. Technical skills and knowledge may be required in some instances.

More general information about using certificates can be located at *https://letsencrypt.org/docs/*

Advanced
This covers more advanced topics. Many users will not need to worry about this tab, which addresses some more specialized areas:

HTTP Compression - tick the box to improve performance when connecting to the server via HTTPS.

TLS/SSL Profile Level - used when working with cipher suites. The default option of **Intermediate compatibility** is suitable in most scenarios.

Spectre and Meltdown Protection - provides protection against vulnerabilities in certain processors but will reduce overall performance of the DiskStation. Note: this section may not be present on some models.

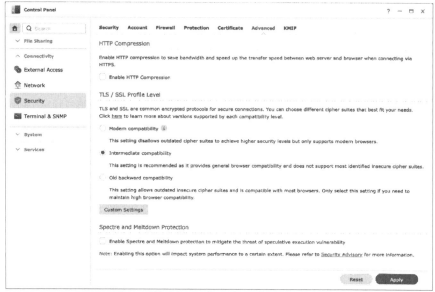

Figure 97: Advanced section within Security

KMIP

When creating encrypted volumes on a DiskStation, as described in section **2.5 Setting up Storage**, a copy of the encryption key is downloaded and which can be stored in a safe location, such as a removeable USB memory stick. In a home or small network, this is sufficient, but in a larger network containing dozens or hundreds of servers, which may be dispersed geographically, a more practical solution is required. The *Key Management Interoperability Protocol* (KMIP) service enables a DiskStation to be designated as a repository (Remote Key Server) for storing the encryption keys of other DiskStations (Remote Key Clients). For instance, the Remote Key Server might be located at an organizations head office, with the DiskStations at the branch offices configured as Remote Key Clients.

6.4 Antivirus Protection

The chances of a DiskStation becoming infected with malware are low, as DSM is based on a customized version of Linux and is not particularly susceptible, although it is possible. However, the files being stored on it by Windows computers and other clients may be infected and these need to be checked to prevent further distribution. Synology's *Antivirus Essential* is a free download from the Package Center and runs on the DiskStation itself. Separate provision still needs to be made for the workstations using an anti-virus program such as Microsoft Security, AVG, McAfee etc., as there is no linkage between them and the server, nor is this intended as a replacement for security software on desktops and laptops.

Having downloaded and installed Antivirus Essential from the Package Center, an icon will appear in the Main Menu - click it to display the console.

Figure 98: Antivirus Essential Overview screen

Three types of on-demand scan are available:

Full – All files on the NAS are checked. Synology recommend a full scan if you think the NAS is infected with a virus.

Custom – Specify the folders to be scanned. This will be faster than a full scan.

System – Scans the system partition only and does not scan the data volumes. Useful as part of a general health check of the NAS.

By default, the latest anti-virus signatures will be downloaded before the scan commences, although this behavior can be changed from the **Settings** option. You can also click **Update** at any time and it is suggested you do this before running your first scan.

Scanning can result in high CPU and memory utilization, particularly on DiskStations with less than 512MB RAM and, depending on the amount of data stored on the DiskStation, can be time consuming. Partly for this reason it is best done as a scheduled task out of hours, such as during the middle of the night or at the weekend. To schedule a scan, click on the **Scheduled Scan** option followed by the **Create** button.

The results of scans and other activities are recorded in log files, which can be found by clicking on the **Logs** option. If infected files are found on the server, go to the *Quarantine* section within Antivirus Essential and delete them, try to identify the source of the infected files (i.e. the computer they came from) and clean-up that computer using anti-virus and malware tools appropriate to the platform.

There are also commercial anti-virus/anti-malware products for the DiskStation produced by third parties, for instance, *Antivirus by McAfee* is available through the Package Center.

Note: Antivirus Essential is based around a free product called Clam AntiVirus. One limitation in the package is that it cannot scan individual files which are larger in size than 2GB.

6.5 Password Settings

When a user account is created on the DiskStation, a password must be specified. Passwords should be non-obvious – under no circumstances should words such as 'password', 'secret', 'diskstation', 'synology', 'admin' and so on be used as these are easily guessed, nor is it a good idea to have the password the same as the user's name or a close variant thereof (and by default DSM will prevent the use of many such passwords). The best passwords combine a mixture of upper and lower letters, numbers and punctuation and are not too short in length. For instance, a password such as *!N3y!YoRk!* would be quite difficult for someone to guess, although as thousands of copies of this guide have been sold you probably don't want to use that particular one. By default, DSM requires passwords of at least eight characters in length, but can be configured to enforce 'stronger' passwords. A judgement must be made regarding how strong the passwords should be; by way of guidance, businesses generally require stronger passwords than home systems and if the server is to be accessed remotely then the passwords should be as strong as possible. Conversely, in a primary or elementary school it might be better to use simple passwords for the pupils.

To manage password characteristics, go to **Control Panel** and click the **User & Group** icon. Click the **Advanced** tab to display the following panel and expand the *Password Settings* and *Password Expiration* sections:

Figure 99: Password Settings and Password Expiration

Tick the **Apply password strength rules** box and tick the conditions to apply. In the above example: the user name and description cannot be part of the password; a mixture of upper- and lower-case letters have to be used, along with numbers and special characters (punctuation); the password must be at least 8 characters long; the user cannot use the same password again. Click **Apply** to make the changes.

Automatic password expiration can be enabled. For instance, passwords can be set to expire every, say, 30 days and/or the users prompted to change their password at that time. Having passwords that expire in this manner is considered good practice from a security standpoint, especially in businesses.

Password settings apply to all users of the system, although it is possible to exclude the administrator user from password expiration. All users must change their passwords after password strength rules are applied.

Forgotten Password

If a user has forgotten their password or it needs to be changed for any other reason:

Within **Control Panel > User & Group**, highlight the user's name on the **User** tab. Click the **Edit** button or right-click the name and choose **Edit**. On the **Info** tab, click **Change Password**. Enter and confirm the new password of choice, else click **Generate Random Password**. Click **Save**.

A user can also change their own password at any time and how to do so is described in **4.7 User Personalization Settings**.

6.6 Improving Sign-In Security

The standard method for signing into DSM is with a username and password. However, it is possible to both simplify this process as well as make it more secure. This is done using the *Secure SignIn Service*, which is app that runs on a separate hardware device, such as a smartphone or tablet. Three advantages are that it removes the need for the user to remember their password, reduces the risk of passwords being compromised, plus reduces support overheads in organizations. In addition, *2-Factor Authentication* (2FA) can be enabled, meaning that two sets of credentials must be provided to sign in. You may have encountered 2FA systems when using online banking: typically, websites will require you to provide a username and password, but additionally send a code to your mobile/cell phone that needs to be entered to complete the process of signing in. Such two-step systems greatly reduce the risks of other people being able to access your account.

Secure Sign-In Service

To use the Secure Sign-In Service, the following conditions must be met:

The administrator has signed into the Synology Account, thus enabling the receipt of push notifications (see **Control Panel > Synology Account**).

A QuickConnect ID for the DiskStation has been setup (see **2.7 QuickConnect: The Key to Remote Connectivity**).

A suitable hardware device is being used. Smartphones and tablets are a popular choice, although the Sign-In Service also supports other mechanisms such as *macOS Touch ID*, *Apple Watch* and *Windows Hello*.

Secure Sign-In Service is configured on a per user basis, meaning it can be deployed as required. For instance, in an educational setting it might be enabled for the teaching and administrative staff but not for the students. To enable it, the user should sign into DSM using a desktop or laptop computer and click the **Options** icon in the top right-hand corner of the screen, followed by **Personal > Security**. Scroll down to the *Sign-in Method* section and click **Passwordless Sign-In**, followed by **Approve sign-in**. The user needs to verify their identity by entering their password and clicking **OK**.

Figure 100: Setting up Passwordless Sign-In

On the resultant panel, click **Next**. Install the *Synology Secure Sign-In* app on the Android or iOS/iPadOS device, and when this has been done click **Next**. On the mobile device, launch the app, tap **Add** to add a new profile, followed by **Allow Camera Access**. Scan the customized QR code from the DSM screen. Once this has been done, a confirmation panel is shown in DSM – click **Finish**. The user will be returned to the **Options > Personal > Account** screen, where they should click **Apply**. The user should then sign out from DSM on the computer. The procedure for sign-in is now as follows:

From the DSM sign-in screen on the computer, type the username and press **Enter**. Instead of being prompted for the password, an 'Approve sign-in' panel is displayed on the mobile device, from where the sign-in request must be approved within a short period. It may also be necessary to enter the mobile device passcode or pass its biometric security mechanism i.e. fingerprint or facial recognition. Having done so, the user will be signed into DSM on the computer.

If the user does not currently have access to their mobile device, they should click the **Other sign-in methods** link on the computer screen. From here, they can choose to enter their password in the conventional manner.

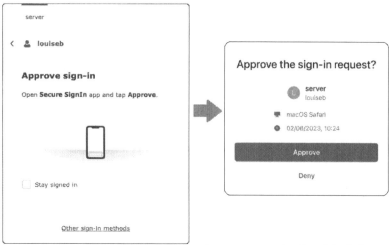

Figure 101: Approve sign-in messages shown on computer & mobile device

Two Factor Authentication (2FA)

As with the Secure Sign-In Service described in the previous section, 2FA is configurable on a per user basis, by the user themselves. The user should sign into DSM using a desktop or laptop computer and click the **Options** icon 👤 in the top right-hand corner of the screen, followed by **Personal > Security**. Click **2-Factor Authentication**. The user needs to verify their identity by entering their password. Click **OK**.

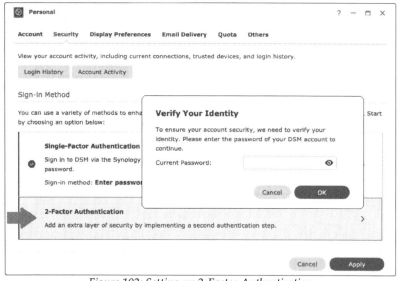

Figure 102: Setting up 2-Factor Authentication

Various options are available, but in this example it is assumed that the user has already configured the Secure Sign-In service, in which case a panel along the following lines will be displayed. The default is to use the device which was configured for passwordless sign-on, alternatively a new device can be added. We will assume the former, so click **OK**:

Figure 103: *Message about configured device*

The subsequent screen is for configuring an alternative sign-in method. Click **Start**:

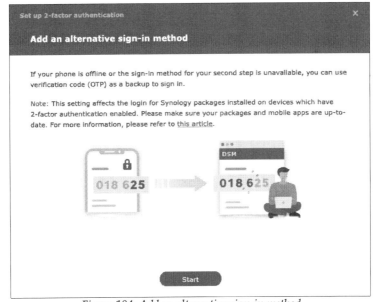

Figure 104: *Add an alternative sign-in method*

The user will be prompted to install the Secure SignIn authenticator app. As we have already done this, click **Next**. Go into the app and click the large plus sign (+) sign to activate the devices camera and scan the QR code which is on the computer screen. A 6-digit code is generated – type it into the computer and click **Next**.

A backup email account needs to be specified; in the event of losing your mobile device, an emergency verification code will be sent to this email address. Enter your email address and click the **Send verification mail** button. After the email address has been verified, click **Next**.

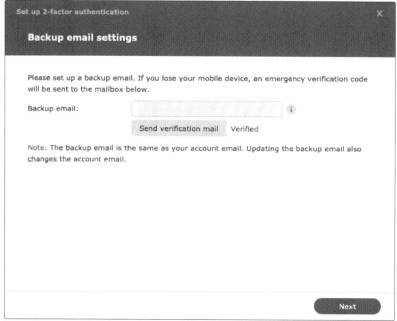

Figure 105: Backup email settings screen

A panel to confirm that 2-factor authentication has been turned on is displayed – click **Done**. Having been returned to the initial Security tab within Personal settings, click **Apply**.

To use, begin the sign-in process to DSM by entering the username and password on the computer. A verification code is generated and sent to the mobile device. Type this code into the panel which has appeared on the computer to complete the sign-in.

If the user hasn't received the code, they can click the **Try another sign-in method** link or use the **Can't sign in with the OTP** link to generate an emergency code, which will be sent to associated email account.

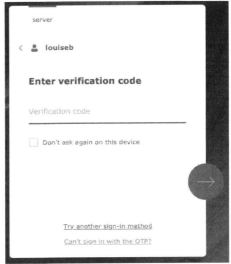

Figure 106: Enter verification code

Checking 2FA Status

Setting up and managing 2-Factor Authentication is under the control of the individual users. However, the administrative user can view the status of who is using it by going into **Control Panel > User & Group > User**:

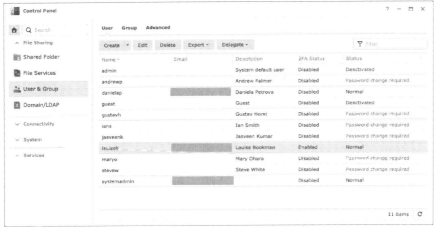

Figure 107: Checking 2FA Status

6.7 Account Activity

DSM maintains an audit trail of when users login in to the system and this can be used to track activity when there are suspected security violations, as well as more general access problems. To access it, login as the user and click the **Options** icon in the top right-hand corner of the screen, followed by **Personal**. On the **Security** tab, click the **Login History** button:

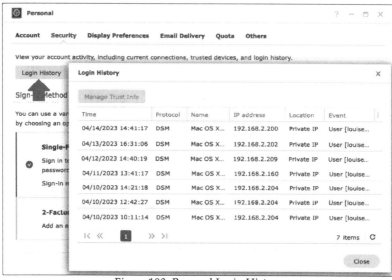

Figure 108: Personal Login History

To view the specifics of a particular login session, highlight it and click the **Manage Trust Info** button:

To forcibly sign-out a user, go to **Control Panel > User & Group**. Highlight the user, click **Edit** and on the **Info** tab click the **Sign Out of All Devices** button.

Figure 109: View Login history

6.8 Changing the Administrator Account

The administrative account on many DiskStations is *'admin'*. If you installed DSM using the Synology Assistant, it will have used this name as it is hard coded into the utility. However, if you installed DSM using Web Assistant or DS Finder, there was an opportunity to specify a different name. It is preferable that *admin* is not used as the main administrative account, as the name is too well-known and hence presents an obvious target for hackers and criminals. One option is to create an alternative administrator account and use that instead, and in this example we will replace *admin* with a different name.

Go into **Control Panel > User & Group**. Highlight the *admin* account, click the downward-pointing chevron on the **Create** button and choose **Copy user** to run the *User Creation Wizard*. Specify the name of the new account, description, and enter and confirm a password. Remember, with administrator accounts the password should be as strong as possible e.g. a mixture of upper- and lower-case letters, numbers, and punctuation. Click **Next** followed by **Done** on the subsequent *Confirm settings* panel:

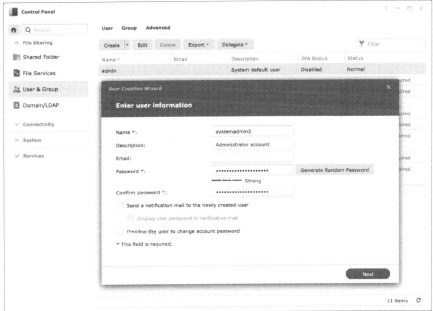

Figure 110: Copying the administrator account

Logout, then log back in using the newly created administrator account. You can now disable the original admin account (it is not possible to delete it). Highlight the account, click **Edit** and on the resultant panel tick the **Disable this account** box, followed by **Save**.

Given the importance of the administrator account, it is essential to make sure that its details are not forgotten. For instance, keep a copy of it and the password in a sealed envelope in a secure environment, such as a safe or lockable drawer.

6.9 Change Port Numbers & Disable Unnecessary Services

Port Numbers

The various network protocols used by computers have port numbers associated with them. For instance, *http*, used by websites, uses port 80. Because these port numbers are so widely used, they are targeted by hackers and hence can constitute a vulnerability. One technique to reduce the risk is to change port numbers from their default value to something non-standard.

An example of this would be Secure Shell (SSH), which is used for secure logins from administrator accounts. It is used, for instance, by *rsync* to support NAS-to-NAS backups (see **7.6 Synology to Synology Backups**). The default port used by SSH is 22, but Synology recommend that you consider changing it. To do so, go into **Control Panel > Terminal & SNMP**. On the *Terminal* tab, the port number is listed underneath the *Enable SSH service* box; if SHH is enabled, enter an alternative port number and click **Apply**.

The alternative port number must be something which is not used elsewhere – you cannot simply choose a random number. A comprehensive list of port numbers can be found at:

> https://en.wikipedia.org/wiki/List_of_TCP_and_UDP_port_numbers

So, you would search the list to identify a gap or an obscure port choose that number.

If this is done, any applications which use the port need to be reconfigured e.g. *rsync* in the above example.

Services

As the server is connected to the internet, there is a risk that it can be attacked by external hackers and cyber criminals. One way to reduce this risk is to turn off or disable services relating to connectivity that are not used or are only used infrequently or under special circumstances, thereby reducing the available 'attack surface'.

One way to do this is to stop and start services according to a timed schedule. For instance, consider a company that uses VPN to provide remote access to a branch office. The branch office is open from 9am-5pm (0900-1700) Monday to Friday and outside of that time there is no need for the connection, so a schedule can be setup to enable the VPN at, say, 8.45am/0845 and disable it at 5.15pm/1715 each day. To do so:

Go into **Control Panel** and click **Task Scheduler**. Click the **Create** button followed by **Scheduled Task > Service**. On the **General** tab give the task a name e.g. *Start VPN*. Click the **Schedule** tab and set the days and time it will run. Click the **Task Settings** tab. Choose the **Start Service** option and click the entry for **VPN**. Click **OK**. Repeat the above process, but this time create a complementary task to **Stop Service** at the desired time.

Note: Further information on working with the Task Scheduler can be found at **15.8 Task Scheduler**.

If a service is not used at all e.g. FTP, then disable it altogether (in this example it is done from **Control Panel > File Services > FTP**).

To quickly see which ports and services are in use, go into Info Center and click the Service tab (see **8.3 Info Center**).

7 BACKUPS

7.1 Overview

The importance of backing up data on a regular basis, to cope with the problems that can arise with computer systems, cannot be over-emphasised. Examples of things that can go wrong include deleting files by accident, virus and malware infections, data corruption, computer failure and equipment being lost or stolen. Usually, the value of data far outweighs the value of computers; for instance, what price could be attached to the irreplaceable photos of a Wedding Day or children's first steps, or a company's accounts or customer database? In the case of businesses, around half that have a serious data loss subsequently cease trading within twelve months, plus there may be statutory requirements to retain certain data and be able to produce it when required. The assumption to follow is that it is a question of *when* rather than *if* data will be lost at some point, which is when the backups will be needed.

Backups are like pay rises or happy memories: you cannot have too many of them. A NAS system such as a DiskStation forms the ideal heart of any backup solution and enables you to take a multi-tiered approach, meaning there are multiple backups to multiple places, ensuring that there is always a fall-back option in the event of problems. For example:

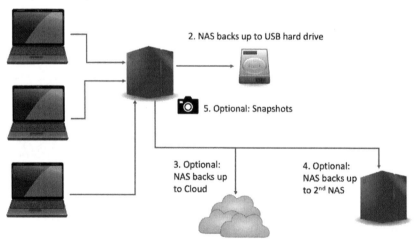

Figure 111: Example of multi-tier backup

The computers in the home or office are backed up to the NAS. The NAS in turn is backed up to a local USB hard drive. Optionally, the NAS or at least the most important data on it are backed up to a Cloud-based service, such as Synology's C2. Additionally, the NAS may also be backed up to a second NAS located on or off the premises.

DSM can handle all these types of backups. Various backup apps are available from Synology and third parties, but the standard one is Synology's *Hyper Backup*, which should be downloaded from the Package Center. As part of the installation, other supporting components such as PHP might also be downloaded.

The most common scenario is to backup the DiskStation to an external drive, so this is what we will concentrate on first. As an additional level of backup, consider using a cloud service, as described in section **7.5 Backups with Synology C2 and Cloud Services**. For backing up to another DiskStation, see section **7.6 Synology to Synology Backups**.

Besides the comprehensive facilities available through Hyper Backup, DSM also features *Snapshots*, whereby data is effectively 'photographed' at regular moments in time. This enables it to be quickly recovered/restored if required, but as it cannot cope with a drive failure it should be viewed as an additional tool rather than as a replacement for backing up to a USB drive or to the Cloud.

All the above mechanisms are suitable for home and small business users. Additionally, Synology have a suite of products under its *Active Backup* category. These are targeted at larger business users, but the main one is overviewed in this chapter to help determine if it might be applicable to your network.

7.2 Backing Up to An External Drive

This backup solution requires an external USB hard drive. The drive should be of sufficient capacity to hold all the data but preferably larger as that will permit multiple backups e.g. if there are 3TB data then use at least a 3TB drive, but a 4TB drive would be better. Portable drives are a good option, as they do not require mains power and are more convenient to store, but there are limitations to their maximum capacity.

To prepare an external drive for backup usage, plug it into a spare USB socket on the DiskStation. On some DiskStations, some of the USB sockets may only be of USB 2.0 specification, which might limit the speed of the backup. Wait 20-30 seconds, then click **Control Panel** followed by **External Devices**. The drive should appear after a few seconds; highlight it and click **Format**. Choose to format the **Entire disk**, using the file system type of **EXT4**. Click **OK** and acknowledge the warning message that is displayed. The formatting may take some time, depending on the capacity, performance and interface of the drive. It is suggested that you do this step, regardless of whether the drive is a new blank one or one that was purchased pre-formatted, as often such drives will have been formatted with the Windows exFAT or NTFS filing systems, which are unsuitable here:

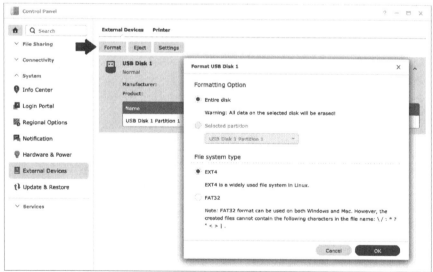

Figure 112: Format external drive for backup

When the external drive has been formatted, quit External Devices, go to the **Main Menu** and launch **Hyper Backup**. You are most likely wanting to backup Folders and Packages (i.e. data); the other option, LUNs, is for users of iSCSI (see section **12.9 SAN Manager and iSCSI**). Click **Next**:

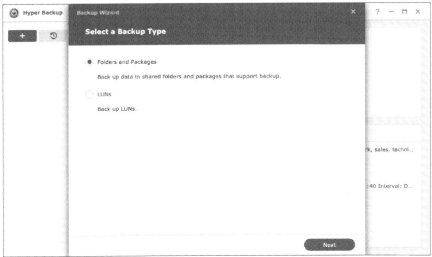

Figure 113: Choose Folders & Packages and click Next

Specify a *Backup Destination*: there are multiple choices, but for backing up to an external drive highlight the first **Local Shared Folder & USB** option and click **Next**.

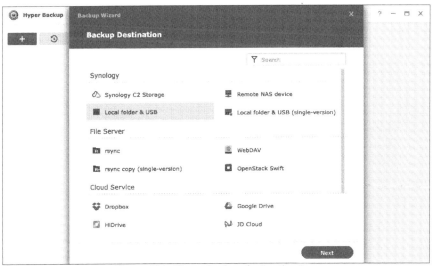

Figure 114: Choose backup destination type

On the following panel, choose **Create backup task** and from the *Shared Folder* drop-down select the external backup drive, which is *usbshare1* in our example. The *Directory* entry, which is derived automatically from the name of server, is inconsequential, so just click **Next**:

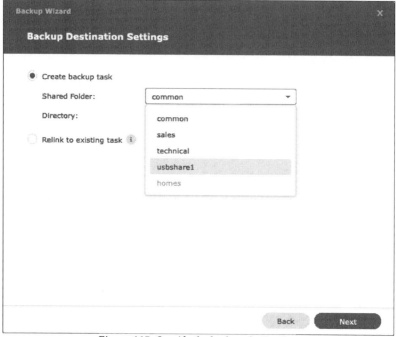

Figure 115: Specify the backup destination

On the subsequent panel, choose the volumes/folder to be backed up. A common requirement is to backup everything, and if you want to do this tick all the folders (a quick way to do this is by clicking the Volume name at the top), otherwise make your selection. Click **Next**. If you have multiple volumes on the DiskStation, they will be listed and can be included in the backup if required. If you want to exclude or include certain file types, click the **Create file filters** link and specify them there.

Figure 116: Select folders to be backed up

A panel listing installed applications which store settings on the NAS is displayed, enabling you to include them in the backup. Select as required - if in doubt, tick everything - followed by **Next**. Note that in some cases, an application will temporarily stop running whilst it is being backed up.

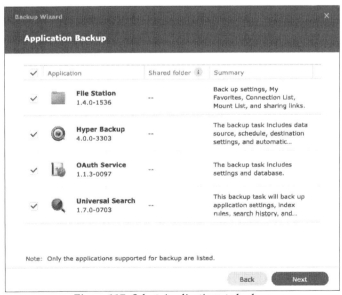

Figure 117: Select Applications to back up

The subsequent panel enables you to set a schedule and specify additional settings. Working through it:

Change the name of the *Task* to something more descriptive, for example in this case we have called it *Dailybackup*.

Remove the tick from *Enable task notification* if you have not yet setup notifications as described in section **8.9 Notifications**.

Remove destination external device when backup task has successfully finished - if the backup drive is left permanently connected to the DiskStation do not tick it, but if it is removed after a backup and kept in a separate location then tick it.

Compress backup data – this is optional. Compressed data takes up less space on the external drive, but the backup and restore processes will be slower.

Enable backup schedule - the backup should preferably run at a time when the server is not being used or at least is not busy, which will depend upon the circumstances of your household or organization. In this example the backup is set to run every weekday at 3:00am (0300 hours).

Enable integrity check integrity – tick all the boxes to enable Hyper Backup to check the integrity (i.e. accuracy and usability) of the backup. In this example it runs weekly on Sunday mornings.

Enable client-side encryption – tick to encrypt the backup. You may want to tick and specify a password if you are backing up encrypted folders, confidential data, and/or to comply with local data protection requirements.

Having specified all the parameters, click **Next**.

Note: if you are backing up any encrypted folders you may receive reminder messages during these screens.

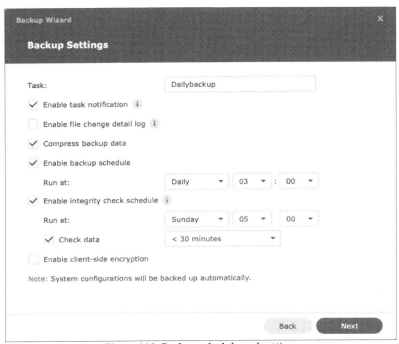

Figure 118: Backup schedule and settings

The subsequent screen defines *Rotation Settings*. With some computer backup systems, you can keep only a single backup. But suppose you are performing daily backups, have a problem and need to revert to a copy of a file made, say, a week ago – what happens then? With backup rotation, Hyper Backup will maintain multiple backups for as long as it can; eventually, when the backup disk is full, it will start to overwrite the oldest backups to free up the space (if you are a macOS user you may be familiar with Time Machine, which operates in a similar manner). To turn on this feature, tick the **Enable backup rotation** box. There are some optional settings, but most people will not need to worry about them as the defaults are generally fine. The timeline at the bottom is an estimate as to how long the system might be able to store backups, based upon your parameters:

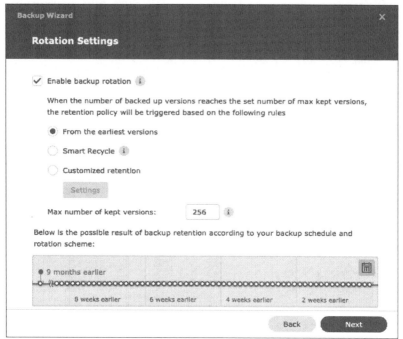

Figure 119: Rotation Settings

Click **Next** and a Summary panel is shown. Click **Done** and you will receive a message asking whether you wish to 'Back up now?'. It is suggested that you reply **Yes**, to both test the newly defined backup job and generate the first backup.

Once the backups have been setup and are working, the main Hyper Backup screen can be used to manage them. To perform a backup at any point, rather than wait for the schedule, click the **Back up now** button. To check the list of completed backups, click **Version List**. To change the parameters of the backup, click **Task Settings**:

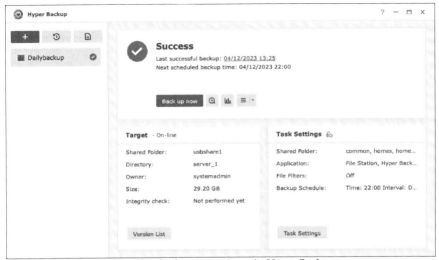

Figure 120: View backup status in main Hyper Backup screen.

Although the first backup may take some time, depending on how much data there is, subsequent backups should be quicker. This is because Hyper Backup uses *incremental backups*, meaning it only backs up the items that have changed since the previous backup.

To make a change to an existing backup task, click the right-hand icon followed by **Edit**. To remove an existing backup task, click **Delete**. You can also run the optional Backup Integrity test from here.

7.3 Restoring Files from a Backup

There are two methods for restoring files from backups made using Hyper Backup: *Backup Explorer* and the *Restore* option.

Restoring Using Backup Explorer

In the middle of the main Hyper Backup screen, to the right of the blue *Back up now* button, is an icon that looks like a combination watch/magnifying glass (if the icon is grayed out, it is because the backup drive is not currently connected). Click the icon to launch *Backup Explorer*:

Figure 121: Backup Explorer

As the name implies, it allows you to 'explore' the backups, effectively stepping back in time until you find the one you want. This can be done using the timeline at the bottom of the screen, otherwise click the small calendar icon; dates for which backups are available will be shown in bold. The backups are displayed in a regular volume/folder/file format, in a similar manner to File Station. Click a file to select it, or to select multiple files, hold down the Control key (Windows) or Command key (macOS) and click them in turn.

Having marked the required items, click one of the buttons at the top of the screen or right-click a file or folder:

Copy to – the items are restored to a location that you specify. For instance, you might have a particular file but wish to check if an older version is more useful. By restoring to a different location, you do not have to overwrite the current one.

Restore – the items are restored to their original location. If you had deleted a file or folder, using this option you could recover it from the backup.

Download – the items are restored, but are downloaded to your computer rather than to the DiskStation.

Using the Restore Option

On the main Hyper Backup screen, click the **Restore** icon and choose **Data** or **LUN** as required. On the resultant panel, select the task that was used to create the backup and click **Next**:

Figure 122: Select Restoration Task

On the next panel, decide whether to restore the system configuration – if you just want to restore data then you would not, but if you are rebuilding the system then you probably would. Click **Next**. On the subsequent panel, choose the backup and the shared folder(s) to be restored. The small triangle icons against the folder names indicate that the restored data will overwrite the original. Click **Next**.

On the next panel, specify any applications to be restored and click **Next**. A summary screen is displayed – click **Done** and the restoration will commence. When it has completed, click **OK**.

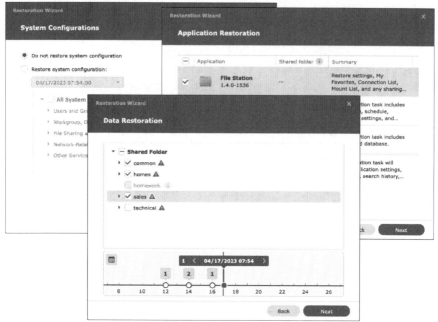

Figure 123: Choose items to be restored

7.4 Quick & Easy Backups Using USB Copy Utility

The *USB Copy* utility can be used in several different ways: to import photos and videos from a USB drive; to import data from a USB drive; to export data from the DiskStation to a USB drive. Some DiskStation models have a front-mounted USB socket or SD socket, along with a dedicated copy button, enabling data to be transferred as required. If the DiskStation does not have a copy button, the power button can be used instead. The USB Copy utility can be configured to execute through the act of plugging in a drive, and this creates a simple method for performing backups. However, the limitation is that it can only backup a single shared folder.

If the DiskStation has the appropriate hardware, the *USB Copy* utility will have been loaded during the installation of DSM, otherwise it can be loaded from the Package Center. Connect the external USB drive or SD card to the required socket; after a few seconds, it should appear as an icon at the top of the screen. The drive needs to be first formatted using a file system that the DiskStation understands, such as EXT4 (recommended) or FAT32 and how to do so is described at the beginning of section **7.2 Backing Up to An External Drive**. Note: the external drive must be connected when creating the backup task described below. Launch the *USB Copy* app from the Main Menu and click **Data Export**:

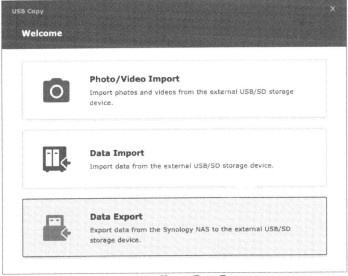

Figure 124: Choose Data Export

On the subsequent panel, specify a *Task name*. For the *Source*, choose a folder to be backed up and in this instance we have specified the *common* folder. For the *Destination*, choose the external USB drive, which on this system is *usbshare1*. Using the *Copy mode* dropdown, three options are available:

Multi-versioned – a separate backup folder is created each time the copy task is run. As there will be multiple backups, it is possible to roll back (restore) to earlier ones if required.

Mirroring – the backup will be an exact copy of the source folder.

Incremental – each time the copy task runs, newly added and changed files from the source folder will be copied to the backup. Subsequent backups will quicker.

In this example we are using Mirroring, so select it and click **Next**. Acknowledge any warning message which might appear.

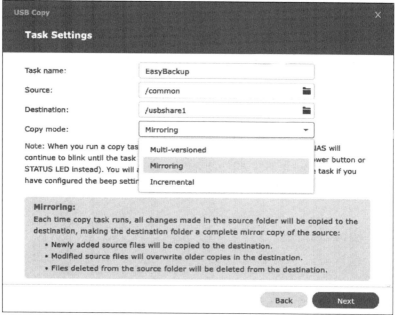

Figure 125: Specify task settings

The following panel is called *Trigger Time* and controls the circumstances under which the backup takes place. It can be scheduled, but in this example will we set it such that the act of plugging-in the external drive will cause the backup to run (in fact, you can have both options simultaneously).

Tick the **Copy data whenever the USB/SD storage device is plugged in** and **Eject the USB/SD storage device when copy completes** boxes, followed by **Next**. If you took a different approach, where the backup drive is left permanently connected, then you would not tick the Eject option. On the next panel, select the types of file to copy, based on your requirements. In this example we will choose all types. If required, custom filters can be created to backup more specific file types. Click **Done**:

Figure 126: Trigger Time & File Filter

To test, eject the external hard drive using the small external devices icon at the very top of the screen, then unplug it. Wait 30 seconds. Plug the drive back in. Once the DiskStation has detected it, it will beep and then start copying data to the drive. When it has finished, it will beep and the drive can be removed and kept in a safe location.

Any backup tasks created will be added to the USB Copy screen, from where they can be subsequently accessed and modified. There is also an option to view the backup log files, by clicking the middle icon in the top-left hand corner of the screen:

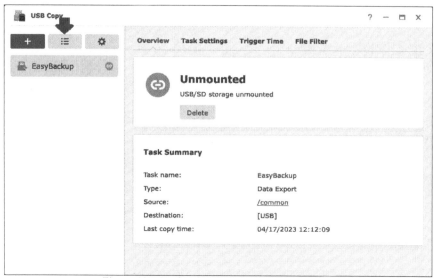

Figure 127: Updated USB Copy Overview screen

As described early, the USB Copy facility can be used in different roles. A common use, for instance, is to facilitate copying photos from a USB memory stick or SD card using the Photo/Video Import option. However, as a simple and straightforward backup solution it can be very useful.

To restore files from the external drive, create a new task by clicking the plus sign icon in the top-left hand corner of the screen, but this time start with the **Data Import** option instead.

7.5 Backups with Synology C2 and Cloud Services

DiskStations can be backed up to many popular cloud services, both consumer ones such as Dropbox and Google Drive, as well as professional ones such as Microsoft Azure and Amazon S3 Storage. Synology offer their own cloud service – C2 – which provides different tiers of storage on a paid basis, ranging from options suitable for individuals through to enterprises, with a 30-day trial available to new users. One attraction of C2 is that it is designed specifically for use with DSM. Regardless of the service used, and it is possible to use multiple ones simultaneously, everything is all controlled and managed using the Hyper Backup package.

Go to **Main Menu** and launch **Hyper Backup.** The backup process is largely identical to that described in section **7.2 Backing Up to An External Drive**. In the top left-hand corner of the screen click the large plus (+) sign and select a backup type of Folders and Packages (i.e. data) or LUNs as required, followed by **Next**.

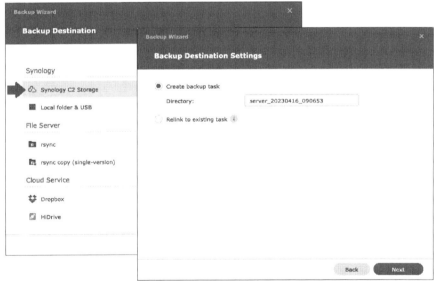

Figure 128: Specify the backup destination & directory name

Select *Synology C2 Storage* or the cloud service of your choice for the Backup Destination, click **Next** and you will be prompted to sign-in to the cloud service and grant access. In this case of Synology C2, you use your registered Synology Account, which you may have created earlier e.g. when setting up QuickConnect.

If you have not used C2 before, you will be offered a free trial; a valid credit card is required, but it will not be charged if the trial is subsequently cancelled. On the next panel, choose **Create backup task** and specify a name for the Directory. The default is the name of the server plus a timestamp, although you can overtype it with a name of your choosing. Note that this directory refers to the cloud side rather than the DiskStation. Click **Next**:

On the next panel, specify the shared folders to be backed up. The tree structure can be expanded as required to include or exclude specific folders; there is also an option to create file filters to include or exclude specific files or file types, for example you might not want to backup large video files to a cloud service. Make your selection and click **Next**:

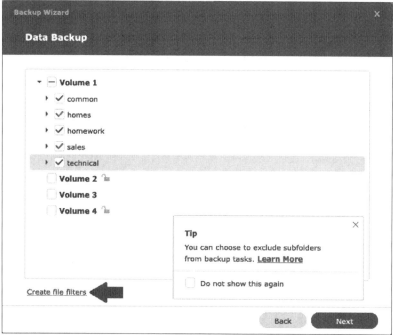

Figure 129: Select folders to be backed up

A panel listing installed applications that store settings on the NAS is displayed, enabling you to include them in the backup. Select as required - if in doubt, tick everything - followed by **Next**.

The subsequent panel is for setting the schedule. In this example, the backup will run daily at 20:00 (8:00 pm), with an integrity check every Sunday at 22:00 (10:00 pm). There is an option to restrict bandwidth, to prevent the backup saturating the connection and impacting on general internet usage. Data travelling over the internet is encrypted, but there is also an option for client-side encryption. Click **Done**. You will be given the option to 'Back up now?'. It is suggested you do so to test the new backup job, by clicking **Yes**.

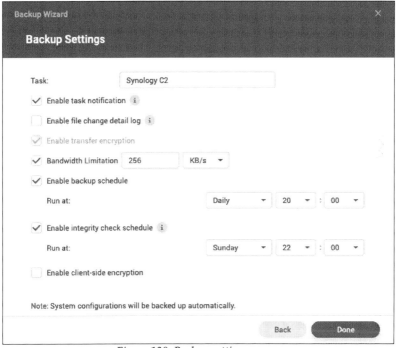

Figure 130: Backup settings screen

Whilst running, the Hyper Backup screen will be updated along the following lines:

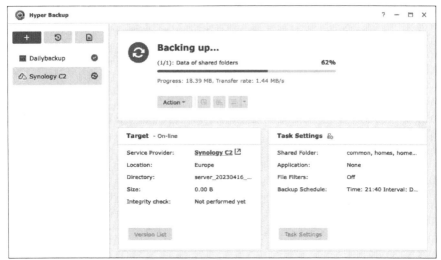

Figure 131: Backup status screen

Restoring data is performed in much the same way as described in **7.3 Restoring Files from a Backup**.

The speed of backup to a cloud service is dependent upon the performance of the internet connection but is typically many times slower than backup to a local drive. For guidance, a backup of 1 terabyte that might take under an hour to a USB drive might take a day or longer over the internet, even with a relatively good upload speed. For this reason, rather than use a cloud backup as the primary backup solution, it might be more appropriate to use it as a secondary backup for a limited selection of important data. Also, cloud services have usage allowances and these should be checked to make sure there is sufficient capacity so you are not, for example, trying to back up 200GB data to a service that has been capped at 100GB.

Managing C2 Online

The Synology C2 account can be managed online from *https://c2.synology.com*. Having logged in, click **Overview** followed by the large **C2 Storage** button in the appropriate section. This will open the *Dashboard* in a new tab, but clicking **Hyper Backup** will provide a more useful summary of usage. The completed backup tasks are listed and highlighting one will cause two mini-icons to be displayed against it. One of these is for deleting the task, to free up space when the backup is no longer required, the other will launch a web-based version of *Backup Explorer*. This can be used for downloading folders and files onto the local computer, which is very useful as it provides a disaster recovery facility. For example, suppose that server and its backups have been lost because, say, the premises have burnt down or been flooded. Provided C2 has been used, the backed-up data can be recovered at a different site and worked upon or used to populate a replacement DiskStation.

Figure 132: Detail screen for C2 Account and Backup Explorer

7.6 Synology to Synology Backups

One disadvantage of using an external USB drive for backups is that it needs to be physically located close to the server. In the event of a disaster such as fire, flood or theft, not only might the server be lost, but the backup drive might be as well. One way to mitigate against this is to use another DiskStation as the backup device. This gives a lot more flexibility as to where it is located; for example, it could be in a different part of the building or even in a totally separate location altogether. The second DiskStation can be in addition to or in place of the external USB backup drive.

We will refer to the DiskStation which is being backed up as the *source* and the one that is receiving the backup as the *destination*, and the first thing to do is setup the destination server. Sign-in to it as an administrator, go to **Control Panel** and click **File Services.** Click the **rsync** tab and on it tick the **Enable rsync service** box. Optionally, you can click **Enable rsync account** and create a dedicated remote backup user account, but this may be less secure and in a home or small business environment you might find it more convenient to use the administrator account on both machines.

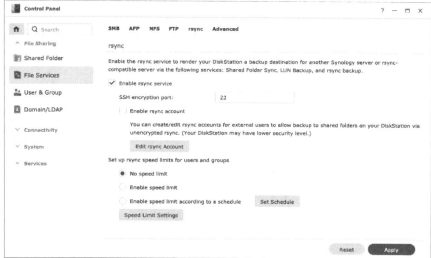

Figure 133: Enabling the rsync service on destination server

A speed limit can be setup to manage network traffic and which can be done according to a schedule if required. Click **Apply**.

As a result of enabling rsync, a folder called *NetBackup* will automatically be created on the destination DiskStation, with R/W privileges for local administrators. Next, go to the Package Center and download, install and run *Hyper Backup Vault*. Once, this is done, the destination DiskStation is ready.

On the source DiskStation, login as administrator. Go to the **Main Menu** and launch **Hyper Backup.** In the top left-hand corner of the screen click the large plus (**+**) sign and select a backup type of *Folders and Packages* or *LUNs* as required and click **Next**. Choose **Remote NAS device** as the Backup Destination. Why this option rather than the specific entry for *rsync*? Because this one is optimized for Synology servers, whereas the latter has settings for use with third party servers running rsync, reflecting the fact that it is a widely used system with its origins in the Unix/Linux world (if you using a non-Synology device as the destination you would choose the rsync option).

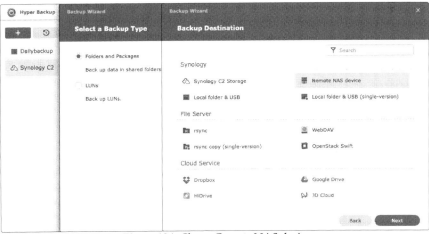

Figure 134: Choose Remote NAS device

Click **Next** and the wizard continues to the *Backup Destination Settings* screen. Specify the *Server name or IP address* of the destination; this can be an internal IP address if the destination is on the same local network, or an external IP address if it is located elsewhere. If you are backing up to a DiskStation on the same local network, the Backup Wizard will have automatically generated a drop-down list showing the backup server(s) it has detected, although this might take several seconds to populate. If you are backing up to an offsite server, set *Transfer encryption* to **On**.

The Port number will default to 6281 and if you are backing up to a NAS that is offsite you should make sure this port is open on the firewalls at each end.

Click the *Authentication* **Log In** button. There may be a warning message about a security certificate – if you click **Yes**, you will be prompted to login to the destination server; if you click **No** you will be presented with a panel for the *Username* and *Password* for the destination server. In both instances the details of the administrative user need to be specified.

The next field is a drop-down which should list the names of the folders on the destination server - you need to set it to *NetBackup*. The field underneath it – confusing called *Directory* – will auto populate, although you could choose to type something different in it as it is unimportant. The rest of the screen can be ignored. Click **Next** to continue:

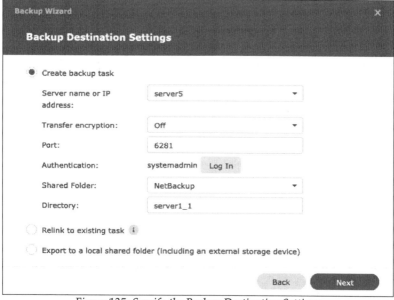

Figure 135: Specify the Backup Destination Settings

On the subsequent panels specify the shared folders to be backed up, any applications to be backed up, the backup settings, including the rotation and scheduling settings. These panels are the same as when backing up to an external USB drive as described in section **7.2 Backing Up to An External Drive**.

Once they have been completed and after a short delay – possibly longer if the server needs to communicate with an external destination server – click **Done** on the summary screen a message appears asking whether you wish to *'Back up now?'*. It is suggested that you reply **Yes,** to test the newly defined backup task.

After the backups have been setup and working, the main **Hyper Backup** screen is used to manage them. To run a backup at any point, rather than wait for the schedule, click **Back up now**. To check the backup log i.e. the list of completed backups, click **Version List**. To change the parameters of the backup, click **Task Settings**. To check data usage at both destination and source, click the **Backup Statistics** mini-icon. From the destination server, the status of backups can be checked by launching Hyper Backup Vault:

Figure 136: Hyper Backup Vault

One capability which may be of interest for larger business and educational users is that one destination server can handle multiple source servers. For instance, consider a school in which, say, each classroom has its own server, all of which could backup to a single server stored elsewhere. Not only is this more convenient, but might be more cost effective than equipping each individual server with its own USB backup drive. If this strategy is used, go into **Settings** in Hyper Backup Vault and review the *Number of concurrent tasks* option. It is also the case that a server can simultaneously be a source and a destination, so two servers can backup to each other.

Non-Synology Destinations

The destination server does not have to be another DiskStation and can be any system running *rsync*. In this case, you would choose *rsync* rather than *Remote NAS* device when setting up the backup job. There is a small amount of variation in the screens and process and, although a non-Synology destination will not be able to run the Hyper Backup Vault package for monitoring, something analogous may be available.

7.7 Backing up the Server Configuration

Although we have discussed how to backup data from the server in this chapter, there is an additional type of backup that is also needed. A lot of customization may have gone into the server in terms of defining users, shares, permissions and other settings. In the event of serious problems with the server - for example, of the sort necessitating a complete re-installation - all this configuration information would have to be re-entered. This can be both difficult and time consuming on all but the simplest of systems. Fortunately, there are facilities to quickly backup and restore the configuration information.

Choose **Update & Restore** from the **Control Panel** and click the **Configuration Backup** tab. Backups can be performed automatically to an online Synology Account, which is the most convenient method, or manually to a local computer.

Figure 137: Configuration Backup screen

Automatic Backup

In the *Automatic Backup* section, tick the **Enable automatic DSM configuration backup** box. If not already signed into your Synology Account, you will be prompted to do so. Choose **Auto encryption** or define your own encryption password. The configuration information will now be backed up automatically on a regular basis. To force a backup at any point e.g. following major changes to the system, click the **Back up Now** button.

Manual Backup

In the Manual Export section, click the **Export** button. There will be a message about the configuration information to be backed up – click **Yes** to acknowledge and proceed. The system will process for a few seconds and then download the backup file it has generated onto the computer you are using, into the Downloads folder. The file has a name of the form *server_yyyymmdd.dss*.

Restoring the Configuration

Should it ever prove necessary to use the backup file, click the **Restore** button in the *Restore DSM Configurations* section. To restore from an automatic backup, choose **Restore from Synology Account** and click **Next**. A list of available configuration backups is displayed; this may take a few seconds to appear, select one and click **Next**. To restore from a manual backup, choose **Restore from a configuration file on your computer**, navigate to the location of the configuration file and select it, click **Next**. A panel is displayed - select the configuration items to be restored (possibly all of them) and follow through the prompts and messages.

7.8 Backing up Computers to the Server

If users store data on their computers rather than on the network, then there is probably a requirement to backup that data; consider, for example, laptop users who take their computers offsite. In the case of Mac users, the built-in Time Machine program of macOS can be used, with the DiskStation taking the place of an external drive. In the case of PCs running Windows Professional, this can be done using its built-in backup program, with the backups stored on the DiskStation. Users of Home Editions of Windows are less fortunate, as the backup programs supplied can only backup to local drives, such as a plug-in USB hard drive or a memory card and they cannot access the network drives (shared folders) of the DiskStation. One way to address this is with use a third-party program that does have such capability, of which several are available, including free ones e.g. *Fbackup* from Softland.

An alternative approach is to use Synology Drive Server, as this works with all modern versions of Windows, as well as with macOS and selected Linux clients. This is described separately in **10 SYNOLOGY DRIVE SERVER, OFFICE & APPS**.

Backing Up Macs using Time Machine

Time Machine is the standard backup solution for Mac users and an integral part of macOS. Mostly used with an external backup drive, support is provided in DSM, thus allowing the server to be specified as a backup destination for Time Machine. This is done as follows:

Begin by creating a shared folder on the server specifically for this purpose (creating shared folders is described in section **3.2 Creating Shared Folders**). Give the folder a meaningful name e.g. *macbackup* and give **Read/Write** access to all the Mac users in the household or organization.

In the **Control Panel**, choose **File Services** and click the **Advanced** tab. In the *Bonjour* section, check the **Enable Bonjour...** boxes are ticked. Click the **Set Time Machine Folders** button, tick the shared folder you just created (*macbackup* in our example) and click **Save** followed by **Apply** on the main screen. If you receive a message about SMB3 being enabled, click **Yes**.

If you are using very old versions of macOS, you will have to enable the AFP service as well (**Control Panel > File Services > AFP > Enable AFP service**) plus the **Enable Bonjour Time Machine broadcast via AFP** option.

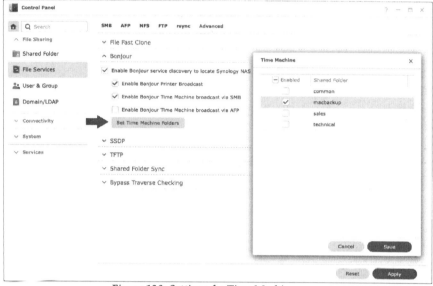

Figure 138: Settings for Time Machine usage

To configure backups for a particular Mac, it needs to be connected to the server, as described in section **5.4 Connecting Macs**. Then, go into settings for Time Machine (these instructions are for recent versions of macOS, for older versions use **System Preferences > Time Machine**):

System Settings > General > Time Machine. Click the **+** (plus) sign, highlight the backup folder we created ("macbackup" in our example) and click **Set Up Disk**. Enter the name and password of the user as defined on the server and click **Connect**. Optionally choose to encrypt the backups. Click **Done**. Thereafter, Time Machine will operate in the normal, expected manner.

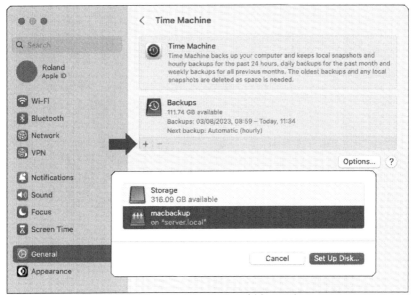

Figure 139: Select the Mac backup folder on the server

Suggestion 1: to avoid the server filling up with backups, apply a quota for each Mac user. Go to **Control Panel** and click the **User & Group** icon. On the **User** tab, highlight a username, click the **Edit** button, then click the **Quota** tab. In the Quota column specify a value for the Time Machine folder, such as 100 GB, 250 GB or whatever value is deemed appropriate. Click **OK**. Alternatively, set an overall quota for the *macbackup* folder when creating it or subsequently by going into **Control Panel > Shared Folder**, highlight the folder and click **Edit**, click **Advanced**, tick the **Enable shared folder quota** box and set a suitable value. Quotas are only available on Btrfs volumes.

Suggestion 2: the folder that stores the Mac backups does not have to be located on the DiskStation. If an external USB drive is connected to the server, that can be specified as the destination when you click the **Set Time Machine folders** button as described above. This enables cheaper USB drives to be used, rather than the more expensive internal RAID storage. If this is done, the external drive needs to be connected permanently.

Suggestion 3: if there are many Mac users, consider using a dedicated volume to hold the backup folder(s).

Backing up Computers running Windows Professional with Built-in Backup Program

All versions of Windows include a built-in backup program that some people may prefer to use, maybe as a simple matter of preference or because of familiarity. However, only Professional and not Home editions are able to backup to network drives. In Windows 7 the program is called *Backup and Restore*; in later versions it is called *File History*. The Windows backup program assumes that you will be using an external USB drive; all that is necessary is to change the backup location so that it points to the user's home folder on the server instead and thereafter it can be used in the normal manner.

Windows 11 Professional Clients

In Windows 11, Microsoft assumes that the *OneDrive* cloud service will be used for backups and hence a small amount of effort is required to find the *File History* program that is needed for backing up to a server. Click the **Search** icon on the Taskbar (it looks like a magnifying glass). Click where it reads **More** and select **Settings**. Start typing in the words 'File history' and it will quickly locate the File History utility on the Control Panel – click to open it. The first panel is to *Select a File History drive* i.e. a destination for the backups. If the mapped home drive (e.g. H:) is not displayed in the list, click **Add network location**. If still not shown, click **Show all network locations**. If necessary, the search path to the user's folder can be entered in UNC format e.g. *\\server\home*.

The subsequent screen will indicate that 'File History is off' – click the **Turn on** button. The screen will update to show that 'File History is on' – click the **Run now** link to start a backup.

To adjust the parameters of the backup, click **Exclude folders** to modify the folders and libraries which are/are not backed up, and **Advanced settings** to adjust the frequency of the backups and their retention period.

Windows 10 Professional Clients

Begin by mapping the user's home drive on the server using one of the techniques described in section **5 CONNECTING TO THE SERVER** if it is not already mapped.

Click **Start** > **Settings** > **Update & security** > **Backup**. Click **Add a drive** and after a few seconds the list of mapped drives will be displayed – click on the user's home drive. Having done so you will be returned to the main Backup panel, where an option to *Automatically back up my files* will have appeared and been set to *On*. That is it – a backup will now run on an hourly basis, copying the user's files from the computer to their home drive on the server.

For greater control over the process, such as controlling the frequency at which the backup runs, click **More options**. From here you can: review the backup status; make the backup run immediately; change the backup frequency (anything from every 10 minutes through to 1 day); change the retention period for the backed-up data.

Windows 7 Professional Clients

Click **Start**, followed by **All Programs**, **Maintenance** then **Backup and Restore**.

Click on **Set up Backup**.

Click the **Save on a network** button. On the next panel, enter the **Network Location**. Specify the user's home folder, using the format \\server\username or click the **Browse** button to navigate to it. Enter the user name and password as defined on the server then click **OK**. The subsequent screen is for choosing what data files are backed up. The default option of **Let Windows choose (recommended)** is suitable in many cases so just click **Next**.

The follow-on screen is a summary of settings; click **Save settings and run backup**.

The backup will run for the first time, during which the status is displayed. Windows will have defined a schedule to subsequently run backups automatically on a regular basis, in this example every Sunday at 7:00pm. If this setting is not suitable it can be altered by clicking **Change settings**.

7.9 Snapshot Replication

Snapshots can be considered as an additional backup mechanism that allows the NAS to record the state of selected data at a moment in time. In simple terms, the system makes a note of what has been altered when a file, folder or LUN has changed, then writes away those details to a different part of the volume or to a different volume altogether. It does not make a complete copy of the file or folder, just the differences, which can then be used to restore the data should that every prove necessary. Snapshots can take place manually or scheduled to run on a regular basis e.g. once an hour, once a day, once a week.

Because only changes are being recorded, the process is very efficient, both in terms of time taken and disk space used. For instance, suppose you had a 10 Mbyte spreadsheet and made a few changes; with a conventional backup the system would create a 10 Mbyte copy, whereas with a Snapshot the backup might only be a few thousand bytes. However, although Snapshots are efficient, the mechanism requires a certain level of hardware support, specifically an x86-based DiskStation or recent ARM-based model, running the Btrfs filing system on a RAID system with a storage pool is required. It should be noted that enabling Snapshots will slightly reduce the overall speed of access to a disk or volume, although there is a worthwhile trade-off between performance and protection.

Clarification: Snapshots operate at the block level rather than the byte level and the above explanation has been simplified to aid understanding.

Setting up Snapshots

Download and install the *Snapshot Replication* app from the Package Center. Click **Yes** to the message about installing the 'Replication Service'. Launch Snapshot Replication by clicking its icon in the Main Menu. There will be a message about *Optimizing Replication Performance*; if you are running a large Synology setup in a corporate environment you may want to make a note about what it says, but otherwise just tick the **Do not show this message again** box followed by **OK**. The *Overview* screen will then appear:

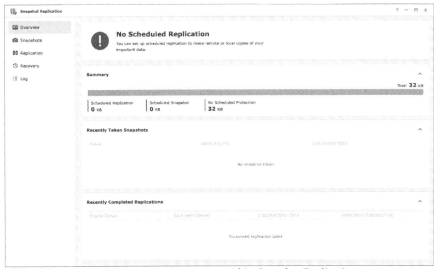

Figure 140: Overview screen within Snapshot Replication

The shared folders or LUNs to be included in the snapshots need to be specified and in this example we are working with folders. Click the **Snapshots** tab and a list of suitable folders (i.e. those on Btrfs volumes) is displayed. Highlight the folder(s) to be included by clicking them; to highlight multiple folders, hold down the **Ctrl** key on Windows PCs or **Cmd** key on Macs whilst clicking. In this example, the *homes* and *common* folders are to be included.

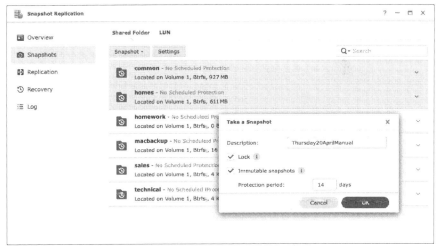

Figure 141: Take a manual Snapshot

Alternatively, if LUNs are to be replicated, click the LUN tab and select from there. Having highlighted the folder(s), to take a manual snapshot click the **Snapshot** button, followed by **Take a Snapshot**. Enter an optional **Description**. If the **Lock** box is ticked, then this snapshot will not be removed automatically during the subsequent creation of any scheduled snapshots. To protect this snapshot being deleted by any means, tick the **Immutable snapshots** box and specify a **Protection Period** e.g. 7 or 14 days. Click **OK**.

Besides manual snapshots, snapshot schedules can be setup by clicking the **Settings** button. On the **Schedule** panel, tick the **Enable snapshot schedule** box and specify the parameters of when replication takes place (you may need to untick the **Keep the original schedule settings...** option to do this). In this example, snapshots will be taken every four hours, each day, between the hours of 0800 and 2000. Again, to protect this snapshot being deleted by any means, tick the **Immutable snapshots** box and specify a **Protection Period** e.g. 7 or 14 days. Click **OK**.

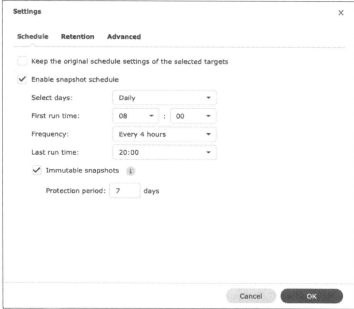

Figure 142: Setting a Schedule for Snapshot Replication

The second tab, **Retention**, controls how long the snapshots are retained. If more snapshots are kept, it becomes possible to roll back further in time to recover data, but there is no one-size-fits-all answer here.

In this example we are choosing to keep 128 snapshots for each folder (the maximum possible is 1024). Alternatively, a time-based policy could be followed e.g. keep all snapshots for 7 days. If the **Advanced retention policy** option is used, a more granular approach can be taken.

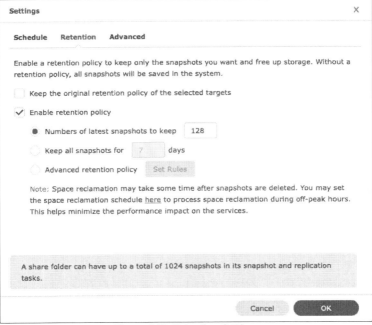

Figure 143: Retention Settings

The third and final tab – *Advanced* – has the useful option to timestamp the snapshots; to enable, tick the **Use the time in the GMT +0 time zone to name the snapshots** box. If the **Make snapshot visible** box is ticked, users can browse the snapshots in the #*snapshot* folder (provided the shared folders are not encrypted).

Having specified the schedule and any options, click **OK**.

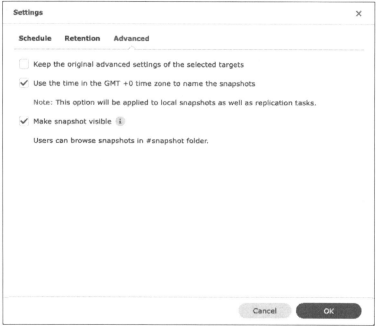

Figure 144: Advanced Settings

Recovering/Restoring a Snapshot

If there is a need to recover data, it is done from within the Snapshot Replication app. On the left-hand side of the screen, click **Recovery** to display a list of snapshot folders/LUN. Highlight the folder(s) or LUN(s), click the **Recover** button, chose the snapshot, click **Action** followed by **Restore to this snapshot**. On the resultant pop-up, tick both the boxes and click **OK**. The time taken for restoration depends upon the amount of data.

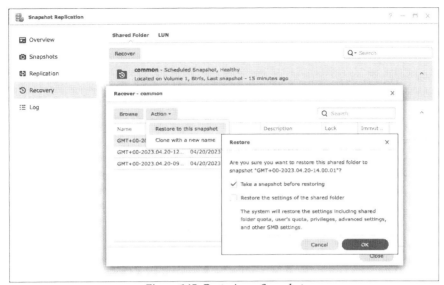

Figure 145: Restoring a Snapshot

Replication

When a snapshot is taken, the data is stored on the same volume. However, if there was subsequently a problem with the volume, it might not be possible to recover the snapshot. To mitigate against this possibility, folders and LUNs can be replicated to separate volumes or different DiskStations altogether, which can be located elsewhere on the network or even offsite. This is a more sophisticated facility, intended mainly for corporate and enterprise users.

Log

As the name suggests, the *Log* section maintains a list of all snapshot-related activities. It can be searched and examined or exported in CSV or HTML format for analysis elsewhere. There is also an option to clear the log file.

Deleting a Folder with Immutable Snapshots

A shared folder which has been configured for immutable snapshots cannot be deleted by any means. To delete such a folder, immutability must first be switched off and the snapshots deleted. With Snapshot Replication, highlight the folder within the *Snapshots* section and click **Settings**. On the *Schedule* tab, remove the tick from the **Immutable snapshots** box and click **OK**.

7.10 Active Backup

In addition to the backup options described earlier in this chapter, Synology offers a range of products under its *Active Backup* category, specifically: *Active Backup for Business; Active Backup for Business Agent (DSM); Active Backup for Microsoft 365; Active Backup for Google Workspace*. As the names suggest, these products are targeted at business users. Collectively, they provide a unified backup system which enables all the computer systems typically used in businesses: Windows PC, Macs, Linux, Windows Servers, Virtual Machines (meaning VMware and Hyper-V, rather than virtual DSM), plus Synology servers of course, to be backed up to centralised Synology NAS using a single method. Data deduplication techniques and compression are used to reduce storage requirements, by ensuring that duplicate files are only backed up once. Furthermore, all these different backups can be managed by the administrator from a web-based portal. Additional capabilities include self-service restoration, enabling employees to browse through backups and recover files and folders that they need, along with bare-metal recovery, which enables a complete image (data and operating system) to be restored to a PC or NAS.

This section is intended as an introduction to Active Backup, to give an idea if it suitable for your circumstances. It is not intended to explore all the available options.

Active Backup for Business

This is the main component of the Active Backup suite and is installed on the Synology box or boxes which will manage and hold the backups. A backup destination machine should be Intel/AMD-based, with at least 4GB RAM, with drives formatted for Btrfs and with sufficient storage capacity to hold the backups. Estimating how much capacity constitutes 'sufficient storage' is a matter of judgement, as it depends on the amount of data held on the computers in the network, the nature of that data, and how many versions of the backups are required i.e. how far back in time data can be restored from.

Because of compression and data deduplication, backups in Active Backup are very efficient, typically reducing storage requirement by a factor of 3x-4x, although it is dependent on the data types e.g. video footage will not compress by that amount. As a starting point, you could simply add up all the storage in the network and use that figure. For example, suppose the network comprises two servers, each with 4TB storage, and 40 computers, each equipped with a 256GB drive. In this case you could use (2 x 4TB) + (40 x 256GB), giving a total storage requirement of 18TB, and then perhaps divide that by two to allow for data compression.

There are several concepts which need to be understood when using Active Backup for Business. Firstly, a small piece of software known as the 'Agent' needs to be installed on the source i.e. the device which is to be backed up. Secondly, the system makes use of *Certificates* as a security measure; these certificates can be self-certified ones or obtained from reputable sources e.g. from organizations such as *Let's Encrypt*. Thirdly, the overall parameters of backups e.g. frequency, encryption, whether the computer should be woken up, are defined by *Templates*. Synology provide initial default certificates and templates and, although useful for getting started, for 'real world' usage in a larger business environment you would need to explore these topics in greater depth.

The installation process will add two icons to the Main Menu: *Active Backup for Business* and *Active Backup for Business Portal*. It will also create a shared folder on the backup server called *ActiveBackupforBusiness*, which should not be edited or changed in any way. Upon running Active Backup for Business for the first time, it must be activated and which requires logging in with a Synology Account. The application is then displayed, with ten options listed down the left-hand side of the screen.

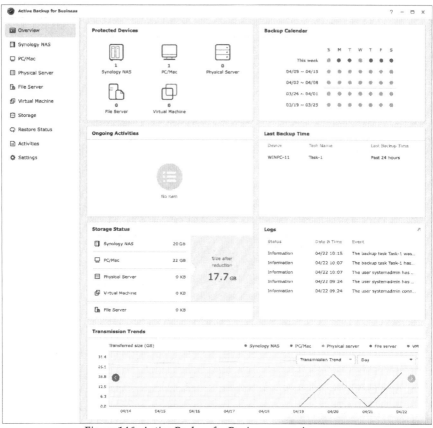

Figure 146: Active Backup for Business, overview screen

Overview – provides an 'at a glance' view of the system. This comprises seven panels, showing a summary of the *Protected Devices* i.e. those which are being backed up; the *Backup Calendar*, showing the dates when backups have been performed; *Ongoing Activities* and *Last Backup Time* show any active and the most recent backups; *Storage Status* shows the amount of space being used to hold the backups – the term 'Size after reduction' is used, illustrating the efficiency of the compression techniques within Active Backup; *Logs* lists the most recent events (the panel can be made full-screen by clicking the arrow in its top right-hand corner); *Transmission Trends* summarises the amount of data backed up by time, and can be filtered by individual device and by day or hour. No settings can be changed from this screen.

Synology NAS – displays information about the DiskStations that are being controlled. To add a NAS, click the blue **Add Device** button. Not all models can be backed up; broadly speaking, only models manufactured during the past five years with Intel or AMD processors are supported, and Virtual DSM instances cannot be backed up. If a particular model is unsuitable, then the Agent software will not be listed in the Package Center on that DiskStation.

PC/Mac – displays information about the Windows PCs and macOS devices which are being backed up. Connecting a PC will be discussed later.

Physical Server – for managing physical Windows and Linux-based servers e.g. Windows Server 2022, Windows Server 2019 and so on.

File Server – file servers running SMB protocol, including Windows, NetApp and Nutanix, can be backed up, as can rsync servers using rsync 3.0 or later.

Virtual Machine – virtual machines based upon VMware vSphere and Microsoft Hyper-V can be backed up.

Storage – displays the status of the storage on the backup server.

Restore Status – details of restoration jobs.

Activities – log files of all backup activities. Reports can be generated and sent to named recipients, on a scheduled basis if required.

Settings – various parameters for the system can be controlled from here, including *Traffic Throttling* to prevent the network being saturated; the number of *Concurrent Devices* (which has implications for the RAM usage on the backup server); the *Certificate*; *User Delegation* (see section **4.6 Delegation** for a broader overview of this topic); *Templates*.

On the following pages, we will setup a backup. In general terms, the process is similar, regardless of the platform.

Backing Up a Personal Computer

Begin by installing the *Active Backup for Business Agent* on the computer to be backed up. It is downloaded from the Synology website and is available for Windows PCs (32-bit and 64-bit), macOS, and selected Linux distributions. When run for the first time, it will prompt for the IP address of the destination server i.e. the one running the main Active Backup for Business package, plus the username and password of an account on the server. Enter the details and click **Connect**. You may receive a message about the SSL certificate: if you are using the Synology-provided one, click **Proceed anyway**, followed by **OK** on the next panel. A Summary panel is displayed, describing the characteristics of the backup, which have been derived from the default template. Click **OK**.

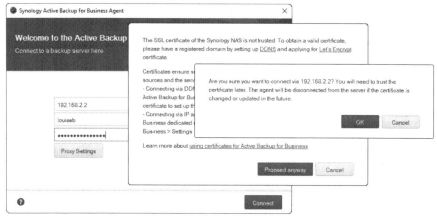

Figure 147: Setting up the Agent on a computer

It is as simple as that. From now on, a daily backup to the server will run. If the computer is not switched on at the time of the scheduled backup, it will take place when it next is. To check the status from the computer, launch the Agent, which will display a screen along the following lines:

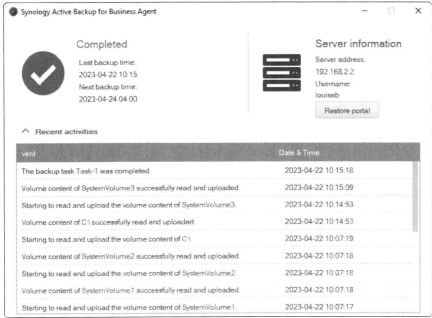

Figure 148: Backup status viewed on a computer

For additional information on a particular platform which has been backed up, click its category on the left-hand side of the screen e.g. clicking **PC/Mac** will display along the following lines. Details of the device(s) and the backup statuses are listed. Various options are available, including adding new devices, creating new backup tasks, restoring data, deleting devices, plus updating the backup agent on devices:

Figure 149: Detailed view of backup status

Active Backup for Business Portal

When *Active Backup for Business* is installed, the *Active Backup for Business Portal* is installed alongside it. This is a restore-only tool which allows administrators, and users who have been delegated appropriate rights, to access, browse, download and restore backups. Admin users can access it from DSM by clicking the Active Backup for Business Portal icon on the Main Menu, or on a machine with the backup agent installed by clicking **Restore Portal**. Delegated users access it by clicking **Restore Portal** on the backup agent and signing-in to the backup server, which will cause the portal to be displayed within the browser:

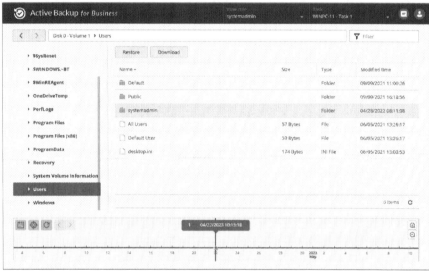

Figure 150: Detailed view of backup status

The screen is similar and operates in the same manner as Backup Explorer (see **7.3 Restoring Files from a Backup**). Navigate to the required backup, highlight the file(s) and folder(s) to be restored, then click the **Restore** button.

8 HOUSEKEEPING & MAINTENANCE

8.1 Overview

Servers must be monitored to check they are operating correctly and there are no problems. In the case of a home system this may only need doing every few weeks, but in a business environment a more systematic approach is better, say once a week at least or maybe even a daily check. Things that should be looked at include disk space; confirmation that backups have completed successfully; the log files; anti-virus scans; results of the regular Security Advisor scan; checking that cloud synchronization is working and up to date; checking for DSM updates. Some of these topics are detailed in other chapters.

Monitoring can be done in a variety of ways: manually checking the DiskStation using Widgets, setting up automatic notifications, using DS Finder on a mobile device, plus using optional downloadable tools such as Storage Analyzer. Most aspects can also be monitored remotely over the internet.

8.2 Checking for DSM Updates

The DSM software is updated on a regular basis by Synology. Updates may be major e.g. from DSM 7 to DSM 8, although typically these only occur every couple of years. Significant updates e.g. from DSM 7.1 to DSM 7.2 are more frequent, typically every 12-18 months. Additionally, there are more rapid updates to fix problems which are made available by Synology as required; as these may be in response to specific security threats it is important that they are applied in a timely manner. Synology have a concept of LTS or *Long Term Support* versions, which is of particular value to business users requiring long-term stability. Typically, most DiskStations are supported with the current version of DSM for around 7 years.

If an update is available, it will usually be indicated by the appearance of a small red marker in the Control Panel against the **Update & Restore** icon. Alternatively, to check for updates at any point, launch **Control Panel** and click the icon.

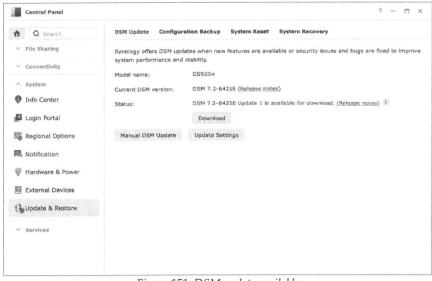

Figure 151: DSM update available

To check if an update is of relevance, click on the **Release notes** link and follow the various Synology forums available on the internet. If the update is required or advisable, click the **Download** button. Once the download is complete, the button will change to read **Update Now**.

As updates invariably require a reboot of the system, it is suggested that they are done outside of normal working or usage hours. Also, the server data and configuration information should be backed up before installing an update.

The settings for DSM updates can be changed by clicking the **Update settings** button. Whilst keeping DSM up to date is recommended in most instances, a more cautious approach to updating may sometimes be appropriate, particularly in a business environment. To control this, click the **Notify me and let me decide whether to install the new update** option.

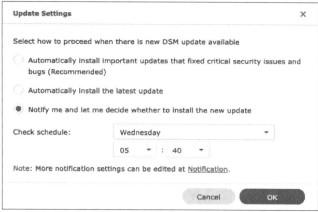

Figure 152: Update settings

Following a DSM update the Package Center should be reviewed, as some apps may also require updating to work with the new version. If updates are available, it will usually be indicated by the appearance of a red marker on the Package Center icon. With some DSM updates, selected packages will automatically be updated; with others, DSM will advise that the package is affected by compatibility issues and will 'Repair' it, or you may have to do so manually. In some instances, DSM may require that an existing package is updated first before it in turn can be updated.

Patch Versions

Although DSM usually advises when a new version is available, in some cases this does not happen and this is intentional. An update might still be available, but it might be optional or in the form of an update patch, downloadable from the Synology website and which must be applied manually.

To see if this is the case, check the release notes for the latest version on the website. To apply the patch, click the **Manual DSM Update** button, navigate to the downloaded file, select and click **OK**.

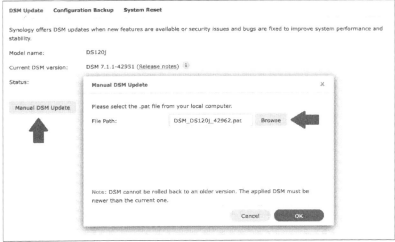

Figure 153: Manual DSM Update

Beta Versions of DSM

Prior to releasing a significant new version of DSM, Synology typically release a beta (test) version a few months beforehand. This enables interested users to gain early experience of the new version, giving them familiarity and the chance to determine its applicability and compatibility with their requirements. It also enables Synology to receive valuable feedback, identifying bugs, usability and other problems. As part of this process, Synology might release further betas and eventually the *Release Candidate*, which is intended to be as close to the final version as possible.

Many users and organisations look forward to beta versions, particularly if they add new and desirable features, whereas others simply like to work with the 'latest and greatest' software. However, there are several considerations when working with beta software:

1. It may be unstable, incomplete in some areas, have compatibility issues and contain bugs. For these reasons, it should be used in a test environment and not on a production or other important machine. There should be no critical or irreplaceable data on the DiskStation.

2. Some applications may need updating to be compatible with the beta version. In some instances, new versions of applications may not be available during the beta phase.
3. It is not possible to downgrade from a later to an earlier version of DSM, and this applies to beta versions also. For instance, if it is decided not to continue testing with the beta version, the DiskStation cannot be reverted to a standard release e.g. back from DSM 7.3 beta to, say, DSM 7.2.

It might be thought that running a DSM beta in a virtualized environment (see **14.3 Installing Virtual DSM**) would be a good option. However, support for Virtual DSM may be absent during the beta phase.

In a larger business environment, the best option for testing beta versions of DSM is to use one or more DiskStations specifically allocated for this purpose.

Downgrading to an Earlier Version of DSM

One question which is sometimes asked is: Is it possible to downgrade the version of DSM which is installed, e.g. from 7.2 to 7.1, using the *Manual DSM Update* option and choosing a previously downloaded version of DSM? The answer is 'No'*. When DSM is installed or upgraded, flash memory inside the DiskStation is updated. As part of the installation, this memory is checked and the process will not proceed if it detects that a more recent version has been installed. It is important to be aware of this if you want to try installing a beta version of DSM, as you will not subsequently be able to revert to an earlier release.

Technically it is sometimes possible, but requires specialist skills and tools to modify the flash memory and may result in the DiskStation being 'bricked' and unusable.

Checking for Updates with DS Finder

DSM updates can be managed from within the DS Finder for mobile devices. To do so, tap the **Update settings** option from the General screen, which will result in the following screens. If you are using DS Finder on an iPhone and have an Apple Watch, notifications will also be received on that.

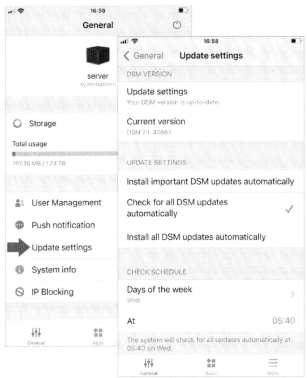

Figure 154: Update options from within DS Finder

8.3 Info Center

Info Center provides a quick summary of the status of the DiskStation and some key configuration details. It duplicates much information that can be found elsewhere but presents it in summary format in a single place. Click **Control Panel > Info Center** to display the following screen:

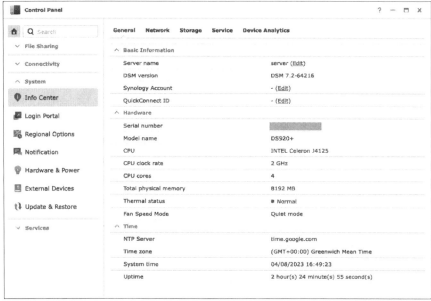

Figure 155: Info Center

There are five tabs in the Info Center:

General – an overview of the hardware and DSM version. The Server name, Synology Account and QuickConnect can be edited from here.

Network – details of the networking configuration, such as IP information.

Storage – status of the drive(s) and volume(s)

Service – summary of services and ports

Device Analytics – controls whether usage and network location information are shared with Synology.

System Info in DS Finder

Within the DS Finder, the *System Info* screen is analogous to the Info Center. It can be accessed by tapping **System Info** on the **General** (Home) screen, resulting in the following display. Besides the standard System information, key network information can be viewed, although not changed, by tapping **Network Info** and **LAN** at the bottom of the screen (not visible in this screenshot from an iPhone).

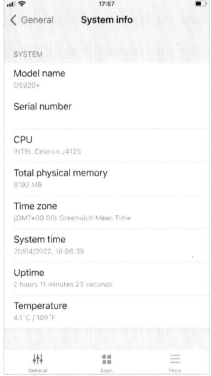

Figure 156: System Info in DS Finder

8.4 Widgets

Widgets are small panels available to administrative users that provide status information, mainly relating to the health of the system. Click the Widget icon in the top right-hand corner of the screen; the resultant panel can then be customized by clicking the plus sign in its top left-hand corner. There is a selection of widgets and the number that can be shown simultaneously depends upon the resolution of the screen, the size of the browser window and the panel itself, which is resizable. A typical selection might be *System Health*, *Resource Monitor* and *Storage*, for example. The Widgets panel can be dragged anywhere on the desktop.

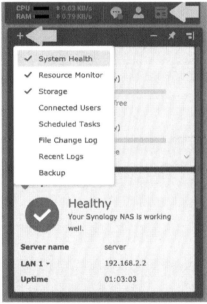

Figure 157: Setting up Widgets to check server status

By hovering the mouse cursor over the top right-hand corner of each widget, mini-icons appear, enabling it to be collapsed so it can be viewed in a more compact format. Additionally, some of the widgets have a mini-icon to transfer them to the task manager e.g. the Resource Monitor. To return a widget from the task manager to the main panel, just click it.

To hide the widget panel, click again on the icon in the top right-hand corner of the screen.

8.5 Checking Disk Health

The health of the disks in a DiskStation should be checked regularly, especially if there appear to be any problems or if the DiskStation has shut down unexpectedly for any reason. There are several ways of doing so: using the Storage Widget (see **8.4 Widgets**), by going into Info Center (see **8.3 Info Center**) and clicking the **Storage** tab, but more comprehensive facilities are available in Storage Manager.

Go to the **Main Menu** and start **Storage Manager**. On the left-hand side of the screen click **HDD/SSD**. Within the **HDD/SSD** tab, highlight the disk drive to be tested and click the **Health Info** button followed by the **S.M.A.R.T.** tab. A *Quick Test* or *Extended Test* can be selected, with the former being sufficient in most circumstances. Click **Start**. The time taken depends upon the number and capacity of the drives but is typically several minutes. If a drive fails, the S.M.A.R.T. test it should be replaced at the earliest opportunity and how to replace a drive is explained in **12.2 Replacing a Faulty Drive**.

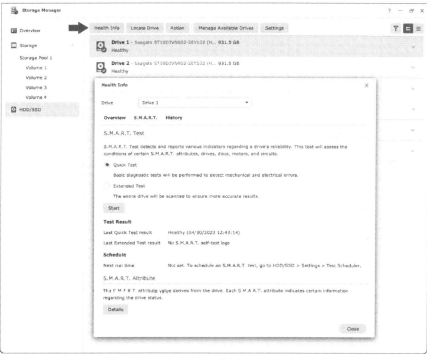

Figure 158: S.M.A.R.T. test for disk drives

To automate the testing, click the **Settings** button within the **HDD/SSD** page of **Storage Manager**. On the **Test Scheduler** tab, click the **Create** button. On the **General** tab, give the task a meaningful name e.g. *MonthlyTest*. There is a choice of *Quick* and *Extended* tests, and all or specific drives only can be tested. Click the **Schedule** tab. Setup a suitable schedule e.g. run monthly, then click **OK**.

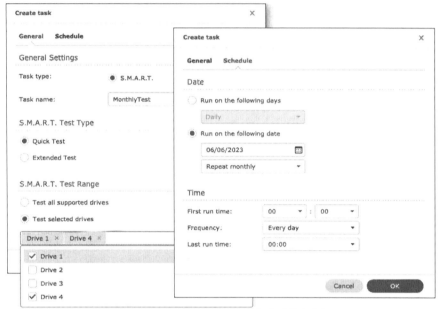

Figure 159: Setting up schedule to test disk drives

8.6 Storage Analyzer

Storage Analyzer is a utility from the Package Center for identifying storage trends on the server and producing reports on usage, enabling you to help answer questions such as: Where has all the disk space gone? How much is being used by particular file types? Who are the largest users? Launching it for the first time will display a message advising that a location for storing reports has not yet been specified; the utility will work without doing so, but for practical purposes you need to click **Yes** and specify a storage location e.g. the *technical* shared folder suggested in **3.2 Creating Shared Folders**. Optionally, specify a schedule for it to run automatically, such as daily or weekly. If required, this report can be automatically emailed to a recipient e.g. the administrative user, provided email notifications have been enabled; if you do not wish to do so, cancel the *Storage Usage Report Wizard* that appears by clicking the cross in the top right-hand corner of its screen.

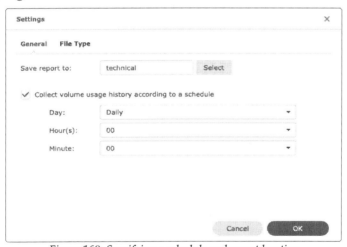

Figure 160: Specifying a schedule and report location

Storage Analyzer is switchable between two screens that provide an overview of volume utilization. The items to be displayed on screen two can be customized by clicking the three-dot menu in the top right-hand corner. To obtain more detailed information, a report can be generated. Click the **Create** button to run the *Storage Usage Report Wizard*. Specify a *Task name*, an optional email recipient and click **Next**.

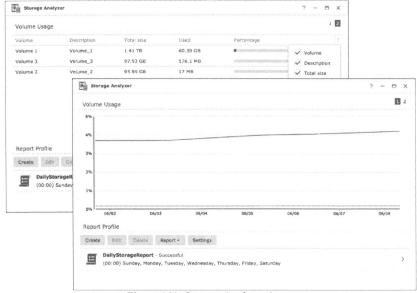

Figure 161: Storage Analyzer in use

Optionally, specify a schedule plus the maximum number of reports to be retained. If emailed reports are required, then email notifications must first be enabled as described in **8.9 Notifications**. On the subsequent panel, tick or untick the required *Report Items*. Click **Next**:

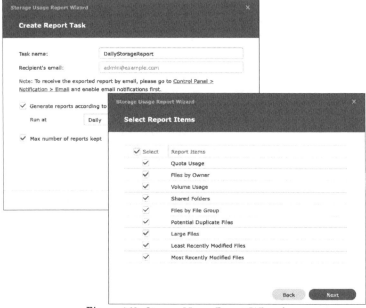

Figure 162: Storage Usage Report Wizard

On the next panel, choose whether all or only specific shared folders should be analyzed. The panel after that is for Advanced Settings, such as finding duplicate files. Eventually you will reach the Summary screen – click **Done**.

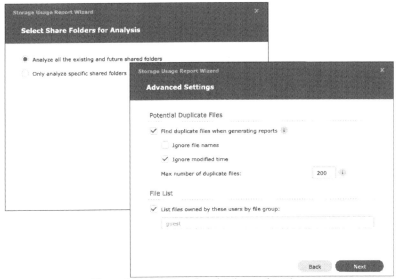

Figure 163: Additional and Advanced settings

If you wish to produce the report immediately, highlight it in the *Report Profile* section and click **Report > Generate reports now**. Reports may take several minutes to generate, depending on the volume of data and criteria specified. Completed reports are listed on the main Storage Analyzer screens. At the right-hand side of the report is a chevron (**>**), which can be clicked to view it at summary level:

Figure 164: Viewing a summary report

The various characteristics such as file type, duplicates and size, can be selected using the options listed down the left-hand side of the screen. When there are multiple reports, they can be selected using the timeline at the bottom of the screen. Clicking **Report Action > View Report** will generate a more detailed report containing all the underlying information, which will be opened in a separate browser tab. From there, it can be downloaded as a CSV file for subsequent analysis in a spreadsheet program.

8.7 Resource Monitor

Resource Monitor is used for monitoring the performance of a DiskStation and is similar to tools provided in other computing environments, such as the Task Manager in Windows or Activity Monitor in macOS. It monitors CPU, Memory, Network and Disk utilization, amongst other parameters. This information can be useful when diagnosing problem or identifying bottlenecks in a poorly performing system and is helpful to IT support staff. To launch Resource Monitor, click its icon in the **Main Menu**. The main topics are listed down the left-hand side, each with their own options and settings.

Performance - Monitors the real-time performance of the DiskStation in seven key areas: CPU, Memory, Network, Disk, Volume, LUN and NFS. The first tab provides an overview, whilst clicking on an individual tab provides more detailed information.

Task Manager – Provides detailed information about the processes and services that are running, such as their CPU and memory utilization. Note: this is replaced by *Processes* on some models.

Connections – Shows which users are currently logged in to the server, along with their IP addresses and which files have been accessed. To forcibly logout a user, highlight them and click the **Kill connection** button.

Speed Limit – Used for monitoring and managing file transfer processes. Connections can also be killed (forcibly dropped) from here.

Performance Alarm and Settings – Allows alarms to be generated for high-load conditions e.g. you could set a rule to generate a warning if Antivirus Essential was running at more than 80% CPU utilization. Note: this is not present on some models.

Settings – enables the utility to maintain historical information in addition to showing live data.

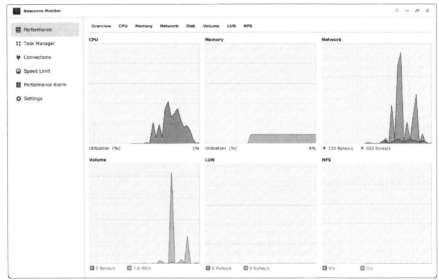

Figure 165: Resource Monitor

8.8 Log Center

DSM maintains an audit trail of all significant activities and events, such as when the system starts and shutdowns, user logins, the creation of shared folders, applications running and more. This information is stored in log files, which can then be examined to monitor and check the smooth running of the system and help identify and diagnose problems using the *Log Center* package.

Log Center is located on the Main Menu. Launching it will display a message about *Advanced Functions*, which are additional capabilities provided by downloading a package (confusingly also called Log Center) from the Package Center. This is particularly useful if there are multiple DiskStations in the network, but if this is not the case then you may wish to tick the 'Do not show this message again' box and click **OK**. Thereafter, the following screen is shown:

Figure 166: Log Center Overview screen

A constantly updated chart provides a visual summary of how many events are being logged and it can be zoomed, unzoomed or paused. Underneath is a list of the most recent events; clicking on **Logs** on the left-hand side of the screen will display a more comprehensive list, which can be scrolled and paged through as required. Entries are color-coded and categorized as *Info*, *Warnings* or *Errors*. The log can be filtered by category, plus there is a search facility. If required, the log file can be exported into HTML or CSV format for analysis with a different tool e.g. Excel.

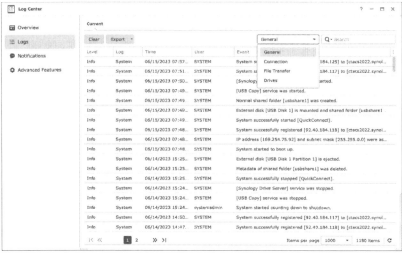

Figure 167: Logs

With time the log file will grow, until it becomes unmanageable. It should therefore be cleared down on an occasional basis, the frequency of which will depend upon the number of users and other factors. For instance, a business system with several hundred users will generate many more logs than a home system with only a few. To do this, click the **Clear** button and acknowledge the prompt. Suggestion: before clearing the log file, create a copy by first exporting it.

The Log Center can send notifications to the administrator (the wider topic of notifications is discussed in the next section). You might want to do this if, for example, to be alerted if the system was generating an abnormal number of logs, suggesting a possible problem. Click on **Notifications** on the left-hand of the screen, use the tick-boxes and fields to specify the conditions, then click **Apply**:

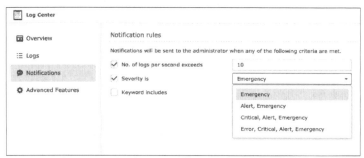

Figure 168: Configure Notifications within Log Center

8.9 Notifications

Notifications provide status information about events that have occurred e.g. backup successfully completed, storage problems, system errors etc. New notifications are indicated by the appearance of a red dot on the notifications icon, which looks like a speech bubble and appears in the top right-hand corner of the DSM screen. If the icon is clicked, the list of most recent notifications is displayed, with the latest at the top. To view a complete list, including older notifications, click **Show All**. To remove a notification, hover the mouse cursor over the right-hand side of it until a small cross (X) appears, then click it. To clear the entire list, click the **Clear All** button.

Figure 169: Notifications, side panel and logs

To customize the notifications, for instance by turning off ones which are not of interest, click the **Notifications** icon followed by the **Settings** wheel, to display the *Notification Settings* panel. When packages are installed, some will add their own entries, so you may have additional or different ones to those shown below. Remove or add ticks against the topics as required. When complete, click **OK**.

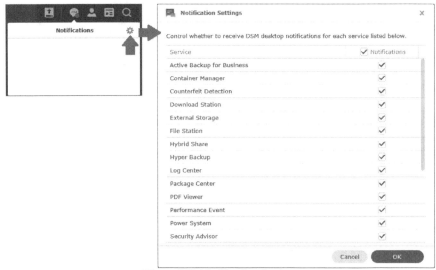

Figure 170: Notification Settings

Automatic Notifications

DiskStations should be checked on a regular basis, but it may not always be possible or practical to do so in person, for instance, the individual who looks after the system may not be located at the premises. Also, it is better to deal with some problems sooner rather than later, and for these reasons DSM can proactively advise when issues occur, using automatic notifications sent out by communication tools such as email, mobile devices, Synology Chat and Microsoft Teams.

From the **Control Panel**, click the **Notification** icon There are five tabs: *Email*, *Push Service*, *Webhooks*, *Rules* and *Events*. The first three are for setting up the notification delivery services and the final two are for specifying the events that generate notifications. Any or all these services can be used, and a selection are discussed in this section.

Configure Email Notifications

Emails can be sent to the address associated with your Synology Account, handled through Synology's email servers, or through third party services such as Gmail and Outlook, or a customized SMTP service such as an in-house email system. To configure, click the **Email** tab within Notification.

To use the Synology Account, tick the **Receive notifications...** box in the *Synology Account* section. The account details will be listed if you are already signed in. Click the **Rule** dropdown and select *All, Warning, Critical* or *Custom*. The first option will generate too many messages, so you probably don't want to use it. How to define Custom rules is described later. Click **Apply.** Click the **Send Test Email** button, wait a few minutes, then check that you have received the test message. This is the easiest method for setting up automatic notifications.

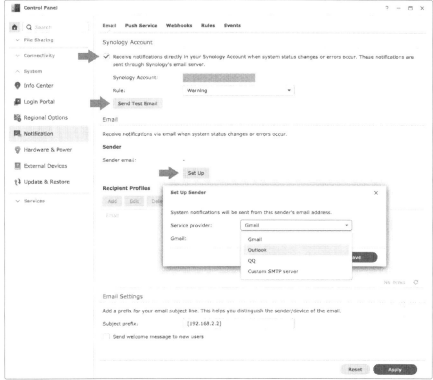

Figure 171: Configuring email

To use a third-party email service, click the **Set Up** button in the *Email* section. Using the dropdown, choose the email **Service provider** – there is a choice of *Gmail, Outlook, QQ* or *Custom SMTP*. If SMTP is used then it is necessary to provide the details of the SMTP server (name, port number, authentication etc.), which should be available from whoever runs or controls the email service. If using Gmail or Outlook, you will be prompted to login to that service and give permission for Synology to access it, which you should do.

Next, you need to define the *Recipient Profiles*, meaning who receives the emails and what types of notifications they receive. Click the **Add** button, choose a Rule, specify the email recipients, click **Save**. Finally, in the *Email Settings* section, you can optionally specify a Subject Prefix for the emails, so the recipients will know what they are. Click **Apply**.

Figure 172: Recipient Profiles

Configure Push Service

The *Push Service* can send notifications to mobile devices running the DS Finder app, directly to supported browsers (Chrome, Edge and Safari), or to Synology Chat, Microsoft Teams, LINE or SMS via the 'Webhooks' feature. The options are not mutually exclusive and you can use a mixture. This section describes how to setup mobile devices and browsers.

Setting Up Mobile Devices

Go to **Control Panel > Notification > Push Service**. Click the blue **Set Up** button and choose **Device** or, if some item(s) have previously been configured, click **Pair > Device**. A pop-up panel appears; if DS Finder is not already installed on your mobile device, you can do so by scanning the appropriate QR code.

Figure 173: Setup Push Service

If you receive a message about permitting notifications, reply in the affirmative, then check within DS Finder that the Push Notification switch on the *General* screen is set to the 'On' position. You might also be prompted to add permissions for notifications within iOS or Android.

Returning to the server, the newly added device should now be visible on the *Push Service* tab. If not, refresh the screen by clicking a different tab and then returning back to *Push Service*. Choose the category of notification to be sent using the dropdown. Click **Send Test Message** and check that it has been received on the mobile device.

Setting Up Browsers
On the computer which is to receive notifications, sign-in to DSM and click **Control Panel > Notification > Push Service**. Click the blue **Set Up** button and choose **Browser** or, if some item(s) have previously been configured, click **Pair > Browser**. A new tab is opened on the browser. The procedure varies, depending on the browser and platform, but you will see a **Pair Now** or **Install Now** button, which should be clicked. With the latter, you may be prompted to download and install a necessary extension for the browser.

After a few seconds, details of the server will be displayed on the *Paired Device* section within the browser. Click the *Event* section and you will see recent events. You should also see a message from the computer's own notifications system i.e. the one in macOS or Windows, which means that messages will be received from the DiskStation and the browser does not actually have to be used or open for this purpose.

Returning to the server, the newly added browser should now be visible on the *Push Service* tab. If not, refresh the screen by clicking a different tab and then returning to *Push Service*. Choose the category of notification to be sent using the dropdown. Click **Send Test Message** and check that it has been received by the computer.

You can configure multiple mobile devices to receive messages. If you ever need to 'unpair' a device, you can do so by going into **Control Panel > Notification > Push Service**. Highlight the device, click **Unpair**, and acknowledge the warning message.

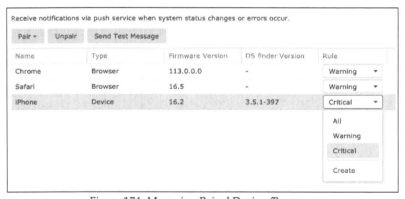

Figure 174: Managing Paired Devices/Browsers

Rules

To specify events that are reported upon, click the **Rules** tab. This screen serves two main purposes. Firstly, it provides a summary of which event categories (warnings, critical, all) are reported upon by the different mechanisms (email, devices, browsers). Secondly, there are dozens of different potential notifications that can be generated, organized into several categories, and these can be customized and/or new rules added.

To create a new rule, click the **Add** button. On the resulting panel, specify a *Rule name*. Expand the list of events and add/remove ticks from the required events. For instance, you could create a rule which reported only on events relating to backups, which would necessitate selecting events in the Hyper Backup category and deselecting events in all the other categories such as Container Manager, Download Station, External Storage and so on. When complete, click **Add**.

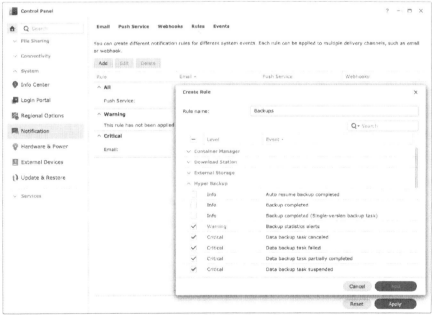

Figure 175: Notification rules

The next step is to apply the new rule to one or more delivery channels. For example, go the *Push Service* tab and against an entry click the Rule dropdown. In addition to the built-in rules of *All*, *Warning* and *Critical*, the new rule will be now available for selection.

Events

The contents of the messages (notifications) that are generated can be customized. Messages comprise a mixture of text and system variables and these can be customized (this might not be a common requirement). To edit a message, double-click its entry on the **Events** tab, or highlight it and click **Edit Message** or **Edit Variables**.

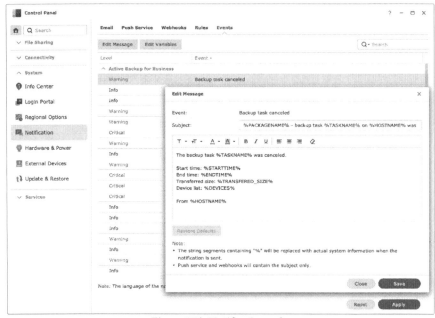

Figure 176: Notification rules

Notification Language

To change the language of the notifications, go to **Control Panel > Regional Options > Language**. The Notification language does not have to be the same as the Display language; for example, DSM might be configured to operate in English but the notifications are sent out in Spanish.

8.10 CMS (Central Management System)

If you work in an environment with multiple DiskStations, you might want to consider Synology's *CMS (Central Management System)* package. This enables you to manage multiple servers from a single DiskStation, known as the *CMS Host*, even if the servers are at disparate locations. The servers can be using different releases of DSM, although they must be DSM 6.2 or later. The capabilities of CMS include:

- Monitoring the status of managed servers.
- The ability to create server groups, then define policies that apply to those groups (analogous to Group Policy Management in a Windows Server environment).
- Install DSM onto new DiskStations.
- Install packages and firmware updates on the managed servers.
- Delegate administrator permissions to specific users and groups, enabling them to manage certain pre-defined settings on their local server(s).

Download and install CMS from the Package Center onto your designated CMS Host. Behind the scenes, the installation will create a new user account, called *SynologyCMS*, and this account should not be modified in any way or used directly.

Begin by adding the server(s) to be managed, starting with the one you have just installed CMS upon. Click **Server** in the left-hand panel, followed by the **Add** button. This launches the *Add Server Wizard*: choose the **Add existing servers** option and click **Next**. On the second screen there are three ways of adding servers. The second method – *Add a server by entering its IP address, FQDN or QuickConnect ID* – is the most flexible so choose that and click **Next**.

Additional information needs to be provided. For instance, if you are adding a single server then you will need to provide its hostname or IP address, plus a username and password i.e. the administrator credentials.

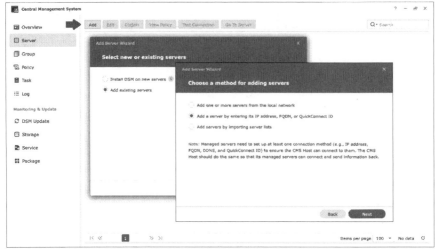

Figure 177: Adding a server to CMS

As DiskStations are added, the *Overview* screen is updated to provide an 'at a glance' view of overall network (server) status. This screen comprises several sections – to expand one of these sections, click the small arrow in the corresponding top right-hand corner, or click one of the options listed on the left-hand side of the screen:

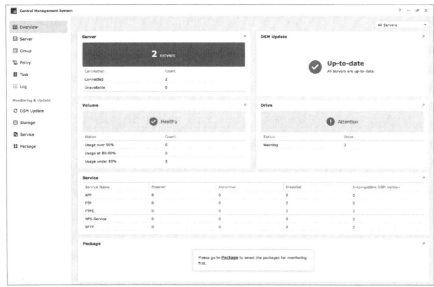

Figure 178: Overview screen

For example, clicking **Server** will display the list of managed servers. The details of the server can be edited from this screen using the buttons at the top of the screen. To login directly, click the **Go To Server** button. On the right-hand side of the listing for each server is a right-pointing chevron and clicking this will expand the details for it, displaying the information that is shown by the *Info Center* on a single DiskStation (see section **8.3 Info Center**).

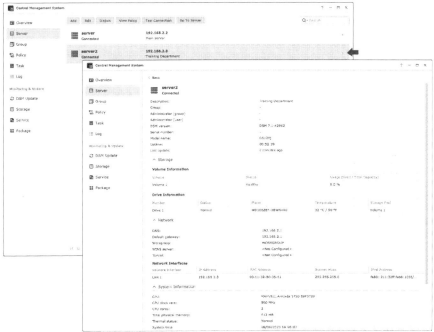

Figure 179: Listing of managed servers

Powerful, additional capabilities are *Group* and *Policy*, which enable settings to be defined that can be applied consistently across the servers or a defined group of servers (for those who are familiar, this is analogous to Group Policy in Windows Server). An example of how they might be used is as follows.

Following a review of security and good working practices, an organization has decided to enforce an automatic logout time of 5 minutes for users who access DSM via a browser. To set this up, click **Policy > Create**. Specify a *Policy name* and *Description* and click **Next**. The subsequent panel contains a complete list of items for which policies can be specified – scroll down to **System > DSM Settings > Security**.

Tick the **Enable this rule (Security)** box and specify the parameters e.g. Logout timer set to 5 minutes. Click **Next** and the Policy will be added. By default, policies apply to all servers, but you can optionally create groups of servers and specify policies for them.

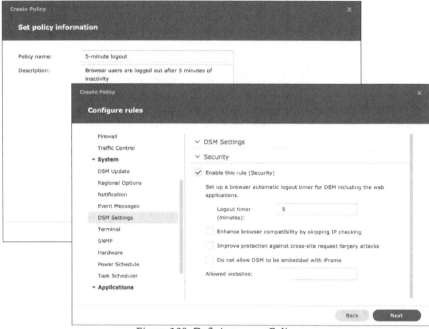

Figure 180: Defining a new Policy

Changes to Control Panel

When a server is added to the Central Management System, an icon for CMS is added to its Control Panel. This can be used to disjoin (remove) the server from the CMS Host. To enable centralized notifications whereby notifications are forwarded from the server to the CMS Host, tick the **Enable centralized notifications** box and use the *Rule* dropdown to specify the type of warnings e.g. 'Critical'. Click **Apply**.

Figure 181: CMS icon in Control Panel

Remotely Installing DSM: Installing on a New Server

CMS can be used to install DSM onto another DiskStation. The DiskStation can be located remotely, maybe as in another part of the premises, provided it is on the same network.

Within CMS, click **Server** > **Add** to invoke the *Add Server Wizard*. Choose **Install DSM on new servers** and click **Next**. On the next panel, select the server(s) and click **Next**. The *Add Server Wizard* will continue, giving the choice of updating to the latest version of DSM provided on Synology's website, or using a .pat file which has previously been downloaded. With both options, a storage location for the .pat files on the CMS server must be specified. Click **Next**.

Figure 182: Add Server Wizard

Enter an administrative username and password, plus a server name prefix for the new DiskStation:

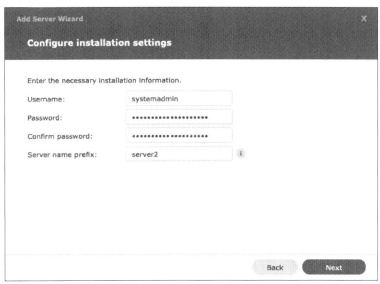

Figure 183: Provide username, password and server name

Acknowledge the message about any data on the disk drives being deleted, then specify the IP details for the server. Click the **Install** button, followed by **Apply** on the summary screen, and the process will commence, during which time a status screen is shown. When the installation status changes to 'Successful', click **Finish** and the newly installed server will be added to the Content Management System, from where it can be managed. At this point, you would need to login to it to configure and setup storage and so on, as described in Chapter **2 INSTALLING DSM** and subsequent chapters.

Remotely Installing DSM: Updating an Existing Server

CMS can be used to update DSM on another DiskStation. The DiskStation can be located remotely, maybe as in another part of the premises, provided it is on the same network.

Within CMS, click **DSM Update** – a list of servers that can be updated is shown. Highlight the one to be updated and click the **Update** button (if there are multiple servers, you could click **Update All**). The *DSM Update Wizard* will commence, giving the choice of updating to the latest version of DSM provided on Synology's website, or using a .pat file which has previously been downloaded. With the first option, a location for storing the DSM files on the CMS server must be specified. Click **Next**, followed by **Update** on the resultant summary screen. The process will now take place without further intervention.

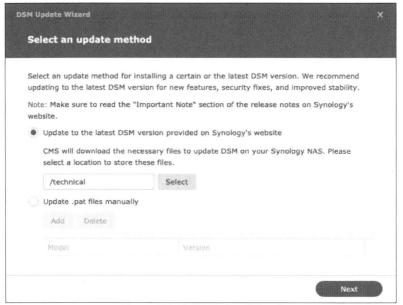

Figure 184: DSM Update Wizard

8.11 Active Insight

Active Insight is a 24x7 cloud-based monitoring service that enables multiple DiskStations to be constantly checked for performance and system anomalies. The DiskStations record and send key information to a secure server at Synology, which can then be accessed via a web portal. When problems occur, notifications are sent by email and/or to the *Synology Active Insight* smartphone app. There are multiple tiers available for Active Insight, ranging from a free, basic one for up to three servers, through to a subscription service with more comprehensive features and for larger numbers of servers ('Premium Plan'). This product is likely to have most appeal to organizations that have multiple DiskStations, especially if they are geographically dispersed. Active Insight is not available on DiskStations with 256 MB of system memory or less, which would generally be older J Series models, or with Virtual DSM instances.

To use Active Insight, it is necessary to have a Synology Account and be signed into it. You may have applied for one during the installation of DSM or subsequently, else have an existing account. Active Insight should have been installed automatically at the same time as DSM, otherwise it can be loaded from the Package Center. Launch it from the Main Menu, tick the **Register this Synology NAS for 24/7 health monitoring** box, and click **Apply**. After a few seconds the service status should change to 'Enabled'. This step is the mechanism by which a DiskStation, referred to as a 'Host', is added to Active Insight and needs to be performed on each DiskStation which needs to be monitored. There will also be a message about the Active Insight Portal.

Figure 185: Enabling Active Insight

The **Settings** button controls whether metrics are collected, which are required for full functionality of Active Insight. Usually the box would be ticked to enable metrics, but this can affect performance on less powerful DiskStations, in which case it can be switched off by unticking the box.

To access Active Insight, go to the portal at **https://insight.synology.com** (there is a link on the Active Insight screen above the Settings button). Login using your Synology Account details and the Overview screen will be displayed. There are seven main sections:

Overview – Provides an 'at a glance' view of key metrics such as CPU, memory, network and storage utilization. Individual servers are referred to as *hosts*. The items to be shown can be specified using the *All Metrics* dropdown on the bottom right-hand side of the screen. Clicking an item will expand that topic to provide more comprehensive information.

Host – Displays summary level information for hosts, of similar level to the information shown by the regular DSM Widgets. Clicking a host will expand the amount of information, allowing Performance, Service Information, Storage and Events to be examined in greater detail.

Figure 186: Active Insight screens

Event – Lists various events which have occurred. These can be categorized as *New*, *Put Aside* or *Resolved*, and any associated Ticket number assigned.

Protection – Comprises three sub-sections. The first is for updating DSM and Packages on monitored hosts and is available on all plans. The second keeps track of backups performed using Hyper Backup, whilst the third records login activity (available for paid plans only).

Report – Comprehensive reports based on the metrics monitored by ActiveInsight can be generated and emailed to named recipients on a scheduled basis. Reports can be in PDF and CSV formats. This feature is unavailable on the Free Plan.

Management – The Management panel provides several functions. These comprise: a list of current and recent login sessions (*Login Session*); the ability to group several servers together for management purposes (*Group*); list of hosts which have Active Insight installed on them (*Host*); send delegation request to host owner and manage on their behalf (*Account Delegation*); the ability to create customized events that generate warning messages (*Custom Event*); Log file of user activities on *ActiveInsight* (*Log*).

Subscription – for handling licensing, plans and payments.

Synology Active Insight Mobile App

Synology offer an Active Insight app for use on mobile devices, downloadable for iOS/iPadOS and Android devices from the appropriate app stores. It provides many of the features of the desktop version. As it can be configured to receive notifications, it is of particular benefit to support staff who may not be on-site and for supporting multiple hosts.

Note: when signing into the app, use Synology Account details, not those of an administrator for the server(s).

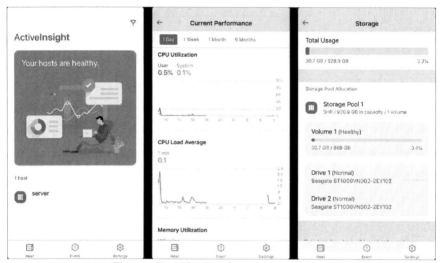

Figure 187: Active Insight running on iPhone

9 MULTIMEDIA & STREAMING

9.1 Overview

One of the most popular uses of a home network is for the storage and playback of media such as photos, music and videos. CDs and DVDs can be 'ripped' into formats such as MP3 and MP4 and these copies played back from the DiskStation, thus protecting the originals against wear and tear. By maintaining a central library, the entire family can access their media from both inside and outside the household. The DiskStation can playback the stored media onto a variety of devices including computers, gaming consoles, tablets, smartphones, smart TVs, streaming TV devices and suitable hi-fi systems.

Synology offer multiple packages (apps) for multimedia. The first one is ideal for a home entertainment system, whilst the other three are optimized for specific media types, offering more capabilities and support for mobile devices:

Media Server – uses the widely used DLNA standard that enables multimedia to be played back on computers, smart televisions, media streamers, gaming consoles and more.

Synology Photos – an application for storing, managing and sharing photographs, with support for mobile devices.

Audio Station – for playing a music collection stored on a DiskStation onto computers and mobile devices.

Video Station – for managing and streaming videos to computers and mobile devices.

Additionally, other apps are available from third parties from the Package Center.

Note that the unauthorized copying of commercial CDs and DVDs is prohibited in most countries.

9.2 Media Server (DLNA)

DLNA is the abbreviation for *Digital Living Network Alliance*. It is a widely used standard for interconnecting home network devices for them to stream and play multimedia, with the design goal that DLNA devices can do so without worrying about passwords, network protocols and other technical issues. Many devices are DLNA-compliant including computers, smart televisions, media streamers, gaming consoles such as the Xbox and PlayStation, smartphones, Blu-ray players, suitably equipped hi-fi systems and more. Synology have an application – *Media Server* – which turns the DiskStation into a DLNA server. It is a good idea to install it on all DiskStations which will hold media.

Media Server is downloadable from the Package Center and might download additional components at the same time. As part of the installation process it will create three shared folders, called *music*, *photo* and *video*. You can store media files wherever you want and create further shared folders, but you may wish to use these folders. Launch Media Server by clicking on its icon in the Main Menu.

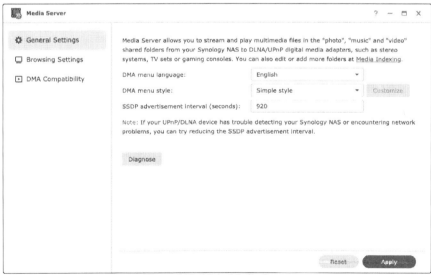

Figure 188: Main Media Server

It is suggested you copy your media folders into the appropriate folders before proceeding e.g. MP3 files into *music*, JPGs into *photo*, MP4 movies into *video* (other media formats are supported for all categories). Depending on how much media you have and the processing power of the DiskStation, there may be a considerable delay as Media Server indexes your files for the first time and makes them available, marked by a progress indicator on the Task Manager at the top of the screen.

You should now be able to connect your DLNA client(s) to the server. As DLNA devices vary considerably there is no single method for doing so: in most cases the client should just 'see' the server, whereas on some devices it may be necessary to explicitly go into its network settings or there may be an option to search for and add media servers (refer to the manufacturer's instructions or website for details).

Media Server 'just works' and it is not usually necessary to change any of its settings. However, there are some options that may be of relevance or interest to some people and on the Media Server screen, there are three sections:

General Settings

There are three items that can be changed:

DMA menu language – choose a language for DMA to work in. There is a choice of 20 widely used ones.

DMA menu style – the default is 'Simple style', but you could choose Advanced or iPod-style or customize your own.

SSDP advertisement interval – the default value of 920 should be suitable. But some devices, such as older smart televisions, may be DLNA-certified but have difficulties connecting to NAS-based DLNA servers. Reducing this value – try going down in steps of 100 at a time – might help.

Having made any changes, click **Apply**.

Browsing Settings

This refers to browsing for media when using DLNA client devices and how the information - titles, sort sequence etc. - will be displayed (this is unconnected with internet browsers such as Chrome, Safari etc). Concerned mainly with visual presentation issues, you can also enable Internet radio and integrate the Video Station database (if you are using *Video Station*) into Media Server.

Having made any changes, click **Apply**.

DMA Compatibility

Besides MP3, other popular audio formats exist, such as *FLAC, APE, ALAC, OGG* and *AIFF* and, although the Synology software can handle these formats, not all DLNA client devices are able to do so. By ticking the **Enable audio conversion** box, the files will be converted into formats that most devices can understand. Similarly, you can tick **Enable video conversion** to do the same for *rm, rmvb* and *mkv* format video files. There may be some restrictions on video conversion on less powerful DiskStations.

You can also restrict access to Media Server for selected DLNA clients in your network if you do not wish people to play media e.g. in a business or other setting.

Having made any changes, click **Apply**.

Media Indexing

When photos, music and videos are added to the DiskStation, you may find that they do not automatically appear in the various media applications, and this problem can be resolved by re-indexing the media.

Go into **Control Panel** and click **Indexing Service**. In the *Media Indexing* section, click the **Re-index** button. To define which folders are indexed and the media type they contain, click the **Indexed Folder** button. On the resultant panel you can create, delete and edit the folders as required. In this example, we are using the default folders created by Media Server.

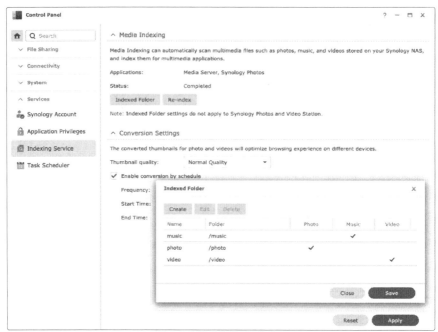

Figure 189: Media indexing

The bottom half of the screen controls *Conversion Settings*. Thumbnails are icons that represent media files as small pictures, giving a quick preview of the files. By default, thumbnails are of *Normal Quality* but you can, if you wish, change them to *High Quality*. This might be important, for instance, to a photography business. The generation of high-quality thumbnails uses a lot of processing power and to help with this, the DiskStation can convert thumbnails on a scheduled basis. To do so, tick the **Enable conversion by schedule** box and use the dropdowns to specify the frequency and times. The term *transcoding* is often used to describe this conversion process.

Whenever you add more media files to the DiskStation, you should go into Media Indexing immediately afterwards and re-index them. Note that the indexing mainly relates to Media Server and may not affect other media apps, such as Synology Photos and Video Station.

Advanced Media Extensions

Synology's *Advanced Media Extensions* package adds HEVC (High-Efficiency Video Coding) support to the NAS, enabling HEVC videos to be viewed. As usual, it is downloaded and installed from the Package Center. For AME to work, you need to be signed into your Synology account on the NAS.

9.3 Synology Photos

Synology Photos is an application for managing photos and videos. It utilizes what Synology describes as a 'deep learning algorithm', enabling it to automatically sort and categorize photos with similar faces, subjects, and places. Synology Photos runs on the server but is also designed to work with iOS/iPadOS and Android mobile devices. Photos taken on smartphones and tablets can be automatically uploaded to and backed up on the DiskStation, also enabling storage space to be freed up on the devices. It is similar in operation to products such as Apple's Photos and iCloud Photo Library or Amazon's Prime Photos, but with the advantages of everything being under your own control and without ongoing subscription costs.

Synology Photos is downloaded and installed from the Package Center. Click its icon on the Main Menu and it will open in a new browser window to display the following screen:

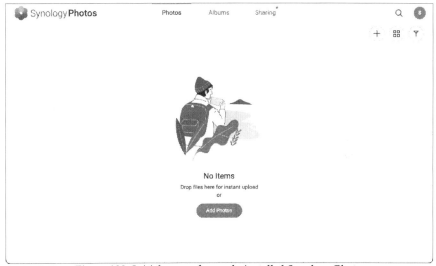

Figure 190: Initial screen for newly installed Synology Photos

Photos can be stored in two locations: in addition to a *Personal Space* for each user, there is also a *Shared Space* that can be enabled and made available to other DSM users, such as members of the household or organization.

Usage

As the description *Personal Space* implies, this is private to a user and their photos are not visible to other users unless they explicitly choose to make them so. The photos are stored in their individual home folder within a sub-folder called *Photos*. To load photos into it from a computer, a user should go into Synology Photos and click the **Add Photos** button or, on subsequent occasions, to add more photos the plus sign (+) icon in the top-right corner of the screen. They can also copy photos directly to their *Home/Photos* folder using File Station.

Depending on the number of photographs and the hardware capabilities of the DiskStation, it may take some time for Synology Photos to organize and index them, after which they will be displayed on the screen. Photos can be viewed as a timeline, or as folders:

Figure 191: Photos displayed in timeline and folder views

In the top-right corner of the screen are menu and control options. There is a greater selection in timeline view, and it is from here that you can switch between timeline and folder views. From left to right:

Change the size of the thumbnails.

To upload further images at any time, or a new folder to hold images, click the plus button.

The third icon enables photographs to be sorted by name, size, time taken and by file type.

The fourth icon toggles between folder and timeline views.

The penultimate icon is for creating links for sharing photos with other people.

The final icon is a filter, enabling photos to be filtered by camera type, lens, geolocation and other parameters.

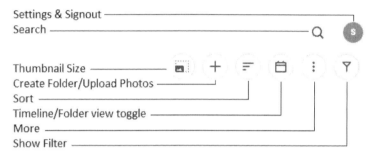

Figure 192: Options and controls

Above the main group are two further icons. The magnifying glass allows photos to be searched based on names, tags or descriptions. The final icon, indicated by the first letter of the user's name ('S' in this example) or their profile photograph, controls various settings and is also used for signing out of Synology Photos.

To view a photo full screen, click it. When viewing, several options become available: you can scroll to the previous and next photos; zoom in; obtain detailed information and add a tag; delete the photo. Clicking the three-dot snowman menu in the top right-hand corner gives additional options: play slideshow; download the photo; add to an album; rotate; move or copy the photo:

Figure 193: Viewing an individual photo

You can share images with other people, and they can be users of your NAS or external people. Click the **Sharing** icon, which will display the following panel. A 'Share Link' will be generated automatically, derived from the server's QuickConnect ID; this can be copied and pasted into an email and sent to the desired recipient. Using the **Privacy Settings** dropdown, the type of access can be specified as: *Private – Only invitees can access*; *Public – Anyone with the link can view*; *Public – Anyone with the link can download*. Optionally, a password can be specified, along with an expiration date. Having made any changes, click **Save**.

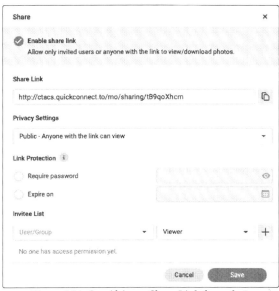

Figure 194: Specifying a Share Link for a photo

Tagging

Images can be tagged (categorized) with user-defined criteria and can then be searched using those tags. Whilst viewing a screen of thumbnail images, click the circles in the top-left hand corner of individual images to select them. A toolbar appears at the bottom of the screen – click the three-dot menu and choose **Edit Tags**. On the resultant panel, type in a new tag, press Enter and click **OK**. A short amount of processing may take place. Thereafter, images can be searched by clicking the magnifying search icon at the top of the screen and typing in the tag name.

Figure 195: Tagging images

Facial Recognition

Synology Photos includes built-in facial recognition technology. To enable/disable it, click the username icon in the top right-hand corner of the screen and choose **Settings**. To control it for the Personal Space photos, click the **Personal** tab and on it tick/untick the **Enable the People Album in Personal Space** option, followed by **Save**. To control it for the Shared Space photos, click the **Shared Space** tab and on it tick/untick the **Enable the People Album in Shared Space** option, followed by **Save**. The server will then process the photos which, depending on how many and the performance of the unit, may take some time.

Click **Albums** to view a list of faces that have been found, with a count of the photos found in which they feature. Clicking a face will show all the corresponding photos found. The system does know who the people are, so click the **Who's this?** link and type in their name or a description.

Figure 196: Facial recognition

Facial recognition technology is never perfect and, as people change their appearance with time or photographs might be taken in poor lighting conditions, the system might generate multiple entries for the same person. To resolve this, click the three-dot 'snowman' menu, click **Merge people**, select the entries by clicking towards the top left-hand corner of the photos and click **Merge**.

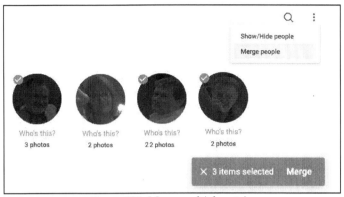

Figure 197: Merge multiple entries

Shared Space

In addition to a personal storage space for each user, there is also a *Shared Space* that can be made available to other DSM users, such as members of the household or organization. This is in the form of a shared folder called *Photo*, which is created automatically when Media Server was installed in section **9.2 Media Server (DLNA)**. If there are already photos in the folder, these will appear in Synology Photos for users who have Shared Space enabled. To enable the shared space, click the user's initial icon or profile photo in the top right-hand corner of Synology Photos and choose **Settings** from the pop-up menu. On the **Shared Space** tab, click the **Enable Shared Space** button, followed by **Save**:

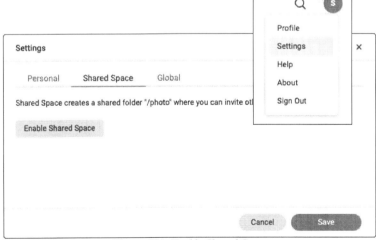

Figure 198: Enable Shared Space

The contents of the tab will change, providing various options – just click **Save**. The user will now be able to switch between Shared Space and Personal Space using the dropdown which will have appeared in the top-left hand corner of the screen.

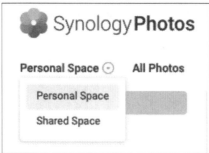

Figure 199: Switching between Personal and Shared Space

Synology Photos App for Smartphones

Synology Photos is also intended for use with Smartphones and tablets and an app of the same name is available from the Apple and Google stores for iOS/iPadOS and Android devices respectively. Having installed it, enter the QuickConnect ID for the server or its IP address, along with a user account name and password. Slide the switch so that HTTPS is used and tap **Login**. The first time it is run a configuration screen is displayed; if you want the app to backup your photos to the server to save storage space on the device, tap **Enable Photo Backup**. However, do not do so immediately, as we will discuss this feature shortly.

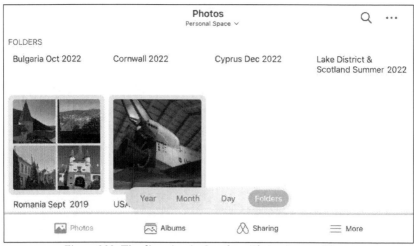

Figure 200: Timeline view in Synology Photos App on iPhone

The main screen is analogous to that of Synology Photos on the server, with the option to view photos in different ways (by folder, by date) and to search them based on tags. Tapping a photo makes it display full screen, from where there are options to share, download and delete. To switch between Personal Space and Shared Space, tap the top of the screen, underneath where it reads 'Photos'.

Several settings in the app can be changed. Tap where it reads **More** at the bottom of the screen. On the resultant screen, tap **Photo Backup Not Enabled** followed by **Enable Photo Backup** on the subsequent panel. If you want to restrict uploads to Wi-Fi only, flip the switch (you may want to do this unless you have an unlimited or generous cellular/mobile data plan). As videos are generally much larger than photos, you may also wish to set the Photos Only switch to the 'On' position.

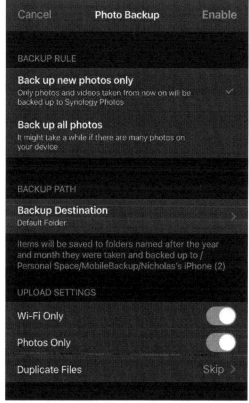

Figure 201: Photo Backup options

9.4 Audio Station

Audio Station is an application from Synology that allows a music collection to be managed on the DiskStation and played back via numerous different devices.

Setup

Start off by copying your music files to the shared music folder i.e. *music*, which was created during the installation of Media Server. The music should be in a supported format, such as MP3, FLAC, OGG etc, and formats can be mixed. Download and install *Audio Station* from the Package Center. Click its icon in the **Main Menu**. The first time it is run it will create a library, index the music and download album artwork from over the internet, which may take some time depending on how much music you have, the performance of the DiskStation and the speed of the internet connection. Thereafter it will load quickly and display along the following lines. The music can be viewed and sorted in various ways, including genre, album, artist, composer and so on, and can be displayed as a text list or as icons derived from the album covers. If the screen is initially empty, it is because the music has not yet finished indexing:

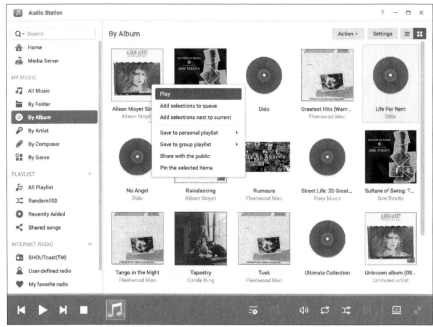

Figure 202: Audio Station running on DiskStation

Access to Audio Station is controllable on an individual basis. Go to **Control Panel > User & Group**, double-click the username, click the **Applications** tab, put a tick against Audio Station in the **Allow** column and click **Save**. To give access to Audio Station for multiple users, you could create a dedicated group for them (see **4.5 Groups**). To make Audio Station available to all users, go to **Control Panel > User & Group**, highlight *users* on the Group tab and click **Edit**. Click the **Applications** tab and place a tick in the Allow column for Audio Station. Click **Save**.

Playback

There are multiple options for playing back music:

Sign-in to the server using a browser. Click on **Main Menu** and launch Audio Station. Choose a track and click to play it. Alternatively, launch File Station, navigate to the music folder and double-click a track for it to play via the built-in mini audio player.

Or, assuming the music folder has been mapped or mounted on the computer, double-click a track and it will playback via the computer's default audio application e.g. Windows Media Player, QuickTime, macOS Music.

Or, music can be played back on devices such as tablets and smartphones, using the *DS Audio* app described below.

Radio

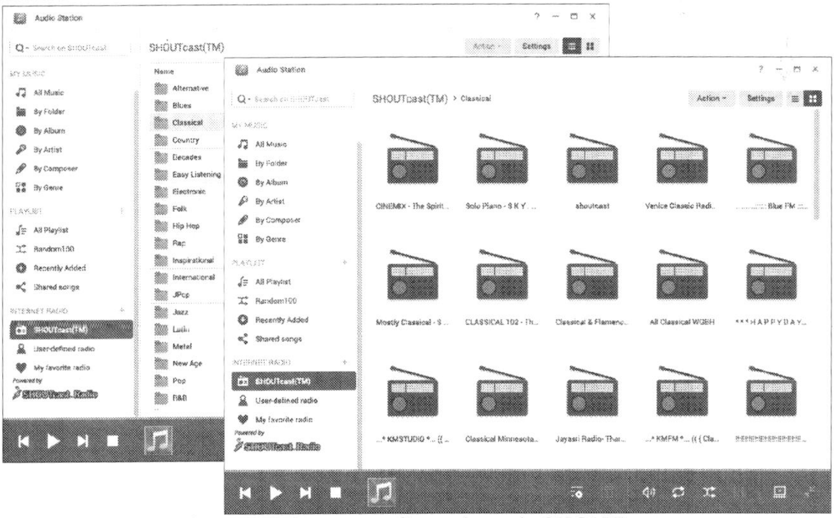

Figure 203: Internet radio stations via SHOUTcast

In addition to your own music held in the library, Audio Station provides free access to thousands of internet radio stations in many genres, powered by *SHOUTcast*.

Settings

The **Settings** button within Audio Station allows greater control and customization:

To enable personal music libraries for users, which will be stored in the *home/music* folder for each user, go into **Settings > Personal Library** and tick the **Enable Personal Library** box. Click **OK**.

To enable Amazon Alexa, go into **Settings > Advanced** and tick the **Enable Amazon Alexa service** box. Click **OK**.

Some DLNA devices do not support audio formats such as FLAC, APE, ALAC, OGG and AIFF. To resolve this, Audio Station can convert them into a compatible format. Go into **Settings > Advanced**. In the *DLNA Settings* section, tick all the boxes except the first one, followed by **OK**.

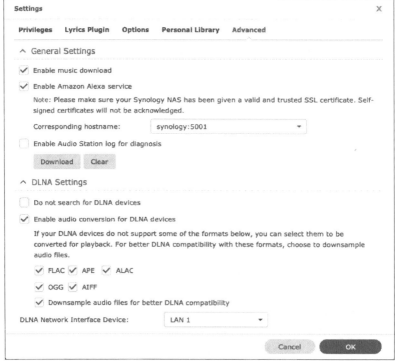

Figure 204: Audio Station Settings

DS audio

DS audio is an app for the playback of music from a DiskStation running Audio Station using a mobile device, and is available for iOS/iPadOS and Android from the respective App stores. It is a comprehensive app that goes beyond streaming and includes the ability to download music from the server, enabling it to be played when offline. Having connected to the DiskStation, DS audio can also stream the music to another player on the network that supports DLNA, AirPlay or Chromecast. It is also supported on the Apple Watch.

When using DS audio for the first time, it is necessary to login. It will offer to search the local network for any servers, else enter the IP address of the server if it is only ever going to be accessed internally, or use a QuickConnect ID if it is also to be used remotely. Enter a user ID and password of an existing user on the DiskStation. These settings can be remembered by the app if required (recommended). If the app detects other suitable playback devices on the network, it will allow you to stream the music to them, as well as being able to play it on the phone or tablet:

Figure 205: Select a player

The user interface is broadly like Audio Station. The music can be organised by album, artist, composer, genre and folder. It is also possible to 'pin' your favourite music for quick access. To download a track to the device for offline listening, tap the three-dot menu to the right of it and choose Download from the pop-up menu.

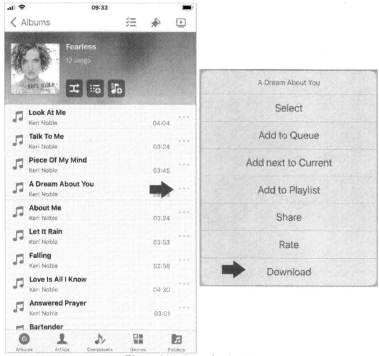

Figure 206: Download option

9.5 Video Station

Video Station is Synology's application for managing and streaming videos. Videos can be played back on computers, devices running iOS/iPadOS or Android, plus popular streaming devices and selected smart TVs. It may be necessary to experiment to determine the video format that gives best results, but MP4 videos created by tools such as *Handbrake, DVDFab* and similar tools work well. The 'ripping' of commercial DVDs is prohibited in some countries and copyright and other legal restrictions should be observed.

Setup

Begin by copying your video files to the shared video folder i.e. *video*, which was created during the installation of Media Server. If you have many videos it might take several hours to copy them to the server, and rather than do this from your computer to the server over the network, it might be quicker to first copy them to a USB drive, then plug the drive into the Synology and copy them using File Station.

Download and install *Video Station* from the Package Center. When complete it will place an icon in the **Main Menu;** click the icon, which will cause it to open in a new browser window. The first time it is run there will be a message about 'Enabling the Video Info Plugin feature'; we will return to this topic later, for now just click the **Got It** button. A short introduction is displayed, which can be worked through or skipped as desired. Click **Movie** on the left-hand side of the screen, then click the resultant message advising you to **Click here to create indexed folders for your videos**. The *Settings* panel is shown; move the mouse to the right-hand side of the Movie area until the small **Add folder** icon is displayed; click it and the screen will appear as follows:

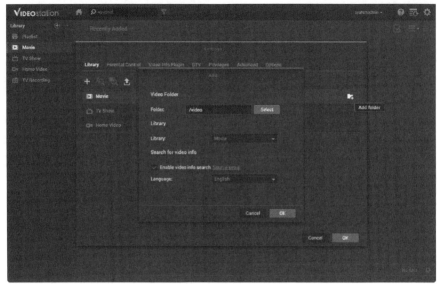

Figure 207: Specifying a library

Click the blue **Select** button and a further panel is displayed, showing the folder structure of the server. Highlight the shared folder containing your videos (i.e. *video* in our example) and click **Select**. Returning to the previous screen, click **OK** and the videos will be indexed. The time taken for indexing depends on the number of videos and the specification of the DiskStation, but might take several hours if you have a large collection. Video Station does not necessarily advise when it has completed indexing; one way to keep track is to have the Resource monitor widget running on the main DSM screen and check for when CPU activity stops or at least drops to a very low level (see **8.4 Widgets**).

When the indexing process is complete, the Movie screen will appear along the following lines, although you might need to refresh the screen. The view can be switched between thumbnails, tiles and lists, using the icon in the top right-hand corner of the screen.

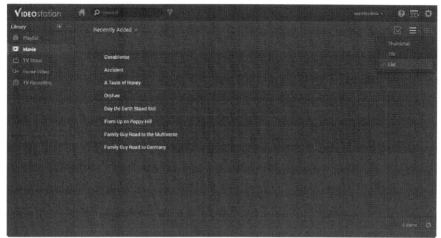

Figure 208: Video Station

Access to Video Station is controllable on an individual basis; go to **Control Panel > User & Group**, double-click the username, click the **Applications** tab, put a tick against Video Station in the **Allow** column and click **Save**. To give access to Video Station for multiple users, you could create a dedicated group for them (see **4.5 Groups**). To make Video Station available to all users, go to **Control Panel > User & Group**, highlight *users* on the Group tab and click **Edit**. Click the **Applications** tab and place a tick in the Allow column for Video Station. Click **Save**.

Playback

There are multiple options for playing back videos:

Sign-in to the server using a browser. Click on **Main Menu** and click **Video Station**, which will open in a new browser window. Choose a video and double-click to play it from within the browser.

Or, assuming the video folder has been mapped or mounted on the computer, double-click on a video and it will playback via the computer's default video application e.g. Windows Media Player or macOS QuickTime.

Or, videos can be played back on portable devices such as tablets and smartphones, using the *DS Video* app, available for iOS/iPadOS and Android. It includes a comprehensive set of options for organizing and sorting videos.

It is AirPlay and Google Chromecast compatible, enabling videos to be streamed to a connected television. In addition to streaming, it can download and save videos onto the portable device, enabling movies to be watched offline, for example when travelling. When running DS video for the first time, it is necessary to login. Enter the IP address of the server if it is only ever going to be accessed internally, or use a QuickConnect ID if it is also to be used outside the premises. Enter a user ID and password for an existing user on the DiskStation. These settings can be remembered by the app if required (recommended). The user interface is analogous to that of Video Station. The DS Video app is also available for Apple TV, Android TV and Samsung Smart TV.

Adding Video Information and Artwork

Be default, the Video Station screen looks bland in comparison to products such as Netflix, Amazon Fire Stick and Apple TV, as titles are simply listed in a textual format, without artwork, synopsis, credits and so on. There are two ways to change and improve this.

Manually add the Info ('Metadata')

Hover the cursor over a movie, click the mini-menu indicated by three dots (...) and choosing **Edit video info** from the pop-up to show a panel with three tabs. On the first tab – **Video Info** – type in the details of the movie. You might find these on the packaging of the DVD, or they can be found on a website which sells movies, such as Amazon. On the second tab – **Poster** – an image can be associated with the video. One way to do this is by searching the internet for suitable pictures and then downloading them into a designated folder on the server e.g. you could create a folder called *video/artwork*. Alternatively, you can specify the URL of a suitable image on the internet.

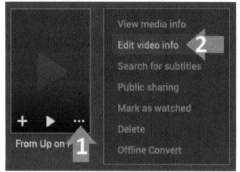

Figure 209: Edit video info

Install the Video Info Plugin Feature

Manually entering the information is tedious and error prone, however, there is an official method to automate the process. This consists of applying for an API key for the Video Info Plugin feature, which will then retrieve metadata from The Movie Database (TMDb).

The procedure is as follows:

Go to the *www.themoviedb.org* website and create an account. This process requires a valid email address, which then has to be verified. Under the **Profile and Settings** icon click **Settings**. Click **API** and on the API page, click the link next to *Request an API Key*. Register your API key as a 'Developer' if you are an individual or home user, or 'Professional' if you represent a company. Read and **Accept** the Terms of Use.

Complete the form. Specify: the *Type of Use* as 'Personal'; the *Application Name* as 'Video Station'; provide the external IP address of your DiskStation as the *Application URL*; describe how you will use the API key in the *Application Summary* section (e.g. "To watch videos using Video Station on Synology NAS"); provide your contact details.

An API key will be displayed in the *API Key (v3 auth)* field. Highlight and copy the key (**Ctrl C** on Windows or **Cmd C** on macOS).

Switch to Video Station and go into **Settings > Video Info Plugin**. Tick the box against the entry for **The Movie Database (System default)**. On the pop-up panel, paste the API key (**Ctrl V** on Windows or **Cmd V** on macOS. Click **Test Connection** to check that it is recognized. Click **OK** and then **OK** again on the previous panel.

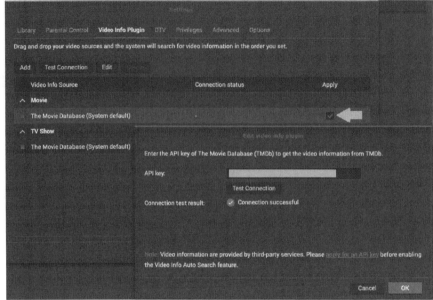

Figure 210: Video Info Plugin settings

The metadata can now be added to individual videos. Hover the cursor over a video, click the mini-menu indicated by three dots (…) and choosing **Edit video info** from the pop-up to show a panel with three tabs. On the first tab – **Video Info** – click **Search from Video Info Plugin**, followed by **Search** on the resultant panel.

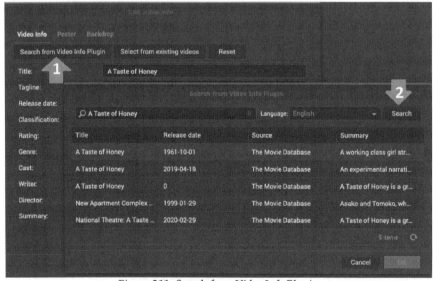

Figure 211: Search from Video Info Plugin

After a short while, a list of possible matches is displayed. Highlight the correct one and click **OK**. The video will now be listed in the main Video Station screen with its details.

Figure 212: Movie with metadata

10 SYNOLOGY DRIVE SERVER, OFFICE & APPS

10.1 Overview

Most people will be familiar with public cloud-based services such as Google Drive, Microsoft OneDrive, Apple's iCloud and others. The basic concept is that somewhere on the internet is an amount of private space for your usage, which you can think of as analogous to a USB memory stick or hard drive in the sky. Data stored on the cloud can be accessed in two ways: the first method is by logging in to the website and working within a browser; the second method is to have a folder on your computer or device corresponding to that space, along with client software or an app. Anything you put in that folder is automatically copied ('synced') to the space on the internet and vice versa, such that whenever anything changes on one computer, the change is reflected automatically on the other.

Some cloud services specialize in providing provide storage (for example, Dropbox), whereas others supplement storage with tools for creating and editing documents (for instance, Microsoft Office Online & OneDrive or Apple's iCloud). Whilst incredibly useful and deservedly popular, these services do have some limitations. Firstly, although they usually give some free storage space, it may not be very much and if you need more you must pay for it. And, whilst these services may be relatively affordable, a regular monthly payment over several years may eventually amount to more than the cost of buying a DiskStation. Secondly, most services have restrictions on file sizes and how much data you can store on them. Finally, some people are just not comfortable with the idea of their data being held by Microsoft, Google, Apple or whoever. *Synology Drive Server & Office* get around all these issues: they are free to obtain and use; there are no practical restrictions on space and usage; data is stored on your own server, meaning everything is under your control. Put simply, they are a private alternative to public cloud services and are particularly suitable for people who travel away from home or the office where their DiskStation is located. The following table is a comparison of the features in Synology Drive Server and Office with some popular alternatives:

Function	Synology	Google	Microsoft	Apple
Storage & Sync	Synology Drive Server	Google Drive	OneDrive	iCloud Drive
Word processing	Synology Office (Document)	Docs	Word	Pages
Spreadsheets	Synology Office (Spreadsheet)	Sheets	Excel	Numbers
Presentations	Synology Office (Slides)	Slides	PowerPoint	Keynote
Messaging	Synology Chat	Google+	Skype	Messages
Calendar	Synology Calendar	Calendar	Outlook	Calendar
Contacts	Synology Contacts	Contacts	People	Contacts
Notes	Note Station	Keep	OneNote	Notes

Figure 213: Synology Cloud components versus competitors

Strictly speaking, Drive and Office are separate packages. If you just wanted cloud storage and did not require word processing, spreadsheet and presentation features, you could install Drive Server by itself. However, they are so closely related and tightly integrated that it usually makes sense to install both and that is what we will do.

Synology also offer a suite of collaboration tools that use Drive Server for storing their data. These comprise *Note Station, Synology Chat, Synology Calendar* and *Synology Contacts*, and they can be accessed in a variety of ways, including apps on smartphones and tablets.

10.2 Installing and Configuring Synology Drive Server and Office

Synology Drive Server uses QuickConnect, so if you have not already done so, setup a QuickConnect ID as described in section **2.7 QuickConnect: The Key to Remote Connectivity**. Download and install Drive Server from the Package Center; it requires some other components and these will also be installed if not already in place, so overall the installation may take several minutes. Three icons will be placed in the Main Menu: *Synology Drive Admin Console*, for administering the system; *Synology Drive* for using the system; *Synology Drive ShareSync*, which is a client for connecting another DiskStation. Next, download and install *Synology Office* from the Package Center; again, you may be advised that some additional components need to be downloaded and installed. The installation process will take several minutes.

After installation is complete, launch **Synology Drive Admin Console** from the Main Menu.

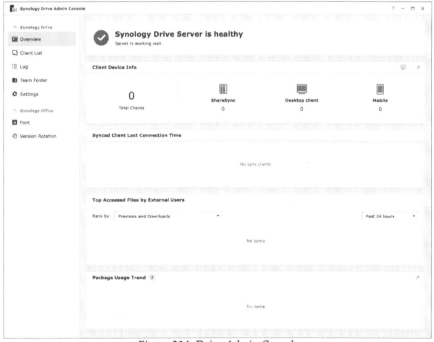

Figure 214: Drive Admin Console

Work through the short introduction; for the moment, ignore the message about setting up *Team Folders*, exit the introduction and click **Overview**, which will display the following screen. This shows the overall status of Drive Server, initially the panels will be empty, but in normal use will become populated. Five options are listed down the left-hand side of the screen: *Overview*, *Client List*, *Log*, *Team Folder* and *Settings*. If you installed Synology Office, two more options – *Font* and *Version Rotation* - will also be listed.

Individual users must be given permission to use *Drive Server*. Go to **Control Panel > User & Group**, highlight the name(s) and click **Edit**. On the *Applications* tab, tick the **Allow** box for Synology Drive if it is not already ticked, followed by **Save**. If you have many users who need access to Drive Server, consider creating a specific group for them and then grant application permissions to that group. If you want everyone to have access, give application permissions to the built-in *users* group.

The default behavior is that each authorized user will have a personal Drive folder inside their individual Home folder on the server, created when they sign-in for the first time following the installation of Drive Server. If this is sufficient for your household or organisation's needs, then proceed to section **10.3 Accessing Drive Server**. However, if you want or need to share additional folders between users, there is the option to setup *Team Folders*. Click the **Team Folder** tab, which will display a list of shared folders on the server; if you need additional folders, create them in the usual manner before continuing (as described in section **3.2 Creating Shared Folders**). To designate a folder for team use, highlight it and click the **Enable** button. A message about *Versioning* is shown; if the **Enable version control** box is ticked, a specifiable number of multiple versions of the folder will be retained so that older copies can be accessed if required. This could be done, for example, for folders containing important data. Adjust the parameters if required and click **OK**. Click **OK** on the subsequent panel that is displayed, noting the warning message that users must have full read/write access to the shared folder(s), otherwise the synchronization will be in one direction only i.e. from the server to the computer. Avoid the temptation to share everything - in this example it is only the folder called *common* that will be synced.

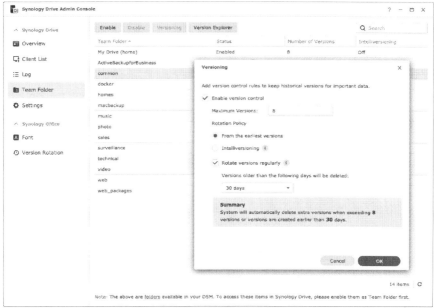

Figure 215: Specifying a Team Folder

The **Client List** and **Log** screens show who is using Drive Server and how it is operating.

The **Settings** screen provides fine control over many aspects of Drive Server. There are multiple options, although the default values are suitable for many home and small business environment settings. It comprises three tabs:

General
Package Usage – keeps track of usage and specifies the volume upon which the Drive Server and Synology Office files are located.

Content Indexing – enables Synology Drive files to be indexed using their content, for more efficient searching.

Direct Access to Hybrid Share from C2 Storage – enables more efficient access to files when C2 Storage is used by reducing bandwidth usage. This must be enabled for specific users and there is a limit to their number e.g. maximum of five users.

Performance – uses spare memory on the DiskStation as a database cache to improve performance.

Email Notification Server – enables email notifications for users. See section **8.9 Notifications**

Display Name – changes the default display name for users from their system username to a nickname.

Enable/Disable Syncing – if this option is unticked, only admin users will be able to use the system.

File Ownership Transfer – enables the ownership of files to be transferred from one user to another. Used, for instance, when a user is deleted.

User Sync Profiles
The file types to be synced can be controlled e.g. you might not want to sync large video files, and this is controllable on a per user basis.

Sharing
Controls whether files can be shared, both internally and externally. Allows password protection and expiration dates for shared files to be enforced.

Figure 216: Drive Admin console Settings

10.3 Accessing Drive Server

Using a Browser

The easiest method to access Drive is using a browser, as it requires no additional software to be installed on the user's device. The user should sign into the server from a browser in the standard manner then, from the **Main Menu**, click **Synology Drive**, which will open in a new tab:

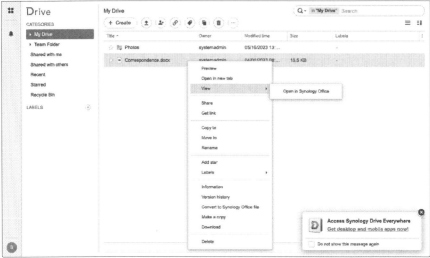

Figure 217: Drive, as viewed within a browser

The folders and items to which the user has access are listed down the left-hand side of the screen, with the corresponding contents of the current location listed in the right-hand panel. If a file is right-clicked, a pop-up menu with a list of options is displayed; this includes file manipulation commands such as Copy, Delete and Rename. Some file types can be viewed by double-clicking them, whilst Word, Excel and PowerPoint documents can be opened in or converted to Synology Office format if it has been installed. To work with a file on the computer using a locally installed application such as Microsoft Word or Excel, right-click it and choose **Download** from the pop-up menu; afterwards the edited file can be uploaded back into Drive.

In the top left-hand corner of the screen is the *App Launcher* icon, which has the same appearance as the icon for the Main Menu on the regular DSM desktop. It provides an easy way to launch other productivity apps that make use of Drive and is found in them, too.

Figure 218: App Launcher

Setting a Nickname and Photo

A user can assign themselves a Nickname for when they use the system, and/or upload their photo. Click the initial in the bottom left-hand corner of the screen and choose **Settings**. On the Profile tab, enter a Nickname and upload a photo if desired. Click **OK**.

Figure 219: Profile Settings

Signing Out

When the user has finished using Drive, they should click on their initial or photo in the bottom left-hand corner of the screen and choose **Sign Out**.

Using the Drive Client

Using the *Synology Drive Client*, files on the DiskStation can be accessed in the same way as files stored locally on a computer. It is available from the Download Center section of the Synology website for Windows 11 & 10, macOS, and Ubuntu Linux 64-bit. All versions look and behave in a consistent manner.

Having installed the Synology Drive Client, run it and click **Start Now**. If required, you can change the language of operation by clicking the small globe icon to the right of the button. On the first screen, enter the *QuickConnect ID* name that was previously registered with Synology (recommended) or, if Drive Client will only ever be used internally, you can enter the IP address of the server or click the magnifying glass to search the network for it. Enter an existing *Username* and *Password*. Make sure that the **Enable SSL data transmission encryption** box is ticked and click **Next** (if a warning message about the SSL Certificate is given, click **Proceed Anyway**). The software will test the connection to ensure it can 'see' the server.

There is a choice of two modes: *Sync* and *Backup* and both will be described here. With the first mode, files are synced continuously between the computer and DiskStation in real time i.e. similar to how Dropbox, iCloud, OneDrive and other services operate. With the second mode, files are backed up from the computer to the DiskStation on a scheduled basis.

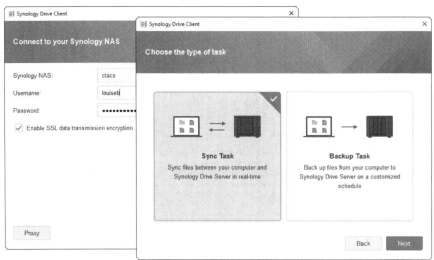

Figure 220: Configuring the Drive Client

Sync Mode

Select the large **Sync Task** 'button' on the task selection screen and click **Next**. The first screen is for setting up the folders to be synchronized. By default, a folder in the user computer's home folder, called *SynologyDrive*, will be created and synced with the user's home folder on the server. If you wanted to change the folder choice you can do so by clicking the **Change** buttons.

Choose whether to tick the **Enable On-demand Sync...** option box. The purpose of this is to save space on the local computer, as files will only be physically downloaded to it when required. This is especially useful on computers with small capacity disk drives, but may not be suitable in all circumstances:

Example 1: a user has a laptop with a relatively small SSD e.g. 64GB. As limited storage space is available, the Enable On-demand option should be used.

Example 2: a user travels frequently. An internet connection is not always available, so to ensure that they always have access to their data, the Enable On-demand option should not be used.

You can fine-tune the syncing process through use of the **Advanced** button. This controls the type of files which are synced, and whether synchronization is bi-directional or in one way only. Having made your choices, click **Done**:

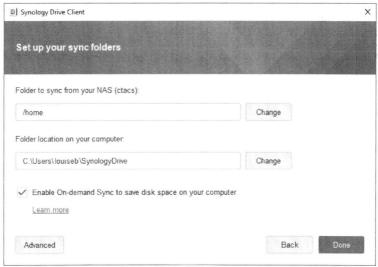

Figure 221: Specify the folders to be synchronized

A short tutorial for Synology Drive is then given, which can be worked through. When finished, click the **Open Folder** button and synchronization will commence. On a Windows PC, an icon for the local Drive folder – called *Synology Drive Client* - is placed automatically on the Desktop for convenience; double-click to open then simply drag files into it. On macOS, the SynologyDrive folder is located in the user's workspace e.g. for a user called *louiseb* it would be */Users/louiseb/SynologyDrive*; if you navigate to this location in Finder you can make an alias for it and place it on the Desktop. In the case of Linux, it is necessary to manually locate the desired folder on the computer, referred to as the *backup source* (the pencil icons for navigating within the client are not present). An icon is also placed on the Menu bar (macOS) or Task bar (Windows), which can be used for monitoring Synology Drive.

Files are marked with one of three small status icons, indicating whether they are available when online only, if they have been downloaded and available offline, or pinned for permanent access anytime. To pin a file, right-click it and choose **Synology Drive > Pin local copy permanently** (Windows 10) or **Shift F10 > Synology Drive > Pin local copy permanently** (Windows 11).

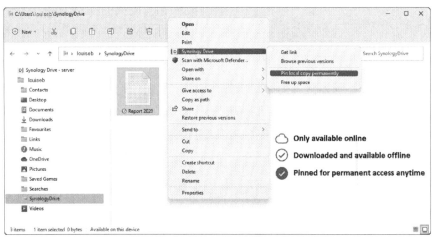

Figure 222: Controlling online/offline status of files

To subsequently adjust the synchronization parameters, launch the Synology Drive Client utility (**Start > All apps > Synology Drive Client** on Windows 11, **Start > Synology > Synology Drive Client** on Windows 10).

Changes to the settings can be made from here by clicking **Global Settings** and the synced folder(s) can be opened by clicking them.

By default, the Synology Drive client generates desktop notification in Windows every time something changes, but if this is unrequired it can be switched off. Within **Global Settings**, click the **Notifications** tab and remove the tick from the **Show desktop notifications for file events** box.

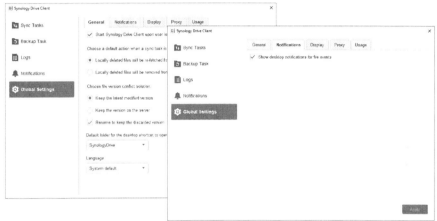

Figure 223: Drive Client Global Settings

Backup Mode

Select the large **Backup Task** 'button' on the task selection screen and click **Next**. If you have already configured the Drive Client for syncing and now wish to add a backup task, launch the app, click the **Backup Task** tab, click the **Create Backup Task** button, then choose the server on the subsequent panel. On the next screen choose the source folders to be backed up i.e. the folders from the computer. By default, the backup destination is called */Backup/name_of_computer* in the user's home folder on the server – this can be to changed, but you might want to stay with it. You can change the parameters of the backup by clicking the **Backup rules** button to include and exclude certain file types, although the defaults may be suitable:

Figure 224: Choose the data to backup

On the next panel, specify the backup mode. There is a choice of *Continuous*, *Manual* or *Scheduled* backup. If the latter is chosen, a panel to set the schedule is displayed and in this example the backup will run daily at 17:00/5:00pm and shut down the computer afterwards:

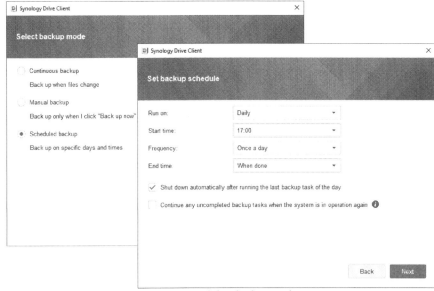

Figure 225: Select backup mode

After clicking **Next**, the system will display the backup settings summary screen. Click **Done** and there will be message asking 'Do you want to run your backup tasks now?' This is a good idea, as it enables the backup to be tested. Click **OK**, the backup will then run and display a status screen:

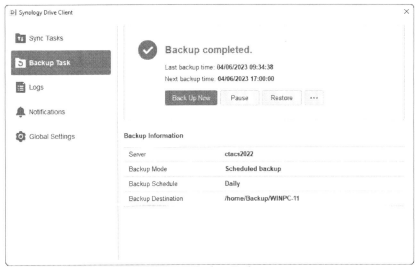

Figure 226: Backup Task screen

To subsequently restore files, click the **Restore** button on the **Backup Task** screen. On the resultant screen, use the calendar and date dropdowns to choose the backup to be restored, expand the folder structure in the left-hand pane and highlight the file(s) and folder(s) in the right-hand pane. Click the **Restore** button.

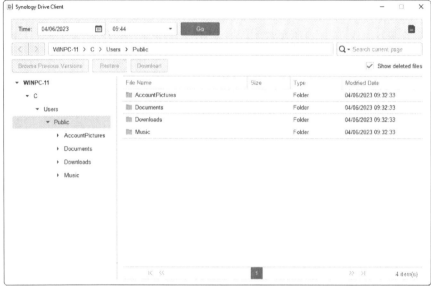

Figure 227: Restore Screen

Using the Mobile Drive Client

Synology provide a mobile Drive client, available from the respective app stores for iOS and Android smartphones and tablets. When running it for the first time, it is necessary to configure it by specifying the QuickConnect ID, user name and password, plus you should enable the HTTPS switch to increase security. The mobile client enables folders and files stored on the DiskStation to be viewed, whilst music, photos and videos are grouped together for easy access. It can also be used for uploading files, folders and photographs from the mobile device to the server.

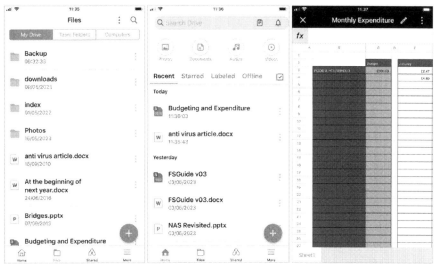

Figure 228: Mobile Drive Client

The default settings in the client will be suitable for most people and purposes, but there are two parameters you may wish to change. Firstly, a user may have more data stored on the DiskStation than will fit on their smartphone or tablet. To cope with this, plus improve overall performance, the mobile Drive client maintains only the most recently used data locally, via a *cache*. If the mobile device has a relatively small amount of local storage, say, 16 GB, then you may wish to minimize the size of the cache. Conversely, if the device has a larger amount of storage e.g. 128 GB, then you may wish to increase the size of the cache.

To do this, tap **More > Settings > Cache management** and choose a value. Secondly, accessing files can use a lot of data. Whilst not an issue on a wi-fi network, if you are connecting via a cellular/mobile network with a limited data plan, then you may want to go to **More > Settings > Download files for offline access** and choose the **Wi-Fi only** option.

10.4 Syncing Between DiskStations

In addition to the desktop and mobile clients described earlier, other DiskStations can be connected as clients, enabling Drive data to be synced between them. An example of where such a feature might be used is an organization with multiple branches which has data that needs to be consistent and available in all locations, for example training and marketing materials.

The first or original DiskStation is referred to as the *host*. Synology Drive Server has already been installed and is up and running. On it, create or choose a shared folder; in our example it is called *training*, to which we will assign *Read/Write* permissions to administrators and *Read Only* permissions to users. Go into Synology Drive Admin Console and enable it as a Team Folder.

A second DiskStation, referred to as the *client*, will now be connected. Download and install Synology Drive Server. When complete, go into the **Main Menu** and launch **Synology Drive ShareSync**. Click the **Start Now** button and on the resultant panel enter the QuickConnect ID or IP address of the host and the administrator's sign-on credentials. It is suggested that you tick the **Enable SSL data transmission encryption** box, especially if the DiskStations are connected at different location over the internet (click **Yes** to any resultant message about the SSL certificate). The connection will be tested and after a few seconds a list of team folders will be displayed. Tick the folder(s) – training in our example – and click **Next**:

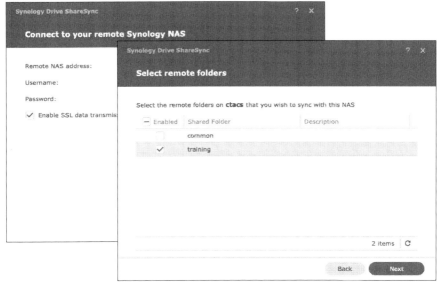

Figure 229: Select the folders to be synced

On the subsequent screen – *Review sync settings* - click **Done** and synchronization will commence. Depending on the amount of data and the speed of the connection between the DiskStations, this may initially take some time.

The above example is intentionally simple. In practical terms, consideration would need to be taken about whether the data could be updated in different locations or distributed for read-only access, along with the types and maximum sizes of files to be synced. This can be done when creating the task by clicking on the **Edit** button on the *Review sync settings* screen. To do so for an existing sync task, launch Synology Drive ShareSync on the client, highlight the task and click **Synced folders**. Highlight a folder and click **Edit**. There are three tabs on the resultant panel. On the **File filter** tab, the file types and maximum sizes can be controlled. On the **Sync Mode** tab, the sync direction can be controlled. Having made any changes, click **OK**, followed by **Apply**.

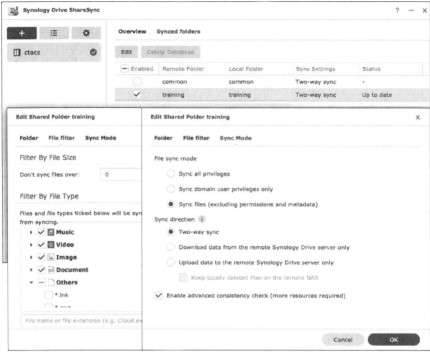

Figure 230: Detailed sync settings

10.5 Synology Office

To use Office, a user should login to the server using a browser as described in section **5.2 Using a Browser and File Station**. There is no icon for Office, as it is implemented is by adding capabilities to Drive, such that users can create and view documents.

Clicking the **Create** button within Drive displays a pop-up menu with six options: new folder; new word processing document; new spreadsheet; new presentation; create a document from a built-in template, of which Synology provide more than 40, suitable for many purposes; create an encrypted file i.e. a document or spreadsheet encrypted with a password:

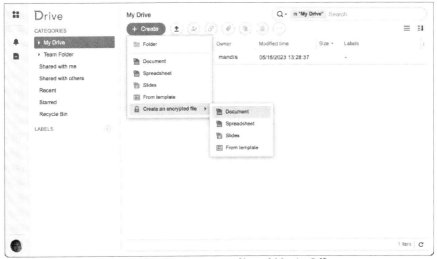

Figure 231: Creating a new file or folder in Office

The word processor, spreadsheet and presentation program function as might be expected, comparable to Microsoft Office Online and Google Docs. When editing files, they do not have to explicitly be saved, as saving happens automatically. To view a file created by the desktop versions of Word, Excel or PowerPoint, double-click it. To then convert the file to Synology Office format, click the **Open in Synology Office** button that will have appeared at the top of the screen.

Once it is open in Synology Office, click the **Import to Synology Office** button that will have appeared at the top of the screen. Choose the location where the imported file will be saved and click **OK**. The saved file will be given an extension of *.oslides*, *.osheet* or *.odoc* as appropriate.

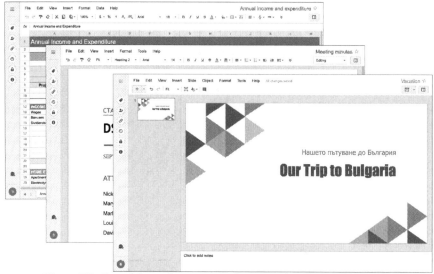

Figure 232: Spreadsheets, documents and presentations in Synology Office

Synology Office is intended as a collaborative tool and there is the capability to share files. Files can be shared with other users on the server or with the outside world, from within main screen or whilst editing by clicking the **File Share** icon.

When finished, the user should sign out by clicking their initial or photograph in the bottom left-hand corner of the screen and choosing the **Sign Out** option.

Tip: to rename a document whilst working in Synology Office, click the current name in the top right-hand corner of the screen and type a new one in the resultant dialog box.

10.6 Synology Chat Server

Synology Chat is an instant messaging and collaboration system, similar to products such as *WhatsApp, Telegram, Viber* and *Skype*. It is aimed at customers who want a private, in-house messaging system that is completely under their own control. Synology Chat can be accessed from a browser, using desktop clients for Windows, Mac and Linux, and with apps for iOS/iPadOS and Android smartphones and tablets.

Begin by downloading and installing Synology Chat Server from the Package Center; installation typically takes a minute or two. Two new icons will be added to the Main Menu: *Synology Chat Admin Console* and *Synology Chat*. The first icon is for administering the system and enables control over when old messages are deleted, whether file uploads and attachment are allowed, plus notification settings. It also maintains log files of all activity. It is not necessary to configure the Chat system before it can be used. The second icon is for accessing the system proper.

Individual users need to be given permission to use Chat. Go into **Control Panel > User & Group**, highlight the user name(s) and click **Edit**. On the Applications tab, tick the **Allow** box for Synology Chat followed by **OK**. If you have many users who need access to Chat, consider creating a specific group for them and grant permissions to that group. If you want everyone to have access to it, give permissions to the built-in *users* group instead.

Note: The Chat application creates a shared folder of the same name on the server. This folder should not be altered or worked with directly in any way.

Browser Access

To use Chat, a user should sign-in to the server using a browser as described in section **5.2 Using a Browser and File Station**. The icon for Synology Chat is on the user's **Main Menu** and clicking it will launch Chat in a new browser tab:

Figure 233: Synology Chat

To change settings, including the overall appearance (theme and wallpaper) of the system, the user should click their initial (or photograph, if they have set one) in the top right-hand corner of the screen and choose **Settings > Themes**. To set a personalized photograph or image, on the **Profile** tab, click the photo panel and in the top-left hand corner, navigate to the desired image and upload it. Click **OK**. On the **Settings > General** tab, settings for notifications and paired devices, date settings and integration with Synology Calendar are controlled.

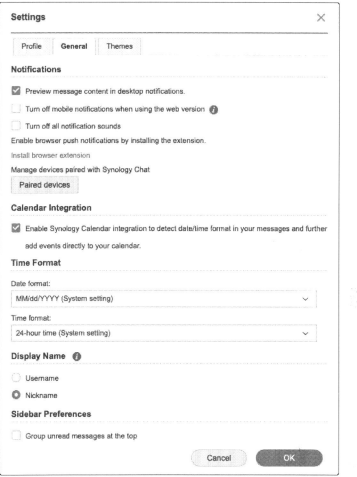

Figure 234: General Settings

Desktop Client

Chat desktop clients are downloadable from the Synology website for Windows, macOS and Linux, and all look and behave similarly. When starting the client, it is necessary to login with the server's IP address or QuickConnect ID, along with the username and password as defined on the server. It is suggested that you tick the **https** box, especially if accessing it externally. Having logged in, the client looks and behaves in a similar manner to the browser version, although some people find it more responsive and fluid in operation.

Mobile Client - Synology Chat

Synology Chat enables smartphones and tablets to access the Chat server and is available for iOS/iPadOS and Android platforms from the appropriate app stores.

Chat Admin Console

Chat Admin Console is for an administrator to manage the system. Clicking its icon in the Main Menu will cause it to launch in a new browser tab. There are four main sections – *Settings, Log, Lookup* and *Channel Management* – of which the first one is the most useful. Within Settings are five sub-categories:

General – controls whether file uploads are allowed and the maximum size of uploaded files, and whether new users are immediately visible to existing ones.

Message Modification – controls whether users are permitted to edit or delete existing messages.

Auto-deletion – if enabled, older messages will automatically be deleted. The elapsed time before this occurs can be defined e.g. 6 months, 1 year, 2 years, 3 years or a custom setting.

Guest – guest users can be enabled. This can only be used if the SMTP service is running, which is enabled from **Control Panel > Notification > Email** (see section **8.9 Notifications**).

Notifications – allows the use of nicknames, and whether notifications are generated by the system and under what conditions.

10.7 Synology Calendar

Begin by downloading and installing *Synology Calendar* from the Package Center; when you do so, you may be prompted to automatically install a dependent package, in which case you should click **Yes**. The total installation will take a couple of minutes.

Individual users need to be given permission to use the Calendar app; to do so, go to **Control Panel > User & Group**, highlight the name(s) and click **Edit**. On the Applications tab, tick the **Allow** box for Synology Calendar followed by **OK**. Suggestion: if you have many users who need access to Calendar, consider creating a specific group for them and grant permission to that group. If you want everyone to have access to it, give permissions to the built-in *users* group.

To use Calendar, a user should sign into the server using a browser as described in section **5.2 Using a Browser and File Station**. The icon for Calendar is on the user's **Main Menu** and clicking it will launch Calendar in a new tab. Some browsers can receive notifications about appointments from Calendar, in which case the user will be prompted as to whether they wish to receive them.

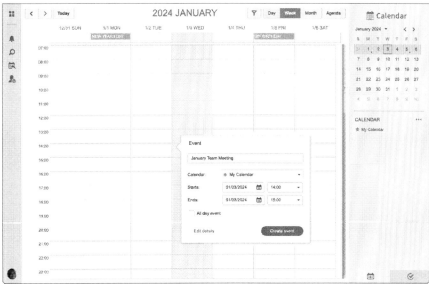

Figure 235: Synology Calendar

The Calendar app has a comprehensive range of features for making and managing appointments. To make an appointment, click in the main grid on the day and time where you want it. To subsequently change an appointment, double-click it or drag to a new time slot. Click **Edit details** to add notes, other information, and invite other people. The main view can be switched between daily, weekly and monthly views. You can import entries from other calendar systems if they are able to export data to *.ics* format, as well as from Google Calendar.

When finished, the user can logout by clicking their initial or photograph in the bottom left-hand corner of the screen and choosing the **Logout** option.

Profile and Settings

To change individual settings and customize the personal calendar, click the initial or user photo in the bottom left-hand of the corner of the screen and choose **Settings**. There are five tabs:

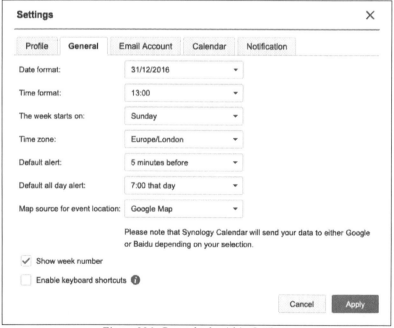

Figure 236: General tab within Settings

Profile – the user can specify their nickname, upload a photo, specify their email address and choose the language they wish to work in.

General – the date and time format, time zone, start day of the week, alerts and mapping can be defined from here. If mapping is used, Baidu is suggested for China, Google for rest of the world, and data will be shared with them.

Email Account – the user can define an email account to be used in conjunction with Calendar. There is a choice of Google Mail, Outlook or a customized SMTP account.

Calendar – the user's personal calendar can be customized here, and whether notifications are received. Calendar data can be exported from here.

Notification – event notifications can be received by email, browser and paired device(s), definable from this tab.

Having made any changes, click **Apply**.

CalDAV Support

Unlike some of Synology's other productivity tools, such as Note Station and Chat, there are no desktop clients or mobile apps available. This is because Calendar has the capability to synchronize events with other manufacturers' products that support the CalDAV standard. How to do this is beyond the scope of this guide, but examples of popular products with CalDAV support include Microsoft Outlook, Thunderbird, macOS Calendar, plus Calendar on iPhone and iPad. For macOS and iOS users, a third-party app called *OneCalendar* is available which connects directly to Synology's Calendar.

10.8 Synology Contacts

As the name implies, *Synology Contacts* is for holding contact information. This can be both personal contacts, unique to each user, as well as centralized team contacts, such as an organization might wish to share amongst its users. Existing information can be imported from Outlook, Google and individual vCards, plus contacts can also be exported for use with other systems. *Synology Contacts* is downloadable from the Package Center and when you do so, you may be prompted to automatically install some dependent packages, in which case you should click **Yes**. Installation takes several minutes.

Individual users need to be given permission to use the Contacts app; to do so, go to **Control Panel > User & Group**, highlight the name(s) and click **Edit**. On the Applications tab, tick the **Allow** box for Synology Contacts followed by **OK**. Suggestion: if you have many users who need access to Contacts, consider creating a specific group for them and grant permission to that group. If you want everyone to have access to Contacts, give permissions to the built-in *users* group instead.

To use Contacts, a user should login to the server using a browser as described in section **5.2 Using a Browser and File Station**. The icon for Contacts can be found on the user's **Main Menu** and clicking it will launch Calendar in a new tab:

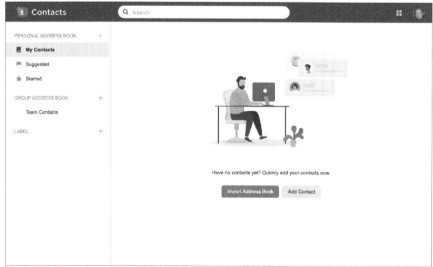

Figure 237: Initial screen in Contacts

To add a new contact, click the **Add Contact** button. The form enables basic information to be entered (name, phone, email etc). To add additional fields (e.g. address, social media chat app), click the **More** button to expand the form. To add a photograph for the contact, click the large gray circle in the top left-hand corner (if doing this, use small JPG files). When complete, click **Add,** followed by **Close**:

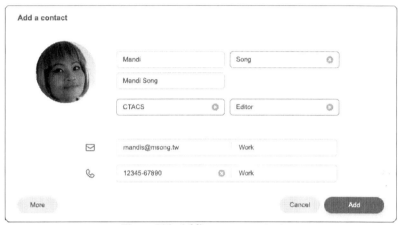

Figure 238: Adding a new contact

The newly added contact will now be listed on the main screen. When finished, the user should sign out by clicking their initial or photograph in the bottom left-hand corner of the screen and choosing the **Sign out** option.

Exporting a Contact

Whilst viewing a contact, click the three-dot menu in the top right-hand corner of the form and click **Export** to generate a vCard. Many applications, including Outlook and macOS Contacts will open vCards and will then sync them to any linked devices.

10.9 Note Station

Similar to applications such as Evernote and Microsoft OneNote, *Note Station* is a flexible personal information management app (PIM) for the DiskStation that allows notes to be created, viewed, managed and shared. Notes can be content-rich, with fonts, formatting, attachments and embedded media. Note Station can be accessed from a browser, or using desktop clients available for Windows, Mac and popular Linux distributions, plus there are apps for portable devices running iOS/iPadOS or Android. Begin by downloading and installing Note Station from the Package Center; installation takes only a couple of minutes.

Individual users need to be given permission to use Note Station; to do so, go to **Control Panel > User & Group**, highlight the name(s) and click **Edit**. On the **Applications** tab, tick the **Allow** box for Note Station followed by **OK**. If you have many users who need access to Note Station, consider creating a specific group for them and then grant permissions to that group. If you want everyone to have access to it, give permissions to the built-in *users* group.

Browser Access

To use Note Station, a user should login to the server using a browser as described in section **5.2 Using a Browser and File Station**. The icon for Note Station can be found on the user's **Main Menu**.

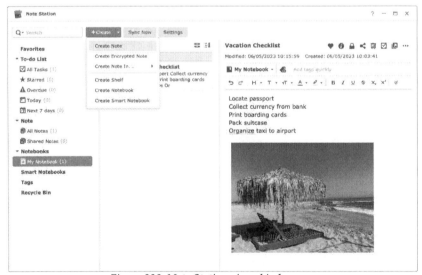

Figure 239: Note Station viewed in browser

To begin a new note, click **Create** followed by **Create Note**, then begin typing in the right-hand panel. On the toolbar there are icons to change the font type, size and color. If the downward-pointing chevron is clicked, options to align the text, add bullet points, insert images and so on become available. There is also a set of icons for encrypting the note, turning it into a presentation, sharing it with local users or external users, and more.

If you are migrating from or also use Evernote, it is possible to import notes from it by going into **Settings > Import and Export**.

Desktop Client

Notes desktop clients are available for Windows, Mac and Linux, downloadable from the Synology website. They all look and behave in a similar manner. When using the client, it is necessary to sign in with the server's IP address or QuickConnect ID, plus a username and password as defined on the server. It is suggested that you tick the **https** box, especially if accessing it externally. Having logged in, the client looks and behaves in an almost identical similar manner to the browser version, although may be more responsive and fluid in operation for remote users. One advantage is that because it syncs data with the server, it can be used offline when there is no internet connection.

Mobile Client - DS note

DS note enables smartphones and tablets to access Note Station. It is available for iOS/iPadOS and Android platforms. Notes entered on the portable device can be synced with the DiskStation in both directions, enabling it to also be used offline.

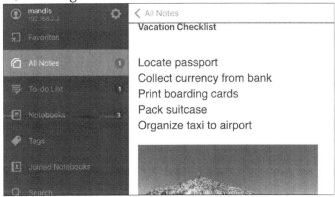

Figure 240: DS Note running on phone

11 OTHER REMOTE CONNECTIVITY OPTIONS

11.1 Overview

Synology Drive – covered in Chapter **10 SYNOLOGY DRIVE SERVER, OFFICE & APPS** – provides an easy and straightforward method for accessing the DiskStation when outside of the home or office. Synology also provide additional options for meeting other connectivity requirements and these are described in this chapter.

11.2 File Station Remote Connection

File Station is used for accessing and manipulating folders and files on the DiskStation. However, it can also connect to remote file systems, providing access to all data in a consistent manner from within a single app. These remote file systems may be other NAS systems or other server types, as well as a selection of popular consumer cloud-based services, which is what we will focus on here. Within File Station, click **Tools > Remote Connection > Connection Setup**. Choose a Cloud Service or Server Protocol and click **Next**.

Figure 241: Choose a cloud service

For a cloud service, you will be prompted to confirm that you wish to grant access to Synology File Station by the provider's website, the specifics of which will vary depending on the provider. Acknowledge the message confirming a successful connection by clicking **Done**.

The connected cloud will now be listed in the left-hand panel of File Station, from where it can be clicked to expand the list of folders and access the data. More than one cloud service can be connected to simultaneously, for instance in this example there are connections to both OneDrive and Dropbox:

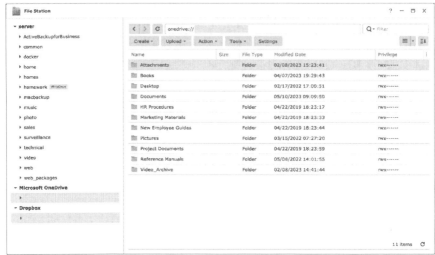

Figure 242: File Station, connected to cloud services

To subsequently connect, disconnect, edit or remove the defined connections, click **Tools > Remote Connection > Connection List**. Select the *Profile Name* (connection) and click the appropriate button at the top of the panel. When finished, click **Close**.

11.3 Cloud Sync

Services such as Microsoft OneDrive and Google Drive are public clouds, whereas Synology Drive Server is a private cloud. Another useful option for DSM is *Cloud Sync*, which gives you the ability to combine the two, thereby creating a 'hybrid cloud'. Why would you want to do this? One reason might be familiarity, for instance you are part of a household or business that uses, say, OneDrive or Google Drive and wish to continue doing so, but in conjunction with the DiskStation.

Begin by downloading and installing Cloud Sync from the Package Center. It will install a new icon in the Main Menu; click to run and the first time it will ask which public cloud service you wish to sync with. There is a choice of many, both business and consumer ones, including such popular ones as Dropbox, Google Drive, OneDrive and Azure:

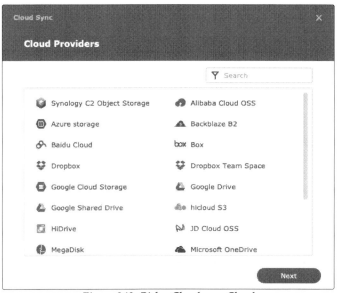

Figure 243: Pick a Cloud, any Cloud

If you do not currently have an account with one of these providers, sign-up first at their website before proceeding (access to these services varies in some parts of the world). Select your service by clicking it, followed by **Next**. You will be prompted to confirm that you wish to grant access to Synology Cloud Sync by the provider's website, the specifics of which will vary depending on the provider.

Having done this, Cloud Sync will prompt for: *Connection name*, which can be left as is or edited; the folder on the DiskStation to be synced (called the *Local path*), which can be specified by clicking the small folder icon and making a choice from the drop-down list followed by **Select**; the *Remote path*, which allows you to specify a folder on the cloud service by clicking the folder icon, otherwise leave as Root folder for everything; *Sync direction*, which would typically be *Bidirectional*. Optionally, tick the *Data encryption* option if required, to enhance integrity and security on the cloud side.

Click **Schedule settings**, which allows you to specify when synchronization occurs. If you are happy for it to take place throughout the day, tick the **Enable schedule settings** box, otherwise drag the mouse cursor to 'paint' the day(s) and hour(s) to define when synchronization should or should not occur. Click **OK**, then **Next** upon returning to the previous screen:

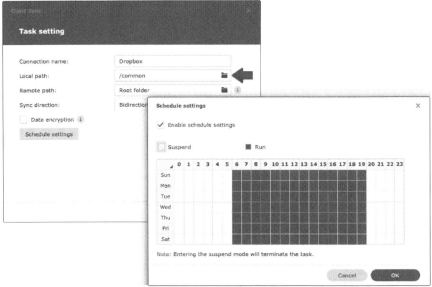

Figure 244: Cloud Sync settings

On the *Summary* screen is a button for optional *Advanced settings*, which can be used to setup File Filters to include or exclude certain file types e.g. you might not want to sync large video files. Click **OK** followed by **Done**, then **OK** to the subsequent message, and syncing should begin immediately. A new icon will appear on the menu bar/task bar allowing the service to be monitored, as well as temporarily paused:

Figure 245: Mini-icon for monitoring Cloud Sync

The main Cloud Sync screen comprises five tabs that can be used to monitor and manage the status of the syncing, although you might find that the default settings are suitable. You can add more public cloud accounts by clicking on the plus sign (+) that is displayed in the top left-hand corner of the screen. There is also a settings icon for administrator controls and adjusting the syncing process:

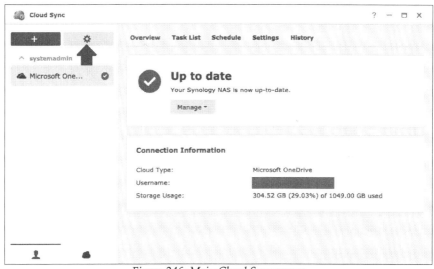

Figure 246: Main Cloud Sync screen

One consideration is that you have sufficient space in the public cloud account, particularly if using free public cloud accounts, as these may only offer a limited amount of storage space. If this is not enough, you may want to consider a paid account.

Another approach is to have accounts with multiple providers and use them for different purposes, for instance Google Drive for general access to files and Microsoft OneDrive for offsite backups.

A further consideration is what happens if you are in a business environment and an employee leaves the company, as if they have the cloud service installed on a home computer they will still have access to company information. In such circumstances you will need to change the main cloud service password, update it on the DiskStation, plus advise remaining employees of the new password. Some cloud services have the useful ability to wipe data from remote devices.

11.4 Hybrid Share Service

The previous section, **11.3 Cloud Sync**, described how to use a public cloud service such as Microsoft OneDrive or Google Drive to create a type of 'hybrid cloud' whereby the DiskStation can store information on it. *Hybrid Share Service* takes this to the next level, allowing shared folders to be created on Synology's C2 cloud service, rather than just using it as a backup destination as described in section **7.6 Synology to Synology Backups**. The key aspects of this are:

C2 can be used to expand the overall amount of storage space. For instance, if the DiskStation was short of space and adding additional (physical) disk storage was not an option, C2 could be used for storing folders.

The system is intelligent in that it only caches the data being used by the DiskStation, rather than maintain a complete local copy, which is how Cloud Sync operates.

A hybrid folder can be accessed safely and simultaneously by multiple DiskStations. It is not necessary to explicitly sync the data between them, such as described in section **10.4 Syncing Between DiskStations**.

Using cloud-based storage can facilitate disaster recovery. If a DiskStation failed or was otherwise out of action, the data stored on C2 is still available.

As implied by the previous two points, Hybrid Share is possibly of more interest to business rather than, say, home or solo users. The requirements and consideration for using Hybrid Share are:

- An account on C2, with an 'Advanced' storage plan, meaning 1TB or greater.
- The DiskStation needs a minimum of 2GB RAM.
- The Btrfs file system must be used on the DiskStation.
- The DiskStation(s) need to be configured to synchronize with an external NTP time server (see **Control Panel > Regional Options > Time Setting**).
- Hybrid shared folders cannot be accessed from Virtual DSM.

- A Hybrid Share folder can be mounted concurrently on up to 10 DiskStations.
- Hybrid Share is not available in China

Support for hybrid shared folders is built-in to DSM and enabled on supported models. To create a folder, go into **Control Panel > Shared Folder > Create > Mount Hybrid Share Folder**. The first time this is done, click **Start** and you will be prompted to sign in to the C2 service and authorize the NAS to access the Hybrid Share folder. Having done so, give the folder a name and set a quota. The quota must be between 500 GB, the minimum permitted value, and the available storage capacity you have on C2. Click **Create**:

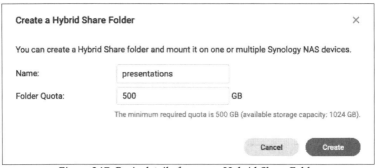

Figure 247: Basic details for a new Hybrid Share Folder

Hybrid Share folders must be encrypted. Specify and confirm the encryption key, click **Next**, acknowledge the resultant message and download and save a copy of the key. The key should not be stored in the folder itself. The download/save dialog box may vary, depending on the browser and platform being used.

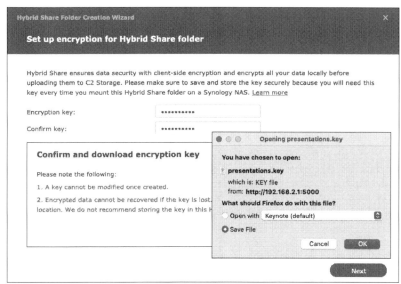

Figure 248: Specify encryption for the folder

On the subsequent panel, leave the folder *Name* as is and specify an optional *Description*. If you have multiple volumes on the system, you can use the *Location* drop-down to define which volume the folder will be on. Tick the **Hide sub-folders and files from users without permissions** box. If you want to be able to recover files that have been deleted, tick the **Enable Recycle Bin** and optionally **Restrict access to administrators only** boxes. Click **Next**.

Figure 249: Specify basic details for the folder

The *Reserved local cache size* needs to be defined and the factors to be considered are that it should be based on the amount of actual data usage in recent weeks, that there is sufficient spare storage space on the server, and that C2 subscription plan has a large enough data allowance. However, the wizard will suggest a suitable value and you may simply wish to use this. Click **Next**.

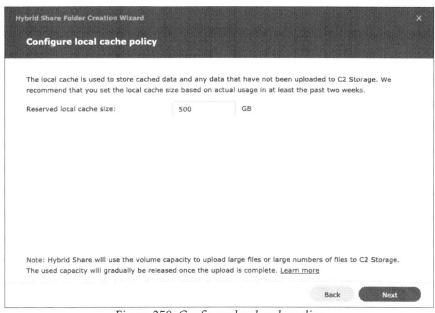

Figure 250: Configure local cache policy

On the *Confirm Settings* panel, click **Next**. On the *Configure user permissions* panel, specify the user access permissions, as with a standard folder. The folder will initialize and then appear in the list of shared folders within the Control Panel. The icon is slightly different than a regular local folder and should normally have a status of 'Connected':

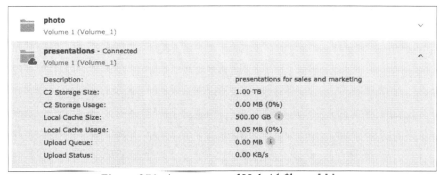

Figure 251: Appearance of Hybrid Share folder

The newly-created folder can now be used in the same manner as any other shared folder.

11.5 DDNS, Router Configuration & Port Forwarding

Connectivity on remote computer servers is frequently done using a combination of *Dynamic DNS* (DDNS) and port forwarding on the router. DiskStations can do this too, and as an alternative to QuickConnect it can be more efficient when simultaneously serving multiple users. A consideration for some people is that this technique does not use the Synology relay servers and, although no data is stored at Synology when using QuickConnect, some people have concerns about such matters. From a technical perspective, the basic requirement is to forward external internet traffic on ports 5000, 5001, 6690 etc. to the internal IP address of the DiskStation, and DSM can be used to configure the router accordingly. If your eyes are glazing over at this point, you might want to skip this section.

The first step is to sort out DDNS. It is easy to find a website on the internet – you simply enter its name e.g. *www.ctacs.co.uk*, *www.synology.com* or whatever you are interested in. But what is the name - or rather hostname - of your DiskStation on the internet? The answer is it does not have one as standard, it just has a number in the form of a public IP address, you might not be aware of what that number is, and your ISP may change it from time-to-time. DDNS services address these issues by giving you a hostname and automatically updating what goes on behind the scenes if the underlying IP address changes. Numerous organisations provide DDNS services, some for free and others on a commercial basis. Examples of suppliers include *No-IP*, *ClouDNS* and *FreeDNS*. Synology also offer free hostnames and signing up for one will be the best option for many home users and small businesses as the process is quick and straightforward. To use the Synology option, you should be signed into your Synology Account.

To setup DDNS, go into **Control Panel** and click **External Access**. Click the **DDNS** tab followed by **Add**. On the resultant panel set the **Service Provider** drop-down to your DDNS provider. If using Synology for DDNS, you can set the Hostname to be the same as your QuickConnect name; the hostname will then consist of *synology.me* prefixed with it. For example, if your QuickConnect name was *ctacs* the hostname would become *ctacs.synology.me*. If you want a different hostname from Synology, or wish to use another provider, click the

Visit DDNS provider's website link and register a name. Then enter the *Hostname* on the original screen.

If all is well, the *Status* indicator will show *Normal* (you can also click the **Test Connection** button to verify matters). Tick the **Enable Heartbeat** box, which will cause Synology to send notifications if the connection is down. Optionally, you can choose to obtain an encryption certificate from the *Let's Encrypt* organization, which will improve security. Click **OK**. You will then be returned to the main External Access screen. In this screenshot some information has been obscured for privacy purposes:

Figure 252: Panel for configuring DDNS

The next step is to configure the router. Remaining in the **Control Panel > External Access** screen, click the **Router Configuration** tab, followed by the **Set up router** button. Click **Start** on the first panel and the wizard will now interrogate the router, during which time a status screen is shown. If the status screen reports a warning/error whilst *Checking network environment,* it may be disconcerting but is not necessarily a problem (frequently, it will advise that it has found two routers, which will probably come as news to you!). When complete click **Next** and then **Next** again on the subsequent panel.

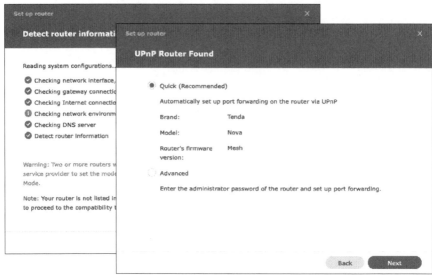

Figure 253: Setup Router screens

After you have been returned to the main screen, click **Apply**. A warning message is given, but just click **OK** to continue and DSM will configure the router. This process takes around a minute, after which the Router Configuration screen is updated.

You will be returned to the previous screen. Click **Apply** - a warning message will be displayed, just click **OK** to continue. When processing has finished, a confirmation screen may be displayed - click **Apply**. On returning to the main screen, click the **Test Connection** button and check that the status is 'OK'.

Assuming all is well you can now test the system. Go to a computer, launch a browser such as Chrome/Firefox/Safari and enter the DDNS hostname that you registered e.g. *ourcompany.synology.me* or whatever it is. You should be greeted with the main DSM logon screen after a few seconds. If it cannot be found or you see the logon screen for your router, do not panic: some routers do not support a feature called *NAT Loopback*, which is required for this type of internal testing. So, the next step is to check if the server can be accessed from outside the premises; if it can then everything is working.

If things are not working, then the most likely cause is that DSM has been unable to configure the router properly, in which case it will have to be done manually. At a minimum this consists of forwarding ports 5000, 5001, 80 and 443 to the internal IP address of the server, though you may need to forward additional ports depending on what applications you wish to run on the server. A full list of ports can be found at:

https://kb.synology.com/en-uk/DSM/tutorial/What_network_ports_are_used_by_Synology_services

Router manufacturers use different terminology to describe this process, such as 'Port forwarding', 'Port triggering' and 'Virtual servers'. As there are thousands of different routers available, it is impossible to describe the specifics here, but instructions for programming most popular routers can be found at the *www.portforward.com* website.

11.6 Virtual Private Networks (VPN)

The purpose of a *Virtual Private Network* or VPN is to securely extend a network to users who are offsite, such as home workers or those in a remote office. Think of it as the equivalent of having a very long network cable that reaches out from the office for 10, 100, 1000 miles/kilometres or more. However, instead of a physical cable the connection goes over the internet, with encryption and other techniques used to maintain security. One advantage of a VPN is that it allows conventional access to files and folders for editing, just as in the office.

Note 1: Some governments block VPN access, particularly to computer systems located outside of their territory.

Note 2: VPN services can also be used to provide anonymous access to the internet, for instance to avoid censorship and geographical restrictions.

Installing VPN Server
Begin by downloading and installing *VPN Server* from the Package Center. From the **Main Menu**, click **VPN Server** to display its *Overview* screen:

Figure 254: VPN Overview screen

VPNs come in several variants, based around different protocols and the Synology VPN Server supports the popular ones of *PPTP*, *OpenVPN* and *L2TP/IPSec*.

These have varying qualities; PPTP is widely supported on many different types of clients but is old and has the weakest security of the three. OpenVPN is popular, especially for Mac users on older versions of macOS, but requires a third-party piece of software to be installed on Windows PCs. L2TP/IPSec has good security, is supported natively by modern versions of Windows and macOS and so will be used here in this example.

Click **L2TP/IPSec** on the left-hand side of the screen. Tick the **Enable L2TP/IPSec VPN Server** box. Accept all the defaults that are offered unless you have specific requirements and technical knowledge about VPNs. The only item that must be specified is the *Pre-shared key* for IKE authentication, which can be thought of as a password and you should choose something non-obvious with a mixture of letters, numbers and symbols. Click **Apply**.

Figure 255: Configuration screen for L2TP/IPSec

After a few seconds a message is displayed, advising that UDP ports 1701, 500 and 4500 need to be forwarded by the router. To do this go to **Control Panel**, click **External Access** and click the **Router Configuration** tab. Click the **Create** button and on the resultant panel choose **Built-in application** followed by **Next**. Find and tick the entries relating to VPN Server with ports 1701, 1723, 500 and 4500 and click **Done**.

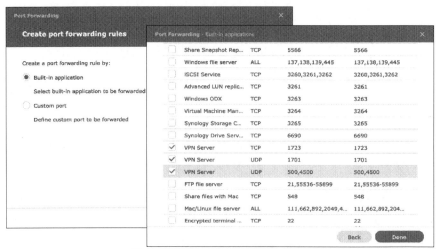

Figure 256: Port forwarding for VPN

Having returned to the previous screen, click **Apply**. A message will be displayed about the port forwarding rules for the router being updated – click **OK**. After a few seconds control will be returned - click the **Test Connection** button to make sure everything seems okay. If it is, then you can proceed to configure the client computers.

VPN Server is now configured and the clients (computers) can be connected. VPN client software is available for most platforms and this section covers installation on three popular ones: Windows 11, Windows 10 and macOS. There may be some minor variations depending on what type of VPN you are using plus any security options you may have chosen (here we are using L2TP/IPSec).

Configuring Windows 11 Clients

Click **Start** > **Settings** > **Network & internet** > **VPN** > **Add VPN** to display the following panel:

Figure 257: Adding a VPN connection (Windows 11)

Click **VPN provider** and choose *Windows (built-in)*, which will usually be the only option available. Specify a **Connection name** e.g. *MyOffice*. For the **Server name or address** enter the external domain address that you registered earlier. Set the **VPN type** to *L2TP/Ipsec with pre-shared key* and enter the pre-shared key you specified when installing VPN server on the DiskStation. The **Type of sign-in info** should be *Username and password*. For security reasons it is suggested that you do not hardcode the **Username** and **Password** and do not tick the **Remember my sign-in info** box. Click **Save**.

The newly defined connection will now be listed on the VPN section. To use it, click the **Connect** button. You will be prompted to Sign in: enter your **Username** and **Password** as defined on the server and click **OK**. After a short while, the status will change to *Connected*. You can now access resources on the server as though you were in the office. For instance, press the **Windows key** and the **R key** simultaneously and in the run box type *server**public* to display and access the shared folder.

When you have finished using the VPN, click the **Disconnect** button.

Configuring Windows 10 Clients

Click **Start > Settings > Network & Internet > VPN > Add a VPN connection** to display the following panel:

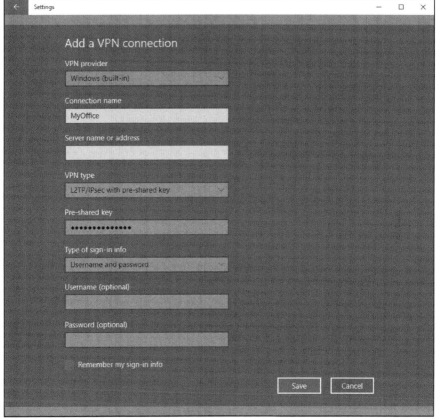

Figure 258: Adding a VPN connection (Windows 10)

Click **VPN provider** and choose *Windows (built-in)*, which will normally be the only option available. Specify a **Connection name** e.g. *MyOffice*. For the **Server name or address** enter the external domain address that you registered earlier. Set the **VPN type** to *L2TP/Ipsec with pre-shared key*, then enter the pre-shared key you specified when installing VPN server on the DiskStation. The **Type of sign-in info** should be *Username and password*. For security reasons it is suggested that you do not hardcode the **Username** and **Password** and do not tick the **Remember my sign-in info** box. Click **Save**.

The newly defined connection will now be listed on the VPN section within Settings. Click it and then click the **Connect** button. You will be prompted to Sign in – enter your **Username** and **Password** as defined on the server and click **OK**. After a short while, the status will change to *Connected*. You can now access resources on the Server as though you were in the office. For instance, press the **Windows key** and the **R key** simultaneously and in the run box type *\\server\shared* to display and access the shared folder.

Configuring macOS Clients

Go into **System Settings**, click **VPN > Add VPN Configuration > L2TP over IPSec**. The *Display name* and *Configuration* can be left as is (assuming this is the only L2TP over IPSec VPN connection being used on the computer). Enter the **Server Address** i.e. the DDNS name created in section **11.5 DDNS, Router Configuration & Port Forwarding**. Enter the DiskStation user's **Account name**, set the **User authentication** dropdown to *Password* and enter the user's **Password**. Set the **Machine authentication** dropdown to *Shared secret* and enter the **Shared secret** i.e. the *Pre-shared key* for IKE authentication, which was defined during the configuration of VPN Server. The Group name can be left blank. Click **OK**.

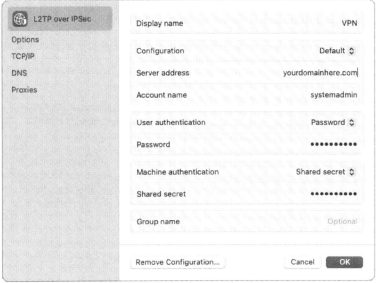

Figure 259: Configuring for VPN

A new entry will have been added to the VPN section of System Settings. To connect to the VPN, slide its button to the 'on' position. To subsequently disconnect, slide the button to the 'off' position.

Figure 260: Enabling/disabling VPN connection

Verify Connections from VPN Server

The status of the VPN and the connections currently in use can be monitored from the server. From the **Main Menu** choose **VPN Server** and click **Connection List**:

Figure 261: Display of active VPN connections

If required, a user can be forcibly disconnected from the VPN by highlighting their name and clicking the **Disconnect** button.

Disabling/Enabling VPN Access for Users

By default, newly created users are automatically given permissions to use the VPN. To change this, click the **General Settings** section in the VPN Server application and remove the tick from the **Grant VPN permission to newly added local users** box. To disable or enable VPN access for individual users go into the **Privilege** section and tick or un-tick the boxes for the users as required, followed by **Save**.

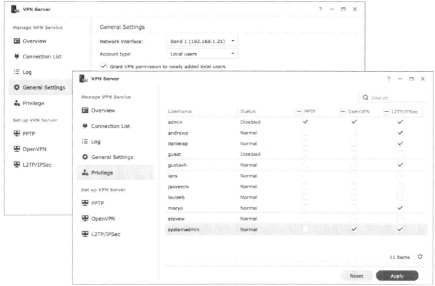

Figure 262: Control VPN access for users

12 STORAGE

12.1 Overview

The key concepts of how DSM handles storage were introduced in section **2.5 Setting up Storage**. This chapter discusses some of the more advanced storage options, including how to configure and manage various storage options, including Snapshots, Caching and iSCSI, plus how to add and replace drives. In addition, there are storage-related housekeeping activities described separately in sections **8.5 Checking Disk Health** and **8.6 Storage Analyzer**.

12.2 Replacing a Faulty Drive

It may be necessary or desirable to replace a drive on the DiskStation at some stage; for instance, a drive may be reporting problems. Provided the correct steps are followed, this can be done without losing data and with minimal disruption to service. In the case of a single drive system, it would be necessary to replace the drive, reinstall DSM and then restore the most recent backup, which would be disruptive and time consuming. However, with a multi-drive system, mechanisms are provided within DSM to replace drives without data loss.

In this example, the DiskStation is a four-bay model holding three drives, which have been configured for SHR-1. However, one of the drives has developed a problem and the storage pool has become what is referred to as 'degraded'. In this situation Storage Manager will look like this; there will also be a notification generated and the system may start beeping (depending on the settings in **Control Panel > Hardware & Power**):

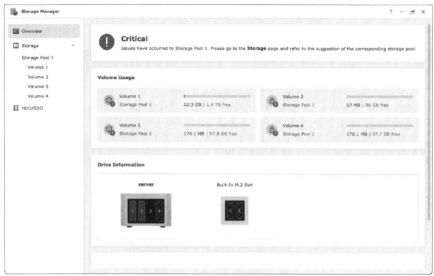

Figure 263: Degraded Storage Pool

Begin by ensuring that the most recent scheduled backup took place, otherwise attempt a complete backup of the system (the topic of backups is covered in chapter **7 BACKUPS**). Having done so, in the *Storage* section, highlight the affected storage pool and click the three-dot menu. The first thing is to try and repair the storage pool, by clicking **Repair**. This process may take some time, but it might resolve matters depending on the nature of the degradation.

Figure 264: Choose Repair option

If the storage pool is not repaired i.e. the status does not eventually revert to Normal, then it will be necessary to replace the drive. If the DiskStation features removeable drive bays, then it also supports hot swapping, meaning the caddy can be pulled out, the drive replaced and then re-inserted back without powering down the unit. If it does not have removeable drive bays and the drives are internal, then hot-swapping is not available, in which case: shut down the unit; disconnect the power cable; install the new drive; restart the server.

Go into **Storage Manager** – the Overview screen will show that the Storage Pool is still 'Degraded'. Clicking on the **HDD/SSD** section should show that the new drive has been recognized, but currently has a status of *Not Initialized*. Highlight the drive, click **Manage Available Drives** and choose the **Repair storage pool** option.

Figure 265: Choose Repair storage pool option

On the next panel select the storage pool (as there may be more than one on the system) and on the one after that select the newly added drive:

Figure 266: Select Storage Pool and Drive

Confirm the settings, click **Apply** and acknowledge the warning message. The storage pool will then repair and return to a status of normal. The time taken for this is dependent on the size of the volume and the amount of data but may take several hours, although the system will be available in the meantime, albeit at reduced performance.

12.3 Adding a Hot Spare Drive

Following on from the example in **12.2 Replacing a Faulty Drive**, where a drive failed and had to be replaced, the decision is now taken to add a 'hot spare'. This is a drive which is physically in place but not in use and is available as a spare; in the event of a drive failure, DSM will recognize what has happened and automatically add the drive to the storage pool to replace the faulty one. In this example we have a four-bay DiskStation with three drives already installed, meaning there is a spare bay to add a further one. Having plugged-in the drive, go into **Storage Manager** and click the **HDD/SDD** section. Highlight the drive, click **Manage Available Drives**, then click the **Assign as hot spare** button.

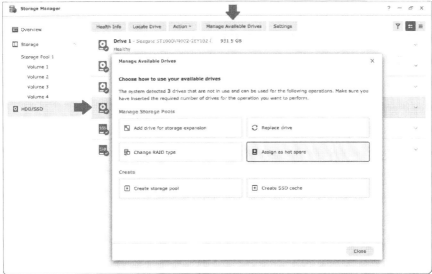

Figure 267: Choose the 'Assign as hot spare' option

The *Hot Spare Creation Wizard* will run. Click the blue **Start** button. On the resultant screen, select the storage pool which is to be protected and the spare drive which will be assigned as the Hot spare. Click **Apply**.

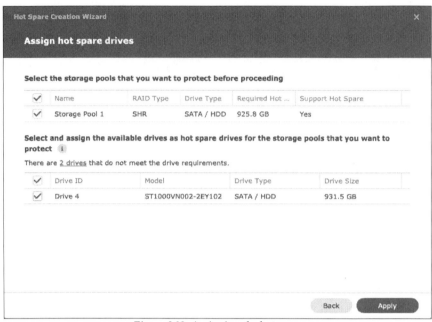

Figure 268: Assigning the hot spare

A few seconds later, the status of the drive, as seen in the HDD/SDD section of Storage Manager, will switch from 'Not Initialized' to 'Hot Spare'. Switch to viewing the Storage Pool information and click the **Hot Spare** button. On the **Settings** tab, tick the **Enable Auto Replacement when the drive status is "Critical" or "Failing"** box and click **Apply**.

Figure 269: Hot Spare settings

No further action is needed and the system will automatically use the Hot Spare in the event of one of the drives failing. Incidentally, it is possible to have more than one Hot Spare drive in a DiskStation if there are sufficient drive bays.

Removing a Hot Spare

Should there be a need to remove a Hot Spare, this is done as follow: View the Storage Pool within Storage Manager. Click the **Hot Spare** button. Highlight the drive, click **Delete** and acknowledge the warning message. Click **Apply**.

12.4 Adding a Drive to Increase Storage

There may be a requirement to expand the amount of storage on an existing DiskStation. Provided it has one or more spare drive bays and the storage pool has been configured as SHR or SHR-2, this is straightforward. The new drive should be of greater storage capacity than the smallest one currently in the DiskStation. Insert it into an empty bay and in the HDD/SSD section of Storage Manager check that it has been recognized. Click **Manage Available Drives** followed by **Add drive for storage expansion**.

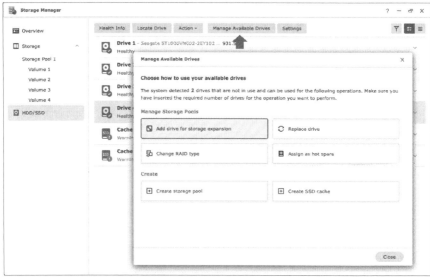

Figure 270: Add drive for storage expansion

On the panel that appears, specify the storage pool to be expanded and click **Next**. On the subsequent one, specify the drive to be added. It is possible to add multiple drives simultaneously, but a safer approach would be to add one at a time in such a situation. Click **Next**.

Figure 271: Select storage pool and drive

On the *Confirm settings* screen, click **Apply**. Acknowledge the warning message by clicking **OK** and the drive will now be added to the storage pool. The time to complete this operation depends upon the capacity of the storage components but may be several hours, during which progress can be monitored from the Storage Pool section of Storage Manager. The system can still be used whilst this is taking place, but the additional capacity will not be available until the process is completed.

Strategy for Replacing All Drives in a Server

There may be a requirement to completely overhaul the storage in a server, perhaps because more capacity is needed or maybe because the existing drives are beginning to age. For instance, the DiskStation may initially have been equipped with low-capacity drives, but it is now desired to install new high-capacity ones to significantly increase storage and prolong the life of the system. One of the advantages of SHR over conventional RAID is that the drives can be of differing capacities plus, using the techniques described here and in section **12.2 Replacing a Faulty Drive**, the drives can be replaced in a piecemeal approach. For example:

Phase 0: Original setup. DiskStation has 4 x 2TB drives, configured for SHR and providing 6TB of protected storage.

Phase 1: One drive is replaced with an 8TB drive. Protected storage initially remains at 6TB.

Phase 2: Second drive replaced with an 8TB drive. Protected storage increases to 12TB.

Phase 3: Third drive replaced with an 8TB drive. Protected storage rises to 18TB.

Phase 4: Final drive replaced with an 8TB drive. DiskStation now has 4 x 8TB drives, providing 24TB of protected storage.

12.5 Data Scrubbing

With computer systems and disk drives, there is always the potential risk of data corruption. Invariably, corrupt data is not detected until an attempt is made to access it, by which time it is too late. To try and pre-empt this problem, a process called *Data Scrubbing* can be used. This is an error detection process whereby data stored in a RAID array is systematically checked for anomalies, which are then corrected using checksums or copies of data. Data Scrubbing can be done manually or scheduled to occur on a regular basis. It is managed from within Storage Manager and is available for use on volumes formatted with the Btrfs filing system (it is not applicable to ext4 volumes).

Launch **Storage Manager**. Within the *Storage* section, highlight the storage pool and expand the details by clicking the chevron on the right-hand side. To manually run data scrubbing immediately, click the **Run Now** button. To setup scheduling, click the **Schedule Data Scrubbing** button, which will display an additional panel.

Figure 272: Data Scrubbing screen

Tick the **Enable data scrubbing schedule** box and select the storage pool (it can only be run on one storage pool at a time). Use the dropdown to set the **Frequency** e.g. every three months. Click **Save**:

The amount of time taken for data scrubbing depends on the amount of storage and data and specification of the DiskStation, but could potentially take a long time and impact the performance of the system. For this reason, it is suggested that it is done out-of-hours or at other times when the server is not being heavily used. To control this, on the scheduling screen tick the **Run data scrubbing only during specific periods** box, click **Set Time Grid** and 'paint' the times on the resultant grid. In the above example, data scrubbing only happens outside of an organization's office hours.

12.6 Global Settings

Space Reclamation Schedule

When shared folders, snapshots or LUNs are deleted, whether automatically by DSM or manually, the system needs to recover the space from the storage pool so it can be re-used (only applicable to Btrfs-formatted volumes). As this is a resource intensive process, it can impact system performance; however, a schedule can be defined so that it only occurs out of hours or during other quiet times. Click the **Set Time Grid** button and on the resultant panel use the mouse to 'paint' the times when space reclamation should be run or paused.

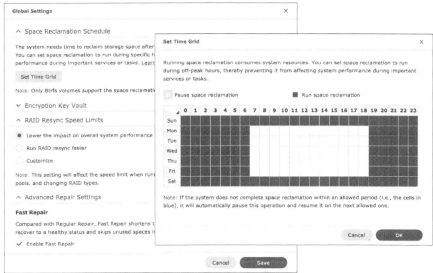

Figure 273: Global Settings in Storage Manager

Encryption Key Vault

When disk volumes are encrypted (see section **2.5 Setting up Storage**), the keys are typically held on the local server. If ever needed, the Encryption Key Vault can be reset and new encryption keys generated. Note that the **Enable Encryption Key Vault** box cannot be unticked if any encrypted volumes exist.

RAID Resync Speed Limits

Most actions associated with repairing and replacing RAID systems are time consuming and, as they are processor intensive, may impact the overall performance and responsiveness of the server. To help mitigate against this, the priority given to the RAID processes of data scrubbing, repairing, expanding storing pools and changing RAID types can be adjusted. In the *RAID Resync Speed Limits* section there are three options, enabling the resync process to run slower i.e. reduce its impact, faster, or with customized values (which requires technical knowledge).

Advanced Repair Settings

There is also an option to **Enable Fast Repair**, which further speeds up the process of repairing a degraded storage pool. It does this by skipping any unused spaces in the storage pool.

12.7 SSD Caching

The principle behind caching is that frequently used data is copied to SSDs, making it quickly available when required, as opposed to it being accessed from the much slower mechanical drives. This process happens automatically and transparently, with DSM keeping track of the data. By using a combination of SSD for performance and lower-priced mechanical drives for capacity, it is possible to obtain the 'best of both worlds' for a reasonable price. Although any amount of SSD will be beneficial, a suggested ratio is 10:1 e.g. if you have 10TB of mechanical storage you should aim to supplement it with 1TB of SSD as cache for good results.

There are three ways to add SSDs for caching:

Some DiskStations feature dedicated M.2 NVMe slots. This is usually the most convenient solution.

Some DiskStations have PCIe slots, enabling expansion cards that hold M.2 NVMe drives to be added. These can be in addition to any drives in M.2 NVMe slots.

Some DiskStations can use regular 2.5" SATA SSD laptop drives. Because of the SATA III interface, these are slower than M.2 NVMe drives, but still give a worthwhile boost to storage performance.

To determine if a particular model supports SSD caching and by which method, refer to the Synology website. At the time of writing, caching is supported only on x86-based models.

Begin by installing the SSD cache drive(s) into a DiskStation that already has DSM installed on it. Launch Storage Manager and click the **Storage** tab. Click **Create** > **Create SSD Cache** (DSM won't let you and says the drives are unsuitable? Go to **HDD/SSD** > **Settings** > **Advanced** and click **Update Now** in the Drive Database section. Then try again). Use the dropdown to associate it with the mount (i.e. volume) to be cached and click **Next**. On the following screen, select a cache mode. If you have two or more SSD devices, there is a choice of *Read-write cache*, which caches both read and write operations and which gives maximum performance, or *Read-only cache*, which caches reads only but still gives a substantial performance boost. If you have a single SSD, then Read-only cache is the sole option. Choose a mode, click **Next** and acknowledge the warning message that is shown.

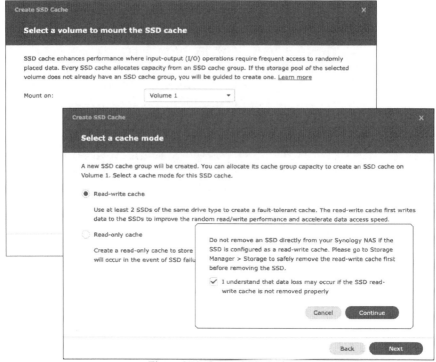

Figure 274: Create SSD Cache

On the subsequent panel, specify the cache RAID type using the dropdown. If there is a single SSD then the only available mode is Basic, whereas with multiple SSDs the cache can be RAIDed to provide fault tolerance to cope with the failure of an SSD. Click **Next**. On the next panel, tick the box(es) to select the SDD(s) to be used in the cache, then click **Next**:

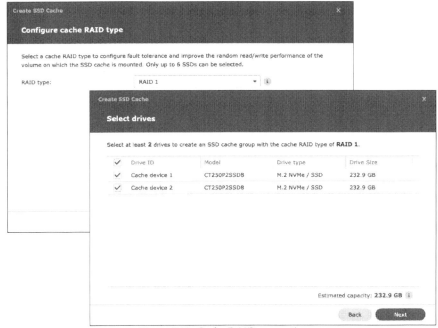

Figure 275: Cache RAID properties

If the SSD drive model is not on Synology's compatibility list, you will receive a warning message to this effect. This does not necessarily mean it will not work, rather that it has not been extensively tested by Synology. In a critical business system, you are advised to use officially supported drives.

On the following screen, specify the size of the cache. One consideration is that a portion of the DiskStation's RAM is used to support caching operations. In this example, we have a 232 GB cache and this will use up 90.6 MB RAM, which is not excessive. However, in a system with large amounts of cache, this could become a consideration. Depending on the configuration there may be a further option relating to Btrfs metadata, which can further enhance performance.

Having decided - and for simplicity you may wish to choose the *Max* option - click **Next**:

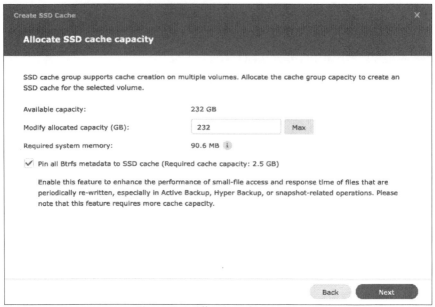

Figure 276: Allocate cache capacity

On the Confirm settings screen, click **Apply** and acknowledge the warning message.

The cache will then initialize, which may take a minute or two, and thereafter will be listed in Storage Manager, underneath the volume that is being cached. By clicking the chevron against the cache drive, it will expand to display more detailed information. At this point, the system will be using the cache.

Note: Whilst the cache is initializing it may display an error condition, particularly if the storage pool that it supports is also in the process of initializing/optimizing. Assuming there are no actual problems with the cache devices, the issue should resolve itself after a short while.

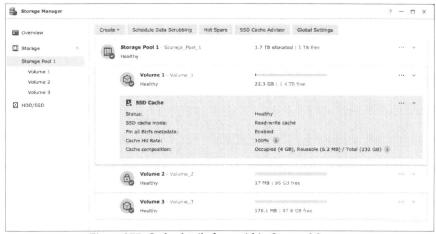

Figure 277: Cache details from within Storage Manager

SSD Cache Advisor

The purpose of *SSD Cache Advisor* is to analyse the performance of the SSD cache, enabling its effectiveness to be evaluated with a view to adjusting the operating parameters if necessary. As this is a specialized facility, it is not commonly used on a home or small business system, but on a large system can be useful for optimizing the system. It is accessed by clicking the **SSD Cache Advisor** button in the Storage section of Storage Manager. Select a volume to analyze and click the **Analyze** button. There will be an advisory message that the analysis will take at least one week. It will automatically stop analysis after 30 days, although it can be stopped manually at any point. It is not necessary to keep Storage Manager open and whilst it is running a progress indicator is displayed at the top of the screen. When complete, the results of the analysis are displayed.

12.8 SSD TRIM

Note: this section is applicable if SSDs are being used for regular storage. It does not apply when SSDs are used for caching.

The SSD TRIM feature improves the performance and lifespan of SSD devices. If a storage pool consisting entirely of SSDs, Synology recommend that TRIM command is enabled. However, the following considerations and limitations apply:

- It is not available on all models.
- Some SSDs do not support TRIM on RAID 5 and RAID 6 volumes.
- Storage pools configured for RAID 0 are not supported.
- SSD TRIM is not supported on storage pools that contain only block-level LUNs.
- If an all-SSD volume is itself supported by an SSD cache, then TRIM cannot be used.
- During the time that TRIM processing is taking place, overall system performance may be impacted, although it can be scheduled to run out of hours.

Assuming these conditions are met, follow these steps to enable TRIM. Within Storage Manager, click **Storage** and select a storage pool that consists entirely of SSD(s). Click the three-dot menu on the right-hand side of the screen and click **Settings**. Tick the **Enable TRIM** box. By default, TRIM processing will take place daily at midnight. To change this, click **Set Schedule**. Click **Save** when finished.

Figure 278: Enabling SSD TRIM

12.9 SAN Manager and iSCSI

iSCSI - *Internet Small Computer Systems Interface* - is a standard for connecting virtualized storage to computers. It is of particular interest to organizations that run multiple servers, have large amounts of storage and require great flexibility when it comes to managing that storage. Servers can be connected using Ethernet or Fiber. In the following examples, we will be creating storage for use with DSM; however, such storage can also be used with products such as Windows Server or VMware ESXi Server.

First, we need to consider how it operates. So far, we have used shared folders on the server. For Windows users, it is possible to map drive letters to shared folders, as described during section **5.3 Connecting Windows Computers**. This enables us to refer to, say, \\server\home as drive H, but it is not a real drive in the sense that the physical C: drive on a Windows PC is and we are simply using the letter H as a form of shorthand. With iSCSI, an amount of space is set aside on the server. The server is referred to as the *iSCSI host* and the space is known as the *iSCSI target* and given a *LUN (Logical Unit Number)* to help reference it. A computer - known as the *iSCSI client* or *initiator* - connects to the LUN (target), which it sees as a complete disk drive. This drive, for most purposes, behaves like a real physical drive and can be partitioned, formatted and used in any way required. There is a one-to-one relationship between target and initiator (in practice, if not in theory), meaning a single target should not be connected to multiple clients. It is possible to move targets from one server to another without unduly affecting the clients, hence its relevance to larger organizations with requirements for redundancy and disaster recovery.

All aspects of iSCSI are managed using the *SAN Manager* utility.

Creating an iSCSI LUN

Go into the **Main Menu** and launch **SAN Manager**. The first time it is run there is a message about loading the optional *Synology Storage Console for VMware/Windows*, although we do not require it here. The SAN Manager Overview screen appears as follows:

Figure 279: SAN Manager Overview screen

Click **LUN** on the left-hand side of the screen, followed by the **Create** button to start the *LUN Creation Wizard*. Enter a *Name* and an optional *Description*. *Location* is a drop-down that allows you to choose the volume that the LUN will be located on if you have multiple volumes. LUNs have more capabilities on Btrfs volumes, so if you have a choice always use a Btrfs volume. Use *Total capacity* to specify how much space will be available – in this example we have allocated 50GB, but it depends on your requirements and available storage. The next field controls *Space allocation* and the choice is between *Thick Provisioning* (better performance and stability, but no support for snapshots) or *Thin Provisioning* (greater flexibility). Thin Provisioning is more efficient and we will use it in this example; however, you need to make sure that there is always going to be sufficient disk space. If using Thin Provisioning, tick the **Space reclamation** box which will appear. Click **Next**. On the following panel choose **Synology iSCSI Target (Recommended)** from the dropdown and click **Next**.

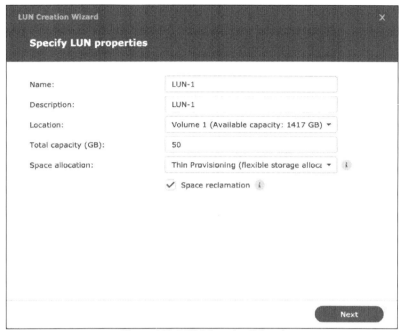

Figure 280: LUN Creation Wizard

The subsequent panel is for assigning access permissions to be defined for iSCSI hosts. This might not be a requirement in a small organization, in which case select the **Allow all** option and click **Next**. Click **Done** on the *Confirm Settings* screen and the LUN will be created and listed in the Overview and LUN sections of SAN Manager.

Figure 281: Newly created LUN listed in SAN Manager

There are several options for managing the LUN(s) on this screen. They can be created, edited (changed), deleted, cloned and defragmented. Defragmentation must be done manually, there is no option to schedule it.

There is provision within Hyper Backup for backing up LUNs. Within it, click the large plus sign (+) in the top left-hand corner of the screen and select **LUNs** as the backup type. This will start the *Backup Wizard*, which enables LUNs to be backed up to a local shared folder, to an external USB drive, or to a separate remote NAS or to another DiskStation altogether. This operates in much the same way as other types of backups, as discussed in Chapter **7 BACKUPS**, and backup tasks can be run immediately or scheduled to run on a regular basis.

Connecting clients

Having set up the LUN(s) on the server, the client computer(s) can now be connected. This section describes how to do so with modern versions of Windows. There is no built-in capability on macOS, although third party solutions may be available.

Windows 11 – click the **Search** icon on the taskbar and search for **iSCSI Initiator**.

Windows 10 - click **Start > Windows Administrative Tools > iSCSI Initiator**.

The first time you do this you may receive a message stating that the Microsoft iSCSI service is not running – click **Yes** to start the service and it will start up automatically on subsequent occasions. In the *Target* field on the Targets tab, enter the IP address of the server and click **Quick Connect** (this name is a coincidence and it is unrelated to Synology's QuickConnect feature). The target should be detected and a status of *Connected* shown. Note: the assumption here is that we are not using any additional security measures for the LUN. Click **Done** and then **OK**.

Go back to **Administrative Tools** and this time choose **Computer Management** and within it click **Disk Management**. You will receive a message about having to initialize the new disk. If the disk is less than 2TB in size choose MBR, if it is greater than 2TB you will need to choose GPT. Click **OK**.

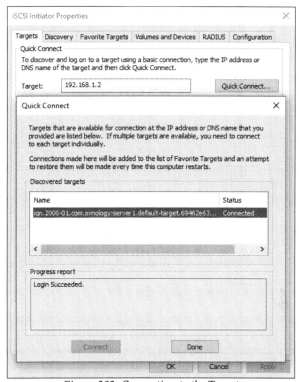

Figure 282: Connecting to the Target

Figure 283: Disk initialization

The new disk will then be visible within Disk Management. Right-click it and choose **New Simple Volume**. Run through the Wizard to assign a drive letter to it and format the volume; thereafter it can be used as a normal disk drive for most purposes.

13 SURVEILLANCE STATION

13.1 Overview

Surveillance Station is one of the most popular packages from Synology and turns a DiskStation into a fully featured CCTV surveillance system and network video recorder. It works with a wide variety of IP cameras and includes features such as real-time monitoring, recording and playback, alarm notifications, plus access from mobile devices. Whether you want a couple of cameras to monitor your home, a sophisticated system monitoring multiple premises with dozens or hundreds of cameras, or any other monitoring requirement, there is a good chance that Surveillance Station is suitable. For home users, one advantage is that there are no ongoing subscription fees, which is commonly the case with consumer surveillance camera solutions. This chapter describes how to get started, but this is a comprehensive product that could easily merit a complete manual of its own.

Suggestion: if you are at the investigative stage, you may want to try out the free Live Demo system, accessible from the *demo.synology.com* website. This allows you to test-drive some aspects of Surveillance Station and see what it is like in operation.

13.2 Installation

Download and install Surveillance Station from the Package Center. If the DiskStation has multiple volumes, there will be a panel asking where recordings are to be stored. Immediately after the download but prior to installation proper, the following panel is shown; this optionally allows the system to be configured so users can login directly to Surveillance Station without having to first login to DSM, and if you wish to do this you should by tick the boxes. It works by adding an extension to the IP address of the DiskStation; for instance, if the IP address is 192.168.1.2 then typing 192.168.1.2/cam in the address bar of a browser will go straight to Surveillance Station (also see **15.5 Customizing the Login & Application Portals**). Click **Next** and then **Done** on the *Confirm settings* screen that follows. The installation process then continues.

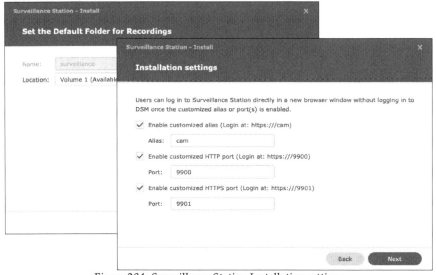

Figure 284: Surveillance Station Installation settings

As part of the installation process, a shared folder called *surveillance* is created on the specified storage location, which is where the recordings will be kept. This folder should not be altered in any way. And if it is not already running, the NTP (Network Time Protocol) service will be automatically enabled.

An icon for Surveillance Station will be placed in the Main Menu – click and it will open in a new browser window; for best results, Synology recommend using the Chrome browser. What you see may possibly surprise you, as it looks like a customized version of DSM designed for running Surveillance Station only, which is basically what it is. It includes its own Main Menu, Application Center ('Package Center') and Help system, along with icons for functions related to surveillance. The Help system will start every time you launch Surveillance Station – if you want to prevent this click **Options > Source > Offline**.

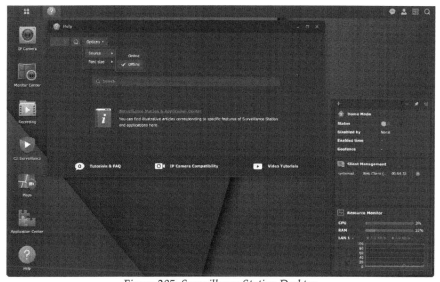

Figure 285: Surveillance Station Desktop

The cameras need to be added. These should first be configured separately for the local network, using the instructions and any software provided by the manufacturer. This process varies depending on the brand and model, but typically it is necessary to provide a username and password for security purposes and assign an IP address to the camera; make a note of these as they are important. All that is needed is that the camera is connected and operational and you do not want to sign-up to any services or install any other software for monitoring and recording.

Within Surveillance Station, launch **IP Camera** and click the blue **Add** button. This starts the *Add Camera Wizard*, which will scan the network for any connected camera(s). Tick the camera(s) and click **Next**. Camera not found? Click the **Add Manually** button, enter a *Name*, specify *ONVIF* (a generic standard for IP cameras) as the *Brand*, and enter the *Camera address*.

On the next panel, type in a *Camera Name*, which could be a physical location or a reference number. Select the storage location from the dropdown. Click the **Authenticate** link and enter the username and password that were used when configuring the camera. Click the **Authenticate** button. If all is well, a thumbnail image from the camera will be displayed alongside its entry.

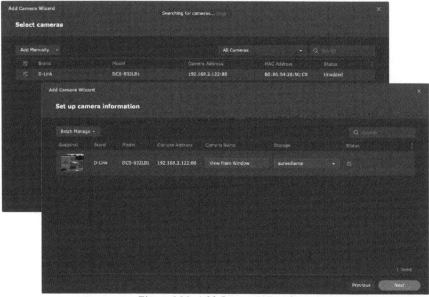

Figure 286: Add Camera Wizard

Click **Next** You will see a panel offering a choice of *Quick Setup* or *Complete Setup*. Assuming there is only one camera, choose the former and click **Next**, followed by **Done** on the Summary screen. You should now be presented with a screen along these lines:

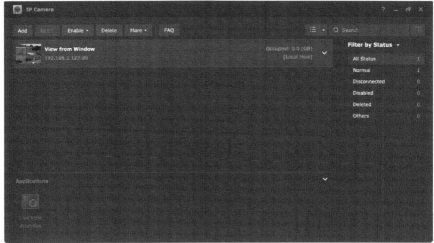

Figure 287: IP Camera screen

To view a live image, click the thumbnail. To change the settings for a camera double-click its name, or highlight and click the **Edit** button. For instance, to change the resolution, frame rate, bitrate and image quality, click **Edit > Device > Video**. Schedules can be setup for cameras, for example, you may have premises that only need to be monitored during night time and at weekends when they are unoccupied. To do this, go into **Edit > Recording > Schedule**. In this example, there is continuous recording from 0800 (8am) to 2000 (8pm) each day, but otherwise recording only occurs when there is motion detection outside of these hours:

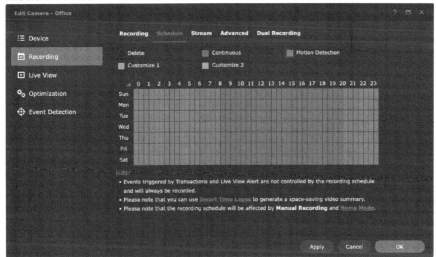

Figure 288: Defining a schedule

To control event detection, use **Edit > Event Detection**. Detection can be under the control of the camera or Surveillance Station, of which the latter offers more comprehensive options. The *Sensitivity* and *Threshold* can be adjusted, and the *Edit Detection Area* defined.

Camera Licensing

Surveillance Station requires that each camera is licensed. For most DiskStation models, Synology grant two free camera licences, although some models are given four. To use more cameras, it is necessary to purchase additional licences, which can be done directly from Synology or through authorized third parties. To manage licenses from within Surveillance Station, click **Main Menu > License**.

Synology's own brand cameras, the BC500 and TC500, do not require licences.

13.3 Usage

There are several icons on the Desktop and Main Menu for using and managing Surveillance Station. *Monitor Center* shows what the cameras are currently viewing, and multiple cameras can be monitored simultaneously. To define the layout, drag the devices (cameras) and tools from the left-hand side onto the main area, plus select a pre-defined layout from the **General Layout** dropdown. A useful feature is the ability to create a map, showing where cameras and other devices are located, and overlay it on the screen. The *Timeline*, along the bottom of the screen, provides an easy mechanism for reviewing the recordings made by the cameras.

Figure 289: Monitor Center

If the mouse cursor is hovered/clicked over the view from a camera, a set of controls appears in the bottom left-hand corner of its screen:

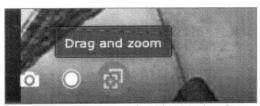

Figure 290: Camera controls within Monitor Center

Working from left to right, the functions of these icons are as follows:

Snapshot – takes a still image of what the camera is currently viewing.

Manual Recording – to instantly begin recording, regardless of any other settings.

Drag and Zoom – for zooming-in (magnifying) part of the image.

When the picture is zoomed, the magnification factor is indicated in the top left-hand corner. To reset it, click the small magnifying glass icon.

The *Recording* icon gives access to the library of recordings, from where they can be managed. Recordings can be played back, exported, locked against deletion, and extracts can be generated. To manage storage, click **Advanced**, tick the **Force to rotate recordings when free storage space is less than** box and specify a value in GB. By default, recordings are stored in a folder called *Surveillance*, with sub-folders for each camera.

The *Application Center* provides access to around 20 apps and extra capabilities for Surveillance Station, grouped into various categories such as Retail, Education, Access Control, Archiving and so on. Some of these will already have been loaded by default and can be enabled if required, whereas others can be downloaded if needed. Application Center is analogous to the Package Center within regular DSM.

When a user has finished working with Surveillance Station, they should logout from it by clicking the **Personal Settings** icon in the top right-hand corner of the screen and clicking **Logout**.

13.4 C2 Surveillance

Overview

C2 Surveillance is an option that enables recordings to be automatically backed up to Synology's C2 cloud service. Besides providing another level of backup, it offers two further advantages: firstly, recordings can be accessed from any location worldwide by logging into the C2 Surveillance portal. Secondly, the recordings are accessible even if the DiskStation is no longer available. For instance, suppose there was a break-in at the premises and the DiskStation was vandalised or stolen, thus making the local data unavailable.

C2 Surveillance is a paid for, subscription service, with different tiers of service available:

Basic: 720p or 1080p resolution recording, footage retained for 7 or 30 or 90 days, event recording.

Advanced: 1080p or 5 MP resolution recording, footage retained for 30 or 90 days, event and timelapse recording.

Professional: 1080p or 5 MP resolution, footage retained for 30, 90 or 180 days, 24x7 continuous recording.

There is an annual charge for each individual camera. At the time of writing, the most basic subscription is €10.70 a year, whereas a professional subscription with 1080p resolution and 30 days storage is €239.99. This approach means that it is possible to mix'n'match to suit specific requirements. For example, an installation with six cameras might choose to use the Basic option with two cameras, an Advanced for one camera, but not enroll the remaining cameras.

Installation and Usage

There is an icon for C2 Surveillance on the Surveillance Station desktop, but it is only an advertisement, inviting you to sign up for a free trial. Visit the Synology C2 portal at *https://c2.synology.com* and choose **C2 Surveillance** from the list of products. Sign-in using your Synology ID. Choose a plan, based upon your requirements. Once this has been done, switch to the DiskStation and launch Surveillance Station. From the Surveillance Station Main Menu, run the C2 Surveillance application. Your subscription details will be listed at the top of the screen:

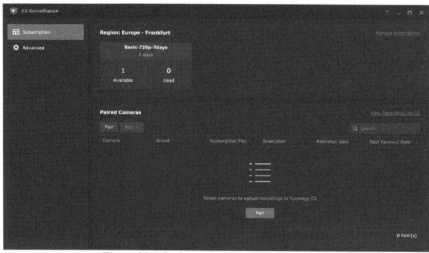

Figure 291: C2 Surveillance Subscription details

Cameras must be 'paired'. Click the **Pair** button and choose an existing subscription plan. On the subsequent screen, choose the camera and click **Next**. In this example, a Basic 720p subscription is being paired to a D-Link camera called 'Office'.

Figure 292: Pairing a camera

A Summary screen is displayed – click **Apply**:

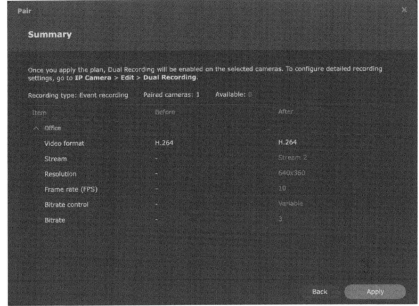

Figure 293: Summary screen

The Subscription section of the main screen will now be updated to show details of the paired camera(s):

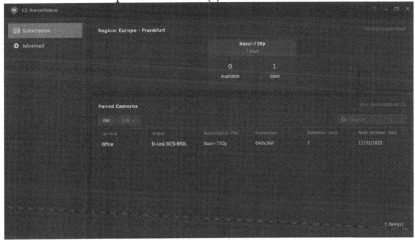

Figure 294: Updated Subscription screen

From now on, any recordings made by the paired camera(s) will be duplicated to C2 Surveillance storage. To view them from there, login to the C2 Surveillance portal. The local versions of the recordings on the DiskStation are unaffected and still available.

13.5 LiveCam and DS cam

LiveCam

LiveCam enables you to use an iPhone or Android smartphone as a webcam with Surveillance Station. This is useful if you only need to use Surveillance Station occasionally or need to setup a temporary system without the overhead of purchasing and installing cameras. It can also be a useful way to redeploy old or unwanted smartphones. When downloading it from the App Store, make sure you specify 'Synology LiveCam'. You will need to give the app permission to use the phone's camera and microphone. Enter the local IP address, along with username and password, and set the HTTPS switch to the 'On' position.

As part of the installation process, LiveCam will automatically add itself to the list of cameras in Surveillance Station i.e. it is not necessary to use the Add Camera feature as described earlier. However, each smartphone will require a licence as with regular IP cameras.

LiveCam includes features such as motion detection and audio. Snapshots can be taken, and recordings played back locally.

Figure 295: LiveCam running on phone

DS cam

DS cam is an app for iOS/iPadOS and Android devices which enables access to Surveillance Station from a smartphone or tablet. During installation, specify the details of the server(s) being used with Surveillance Station, using the QuickConnect ID rather than the internal IP address of the server. This will enable the cameras to be viewed whilst away from the premises being monitored.

13.6 Synology Surveillance Station Client

In addition to managing Surveillance Station using a browser interface, Synology also offer a separate client program, available for Windows 64-bit, Windows 32-bit and macOS. This has two potential advantages: firstly, it can be more responsive and fluid, as browser applications can sometimes be a little bit slow and 'clunky'. Secondly, it removes dependency on browser types and versions (Synology recommend Chrome for use with Surveillance Station, but you may not want to use it). The program can be downloaded from the Synology website downloads section. Having installed it on a suitable computer, two icons will be added: *Synology Surveillance Station Client* and *Monitor Center*. Selecting either will prompt you to enter the IP address or QuickConnect ID of the server, along with a user name and password. The first one gives the standard Synology Surveillance Station 'desktop', in its own re-sizeable window. The second one, Monitor Center, is visually identical to and matches the application described in the previous section.

13.7 Application Center

The Application Center is a version of the Package Center, but containing apps for Surveillance Station and only accessible from within it. Around 20 applications are available; many of these will have been pre-loaded during the installation of Surveillance Station but may be in a stopped condition by default. To activate one of these stopped apps, find it within Application Center, highlight it and click **Run**. One application is *Live Broadcast*, which enables you to stream direct from a camera into YouTube.

The applications are sorted into 11 categories, including Retail, Education, Access Control and PC Utilities. Some applications are listed under multiple categories, the intention being to give suggestions as to which ones are suitable for different needs.

14 VIRTUALIZATION & CONTAINER MANAGER

14.1 Overview

Some DiskStations have the capability to run virtualization software, enabling them to run multiple copies of DSM simultaneously and/or copies of Windows or other operating systems alongside DSM. This provides enormous benefits to corporate users, but virtualization is so accessible with Synology that it becomes available to small business and home users, too. Here are some practical examples of using virtualization:

- A home user can have two discrete systems running on a single DiskStation. For instance, one to provide multimedia and streaming capabilities to the household, the other for experimentation, testing and learning.
- A school has several classes and wishes to provide isolated networks for each of them. By running multiple copies of DSM on a single powerful DiskStation, they can reduce costs, complexity and physical space requirements. It may also be possible to reduce energy costs.
- An organization is running the current version of DSM but still needs access to an earlier version.
- A small business is in the progress of migrating away from Windows Server to Synology but needs to retain a copy of Windows Server to continue running a specialized application for some users. Using virtualization, they can do this on the DiskStation, dispensing with the old server hardware and saving on overall running costs.
- Access to other operating systems, such as Windows or Linux, is required for testing and support purposes.

Virtualization is possible because DiskStations, like most computers, spend much of their time being under-utilized. Although they may be running apps, maintaining communications and serving up files, typically they are sitting there waiting for requests from users and applications. As such, they have a lot of spare time in terms of low processor utilization, which can be used for tasks such as running additional operating systems. Not all DiskStations are suitable, and the facility is only available on a selection of DiskStations equipped with suitable processors and sufficient amounts of RAM.

Synology support two virtualization technologies. The first one is *Virtual Machine Manager*, which can handle many different types of operating system. The second one is *Container Manager* (a renamed version of *Docker*), which can be considered as a 'lite' form of virtualization that runs mainly Linux virtual machines and specific applications; it is also used by Synology to deliver some of its own 'regular' applications from the Package Center. *Container Manager* has less demanding hardware requirements than Virtual Machine Manager.

This chapter is intended only as an introduction to what can be a sophisticated topic. The installation of an additional copy of DSM, referred to as *Virtual DSM*, along with the installation of Windows on a DiskStation, plus the installation of Container Manager, are covered.

14.2 Preparing for and Installing Virtual Machine Manager

Virtualization on the DiskStation is provided by an app from the Package Center called *Virtual Machine Manager* (VMM). Upon starting it for the first time, the *Virtual Machine Manager Setup Wizard* will run. Click **Next** and the *Check Host Settings* panel will show. Usually everything is in order, although the 'Open vSwitch' may be disabled, which will be the case if a bonded interface exists (see section **15.16 Link Aggregation**). On the subsequent screen, select the volume(s) which will be used for storing the virtual machines and click **Next**. The wizard will now create a *Virtualization Cluster* – click **Finish** when it has done so. At this point you can begin creating virtual machines. The Virtual Machine Manager *Overview* initially appears as follows:

Figure 296: Virtual Machine Manager Overview screen

14.3 Installing Virtual DSM

An *Image* of the DSM operating system is first needed - click **Image > DSM Image > Add**. There is a choice of location for the installation file; you might already have downloaded a copy of Virtual DSM onto your computer or NAS, else click the **Download Virtual DSM image** button to download the latest version from Synology. Click **Download** followed by **Next**.

Figure 297: Download Virtual DSM image

On the subsequent panel, select the storage location for the virtual machine. If you intend creating additional virtual machines at some point, you may wish to tick the box at the bottom of the screen to set the volume as the default location. Click **Done**:

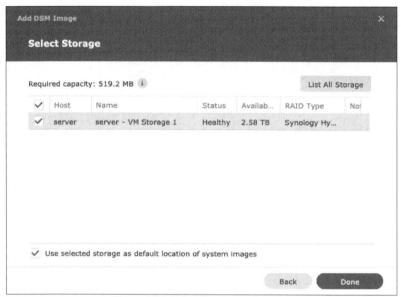

Figure 298: Select the storage location

The image will now be downloaded, which may take several minutes depending on the speed of the internet connection, after which it will be listed on the *DSM Image* panel with a status of 'Healthy'. The virtual machine proper can then be created: on the **Virtual Machine** tab, click **Create**. You will be prompted to choose an operating system and there is a choice of *Microsoft Windows*; *Linux*, such as Debian, Ubuntu or Fedora; *Synology Virtual DSM*; *Others*. In this example we are installing **Synology Virtual DSM**, so select it and click **Next**:

Figure 299: Choose the operating system

Confirm the storage location for the virtual machine on the next panel, and on the one after that specify the general parameters for the virtual machine, such as a *Name* and an optional *Description*. Specify the number of CPUs and the amount of Memory (RAM) – at least 1GB is needed, but more is preferable if available. The *Virtual machine priority*, which will help define overall performance, can be adjusted using the dropdown. Click **Next**.

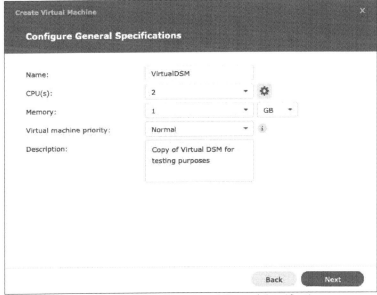

Figure 300: Configure Storage and General Specifications

On the subsequent panel, allocate the size of the virtual disk(s) to be allocated for storage. Click the plus sign (**+**) to add further virtual disks if required - each virtual disk will become a separate volume. Click **Next**. Configure the network to be used; if you have specific requirements, click the control wheel and make changes, else just accept the **Default VM Network** and click **Next**.

Figure 301: Virtual Disk and Network details

On the next panel, use the *Autostart* dropdown to choose whether the virtual machine will autostart when the DiskStation starts up. Click **Next**. On the subsequent panel it is necessary to specify who has permission to power virtual machines on and off; typically, this would be administrative users only:

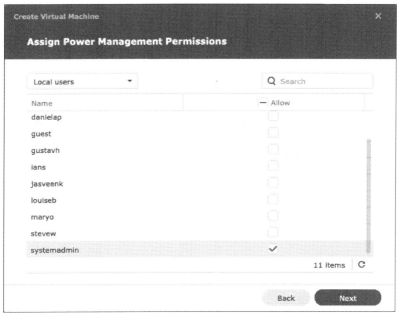

Figure 302: Assign Power Management Permissions

Click **Next** and a *Summary* screen is shown. Click **Done**, and the virtual machine will be created and listed within the *Virtual Machine* tab. To run it, click the **Power on** button and select **Power on;** this button is also used for shutting down, restarting, suspending and resuming virtual machines:

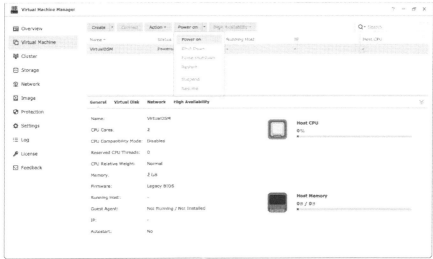

Figure 303: Powering on a virtual machine

The first time a new copy of Virtual DSM is run, the *License Mapping Wizard* will appear. If this is your first and only copy of Virtual DSM, choose the **Use existing license** option. Synology grant a license for one free copy, but if it is a second or subsequent copy you will need to obtain additional paid license(s) from Synology. Click **Next**. On the subsequent panel, highlight the license, click **Next** and then **Done** on the Summary panel.

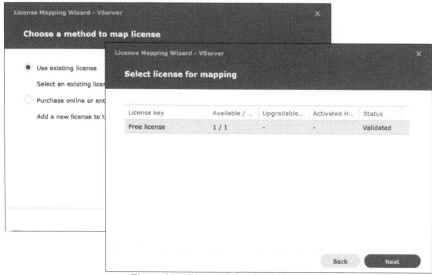

Figure 304: License Mapping Wizard

After a short delay, the virtual machine can be accessed and managed in the same way as a regular DiskStation. The IP address of the virtual machine will be listed on the **Virtual Machine** screen; it will have been assigned a dynamic IP address, although this can be changed during DSM setup if required. To access the virtual machine, highlight it and click **Connect**. A new page will be opened in your browser, from where DSM can be configured in largely the same manner as described in **2 INSTALLING DSM**, with the caveat that the Hardware & Power and External Devices options are not available within Control Panel.

Figure 305: Connect to a Virtual Machine

14.4 Installing Microsoft Windows

The process for installing Microsoft Windows is similar to that for installing Virtual DSM, so you may want to read the previous section if you have not already done so to understand the general principles. To install Windows, you will need an ISO file containing a copy of the software. If the software is obtained electronically, it will be in ISO format. If you have a physical DVD-ROM containing the software, utilities are available to generate an ISO file from it. Trial versions of Windows can be downloaded from Microsoft, which are useful for evaluation and testing purposes e.g. you may wish to check the performance of a virtualized version before committing to a purchase.

Launch Virtual Machine Manager and click **Image > ISO File > Add**. On the resultant panel, navigate to where the ISO file is stored on the DiskStation or local computer. Select it, click **Next** and on the following panel choose the storage location for the virtual machine. Click **Done** and the image will now be uploaded, which will typically a couple of minutes.

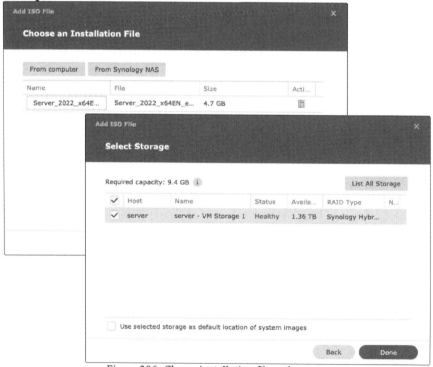

Figure 306: Choose installation file and storage

The virtual machine proper can be created: click **Virtual Machine** followed by **Create**. You will be prompted to choose an operating system: choose *Microsoft Windows* and click **Next**. On the subsequent panel, select the storage location then click **Next**.

On the third panel, specify the general parameters for the virtual machine, such as a *Name* and optional *Description*. From the dropdowns, specify the number of CPU(s) and the amount of memory (RAM); at least 2GB is needed for Windows, depending on the version, but more will give better performance if available. Optionally, specify a video card and priority for the virtual machine. Click **Next**.

Figure 307: Configure general specifications

On the next panel, allocate the size of the virtual disk(s) to be used for storage; to use more than one virtual disk, click the plus sign (+) to add further ones, with each virtual disk becoming a separate volume. Click **Next** and on the panel after that choose the network configuration and click **Next**. If in doubt, use the default values for these settings.

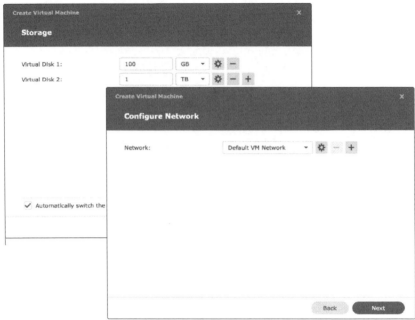

Figure 308: Storage and network options

The *Other Settings* panel will be shown. Choose the *ISO file for bootup* i.e. the Windows image you uploaded. The *Additional ISO file* should be set to the *Synology_VMM_Guest_Tool* (a message may be displayed, prompting you to download it first). Make any changes if required to the other parameters, such as *Autostart* and *Keyboard Layout*. The *Firmware* if often set to Legacy BIOS, but more recent versions of Windows, e.g. Windows 11, require UEFI. Click **Next**.

Figure 309: Other Settings

On the subsequent panel, assign users who will have permission to power the virtual machine on and off; usually, this would be the administrator user(s) only. Click **Next** and a *Summary* panel is shown. Click **Done**, and the virtual machine will be created and listed on the *Virtual Machine* tab. To continue the installation, click the **Power on** button and select **Power on**. After a short while, the **Connect** button will become enabled; click it, and the virtual machine will be displayed in a new browser tab, from where the standard Windows installation screens can be worked through.

Once Windows has finished installing, launch File Explorer. Within the list of devices and drives, there should be a virtual CD drive, typically the D: or E: drive, with a CD called *SYNOLOGY_VMMTOOL* pre-loaded. Open it and run the *Synology VMM_Guest_Tool* application to install drivers and other items to support Windows in the virtualized environment.

The performance of Windows and other operating systems running in a virtualized environment is dependent on the hardware capabilities of the DiskStation. Whereas Virtual DSM has been highly optimized and runs very smoothly, modern versions of Windows can be relatively slow on low-end hardware. If the requirement is to only access Windows on an occasion basis this may not be an issue, but if, say, a copy of Windows Server needs to be kept running permanently then a more powerful DiskStation with plenty of RAM is advised.

Tip: When running Windows in a browser tab, a small set of slide-out tools are available on the left-hand side of the screen. The top one is very useful as it provides access to some specialized keys, including a mini-icon for the **Ctrl+Alt+Del** keyboard sequence.

14.5 Container Manager

Container Manager is downloaded and installed from the Package Center, which results in its icon being placed in the Main Menu. Launching it will display the *Overview* screen, from where containers are created and managed.

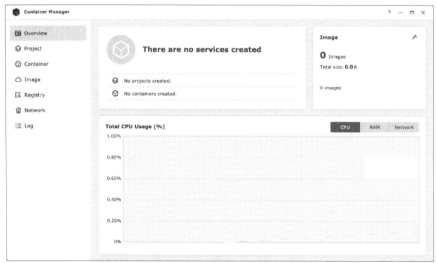

Figure 310: Container Manager's Overview screen

Containers are self-contained applications, largely isolated from the supporting operating system, which in this case is DSM. This approach to virtualization offers good performance and enhanced security. Tens of thousands of ready-to-use containers are available from many different sources; often these are grouped together in hubs/repositories/registries (think 'app store') and Container Station on DSM has been pre-set to the most popular one. If you are new to containers, you might find them slightly underwhelming as many are 'black box' appliances and may not appear to do very much in a conventional sense. The quality of containers varies enormously: a degree of diligence is required and technical knowledge may be required to use some of them.

In this example, we will install a copy of the popular Ubuntu Linux environment. Click on the **Registry** tab, which will display a scrollable list of containers. To search for a particular container or type of container, enter keywords in the search area and having found it, double-click to download.

This may result in an additional dialog box, for instance here we are given a choice of Ubuntu versions. Those with blue ticks against them are Official Images, implying a higher degree of trust:

Figure 311: Downloading a Container

Containers are usually small in size and so download relatively quickly, whence they will appear on the *Image* tab. Highlight the image and click the **Run** button, which will start the *Create Container* wizard. On the first panel, parameters for CPU, memory and auto-restart can be specified:

Figure 312: Creating a Container

The subsequent panel – *Advanced Settings* - contains a wide range of additional settings for controlling the behavior of the container, including network connections, port access, shared folder access and links to other containers. The values for these parameters depend upon your requirements, and supporting information might be available from the publisher of the container. In some instances, the defaults are already suitable and it is not necessary to supply them. Click **Next** and then click **Done** on the Summary panel. The newly created container will now start running and will be listed on the *Container* tab.

To stop or start the container, highlight it and click the **Action** button. You can also double-click a container, which will bring up a detailed panel with four tabs. Using the **Action** button on the *General* tab, a terminal session (command prompt) can be opened. From the Statistics tab, information about CPU, RAM and Network usage can be monitored.

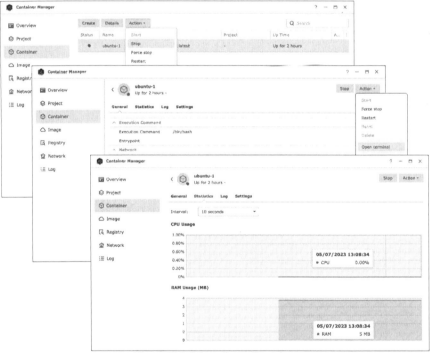

Figure 313: Managing a Container

Note: When Container Manager is installed, it will create a shared folder called 'Docker' on the DiskStation. This folder should not be deleted or altered in any way.

15 MISCELLANEOUS TOPICS

15.1 Overview

This chapter covers a variety of topics to help you get more out of your DiskStation, plus addresses some more advanced and specific technical topics relating to networking.

15.2 Package Center

Whilst the DSM operating system has a huge amount of functionality built-in, it is possible to greatly extend it further through the installation of optional, mostly free, packages ('apps'), and this process is managed through the *Package Center*. Many of these apps have been developed by Synology themselves, whilst others have been supplied by third parties. Some are business focused, others are aimed more at home users, and some are applicable to both. To review what is available, click the **Package Center** icon, located on the DSM Desktop as well as on the Main Menu, to display the following screen (before using Package Center for the first time, it is necessary to accept Synology's terms and conditions statement). There are three top-level groupings: *Installed* - packages which have already been installed on the DiskStation; *All Packages* – a complete listing of what is available; *Beta Packages* - packages for experimentation and testing purposes e.g. new versions.

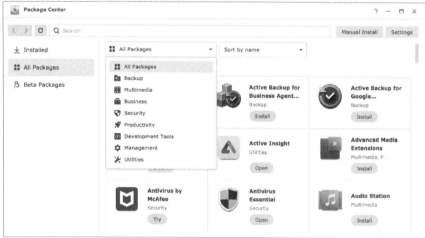

Figure 314: Package Center

At the time of writing around 100 packages are listed in the Package Center, some from Synology and others from third parties, in eight different categories: *Backup*; *Multimedia*; *Business*; *Security*; *Productivity*; *Development Tools*; *Management*; *Utilities*. Not all packages are available for all DiskStations due to hardware requirements, although most are and Package Center will not list ones inapplicable to your model.

To download and install a package, click on its **Install** button. If you have more than one volume in your system, choose which volume it will be installed upon, although it is better that all apps are installed onto a single volume for consistency. Some packages have dependencies, which will result in other components and packages being automatically downloaded and installed alongside them. Most packages will automatically upon installation – if you do not want this to happen, remove the tick from the **Run after installation** box.

The Package Center provides all the mechanisms necessary for downloading, installing, managing, updating and removing packages. Clicking on an installed package within the Package Center will show an Action drop-down where the package can be controlled, with the options available depending upon the package:

Figure 315: Managing an installed package

Control over Package Center itself can be exercised by clicking the **Settings** button. There are three tabs:

General – the default volume that packages are installed on can be specified using the dropdown on systems with multiple volumes. Email and desktop notifications can be enabled which will advise when updates to packages are available.

You can choose to access Beta versions of packages for testing purposes and experimentation; if you do so, you will also have to the acknowledge the terms and conditions when you subsequently click the Beta Packages section.

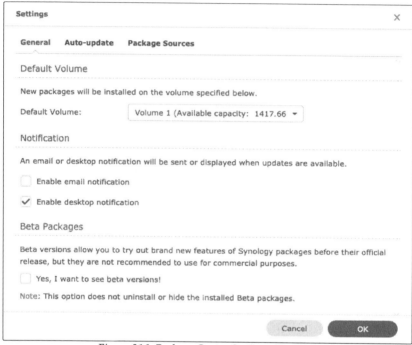

Figure 316: Package Center Settings (General)

Auto-update – choose to have all or specific packages updated automatically whenever new versions are available. Note that when DSM is updated, some packages may also need to be updated (see **8.2 Checking for DSM Updates**).

Package Sources - Although plenty of packages are available through Synology and its partners, there are also many 'unofficial' ones available from other sources. These packages may provide extra capabilities or do things in a different way. Before proceeding, it is important to understand that none of these packages are supported by Synology and if things go wrong then you are on your own. You should only use such packages if you fully understand and are happy with the implications of this.

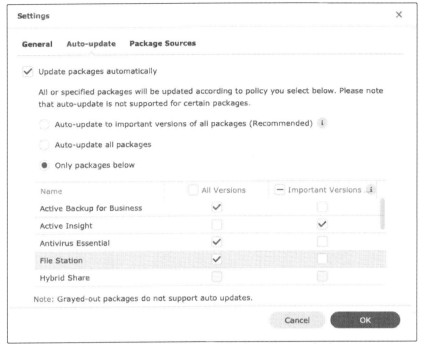

Figure 317: Package Center Settings (Auto-update)

Probably the best-known source of unofficial packages is the Syno Community, who have a comprehensive library. To access it from the Package Center, click **Settings** and on the *Package Sources* tab click **Add**. Specify a *Name* e.g. Community. For the *Location*, enter *https://packages.synocommunity.com* and click **OK**. Having been returned to the previous screen, also click **OK**.

Figure 318: Adding a new Package Source

The entry for 'Community' will now be listed on the left-hand side of the screen and clicking it will cause the available packages to be listed, from where they can be installed in the standard manner.

15.3 Managing Your Synology Account

Using a DiskStation with services such as QuickConnect, C2, and Active Insight requires that you have a Synology Account. Having created an account, it can subsequently be managed online; go to **Control Panel > Synology Account** and click the **Synology Account** link towards the top of the screen, alternatively visit *https://account.synology.com/*. Sign in using your account credentials.

There are seven main sections on the portal:

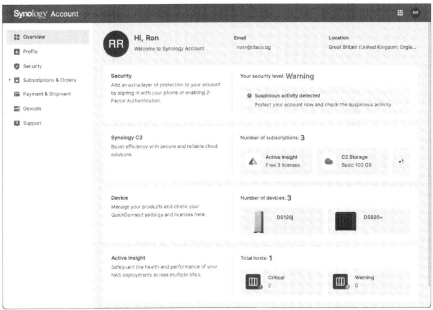

Figure 319: Synology Account portal

Overview – provides 'at a glance' information of the topics listed below, along with additional services such as Active Insight.

Profile – account and contact information can be viewed and edited from here. A recovery email and phone number can be registered. The Synology Account can be deleted from here, should that ever be required.

Security – your Synology Account password can be changed here. 2-Factor Authentication can be specified to improve security. Recent logins to the account are listed.

Subscriptions & Orders – details of C2 subscriptions, DSM/SRM purchases and extended warranties.

Payment & Shipment – payment details and billing information can be viewed and changed.

Devices – details of devices, including serial numbers, QuickConnect settings, plus licenses which have been registered.

Support – support tickets can be raised and viewed from here.

15.4 Support Center

Support Center is located on the Main Menu and enables you to contact Synology directly for support and assistance should you have problems that you cannot resolve yourself. The first tab – **Contact Support** - is for sending a message to Synology Support and to use this you need to login to your Synology Account. The second tab – **Support Services** - is for setting up remote access so that Synology can take control of the DiskStation in order to gather information or apply changes. This is not left permanently enabled, rather you tick the **Enable remote access** box when specifically requested to by Synology and then provide them with the unique and limited life *Support identification key* that is generated at the time. You can specify which items generate log files for diagnosis in the *Log Generation* section (the list of items may vary, depending on your DiskStation model and configuration). The third tab is for use with **Active Insight** (Active Insight is covered in section **8.11 Active Insight**).

Having made the changes, click **Apply**.

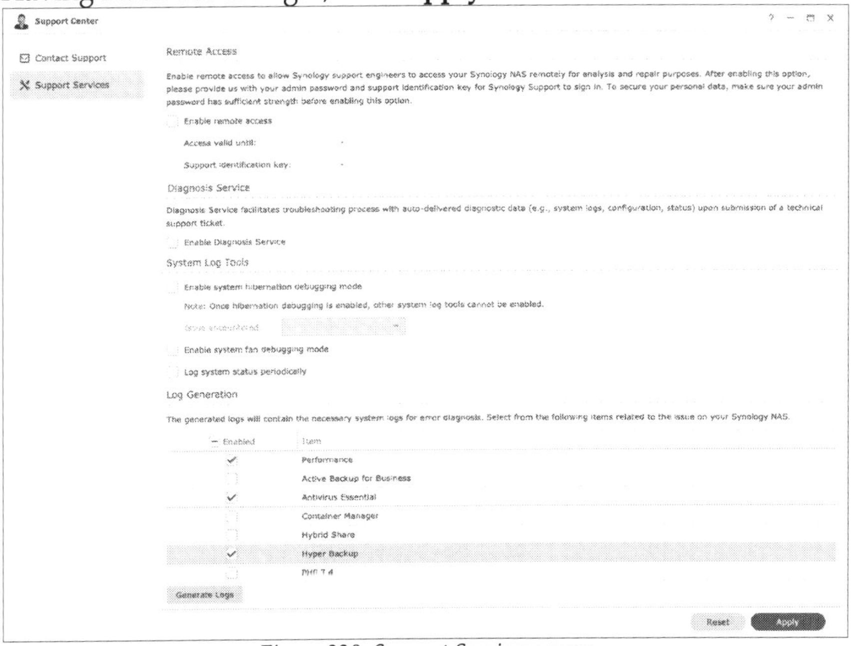

Figure 320: Support Services screen

Once support tickets are raised, they can be viewed and responded to by logging into your Synology Account (they can also be raised from there).

15.5 Customizing the Login & Application Portals

The login portal (screen) for DSM can be changed and customized. You might wish to do this in a business or educational establishment, to enforce 'branding' for the organization. To change the appearance of the login screen, go to **Control Panel > Login Portal** and on the **DSM** tab click the **Edit** button in the *Login Style* section at the top of the screen to show this panel:

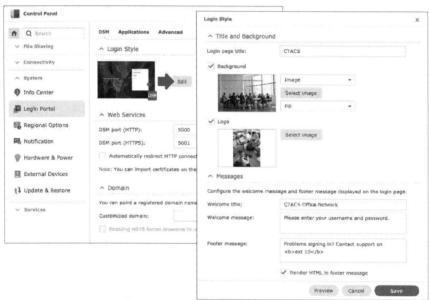

Figure 321: Customizing the Login Style

Several aspects of the login screen can be changed. In the *Title and Background* section, the **Login page title** can be specified – this is the text that appears in the login panel where the username and password are entered. To change the background, tick the **Background** box and use the dropdown to specify an image or a solid color. There is a choice between several built-in images, or a picture on the NAS can be selected, or a file can be uploaded from the local computer (**My Images > Upload**). A **Logo** can be specified and this should be a JPG/JPEG or PNG format file under 1MB in size.

In the *Messages* section, a **Welcome title, Welcome message** and **Footer message** can all be specified. Optionally, HTML can be enabled for the footer message to allow use of attributes such as bold and italics.

By changing these elements, it is possible to create a distinctive login screen. Having customized the screen, click **Preview** to check it or **Save** to adopt it.

Application Portals

Several Synology applications can be assigned their own portals, including Synology Drive, Synology Surveillance Center and Synology Photos. This enables users to sign in directly to the application in its own customized browser window, rather than having to first sign into DSM and then select the app. This can be used to effectively create turnkey systems where DSM is 'hidden' and is particularly useful where users only need access to a single application. For example, consider a deployment where Surveillance Center is in use and several operatives need access to it but do not use anything else.

Go to **Control Panel > Login Portal** but this time click the **Applications** tab. A list of customizable apps is displayed, with the list depending on what has been installed on the DiskStation. Highlight an app and click the **Edit** button:

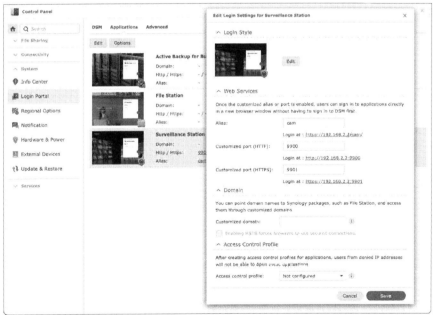

Figure 322: Application portals

Each application portal can have its own background picture. Synology provides a suitable one by default, but if it is not to your liking click the adjacent **Edit** button to change it, plus add your own title, welcome message, logo and so on, the same as when customizing the DSM login portal described previously.

The *Web Services* section is important. This is where the **Customized ports** (IP addresses) are specified. Each application has unique port numbers associated with it, defined by Synology, and although you could potentially change them it is suggested that you do not. Optionally, an **Alias** can be specified – this acts as a shortcut and removes the need for the users to remember the port numbers. The above example shows settings for Surveillance Station. The server has an IP address of 192.168.2.2 and the ports for the app are 9900 (HTTP) and 9901 (HTTPS), plus an alias of 'cam' has been specified. So, to access Surveillance Station directly from a browser the user would type in *http://192.168.2.2:9900* or *https://192.168.2.2:9901*, or simply *https://192.168.2.2/cam/*

15.6 Printing

An advantage of networking is that it allows printers to be shared, thus potentially saving money as well as physical space. There are three methods for sharing a printer on a DiskStation-based network:

USB through DSM – Most USB-only printers can be plugged directly into the DiskStation, with DSM handling the sharing.

Ethernet or wireless through DSM – The printer is connected to the network and DSM handles the sharing.

Ethernet or wireless but independent – Most modern printers have built-in Ethernet or wireless connections, giving them an existence on the network totally independent of any server or computers.

The first technique, sharing USB printers, is described in the next section. The second technique is analogous to the way network printers have traditionally worked, in which print jobs are first sent to the server, which then feeds them out (or "spools them") to the printer. This has advantages in terms of control in a larger business or educational environment with many users and printers, but may be overkill in a household or small business. The third category of printers, ones with built-in network connections, are intelligent devices and can talk directly to computers independently without a server acting as a middleman, and these are the most popular and easiest to use. With such printers, the DiskStation has no significance at all and you simply follow the manufacturer's normal installation procedure on each of your computers.

The exact method for setting up any specific printer type varies, but the following principles can be followed:

Configure the printer with a fixed or static IP address. This should be adjacent to the address of the server and away from the IP address range used by the computers. Suppose, for instance, that the internet gateway is 192.168.1.1 and the server is 192.168.1.2. If two printers were added to the network, then suitable addresses might be 192.168.1.3 and 192.168.1.4. The simplest way to set the IP address is often on the printer itself; alternatively, the technique of a reserving an IP address on the DHCP server, commonly the router in a home or small business setup, can be used (recommended for larger networks).

Download the latest drivers for the printers. The drivers can be stored on the DiskStation, for example in a *technical* folder, so they can readily be copied to the individual computers, rather than having to download them from the internet each time. Printer manufacturers sometimes offer a choice of drivers, for instance a basic one as well as a full-featured one. Use the basic one, as the full-feature ones might have superfluous features mainly designed to capture marketing information and sell you more cartridges. However, be aware that with some multifunction devices i.e. combined printers/copiers/scanners, not all functions may be available in a networked environment or may require additional software from the manufacturer to fully utilize them.

Sharing USB Printers

A decade ago, the ability to share USB printers would have been considered a major benefit. These days all new printers have built-in Ethernet or wireless connections, meaning it is no longer the useful feature it once was, although the ability to share USB printers can be useful in some circumstances. Although it usually works, not all printers are suitable. For instance, all-in-one devices that combine printing with scanning, copying and faxing may not work, or may work for printing only, whilst older obscure brands of printer may prove problematic.

Begin by downloading the latest drivers for the printer from the manufacturer's website and copying them to each computer that will use the printer. Most modern printers have a universal driver i.e. one that will work with any version of Windows, but in some instances it may be necessary to download multiple versions.

Connect the printer to the DiskStation using a USB cable, which must be plugged directly into a USB socket on the DiskStation and cannot be connected via a USB hub. Switch on the printer. Go to **Control Panel** on the DiskStation and click the **External Devices** icon. On it, click the **Printer** tab and the printer will appear, although it may take a short while. Highlight the printer and click **Printer Manager > Setup Printer** to display the following:

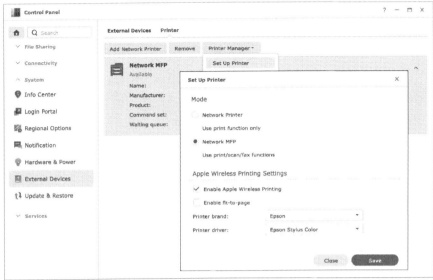

Figure 323: Setup printer

For a regular printer choose **Network Printer**. For an all-in-one printer/scanner/copier choose **Network MFP**, noting the earlier comments about some models possibly having limited functionality. Also, if you are using Windows 10 computers, you might have to choose the Network Printer option, regardless of the actual type. Tick the **Enable Apple Wireless Printing** box if required, which will turn on the Bonjour support required for Macs. Click **Save** and **Close** (this may take a short while if the Apple Wireless Printing option was ticked). The printer status should have a status of *Available* or *Connected*, with the make and model identified correctly in most cases.

Connecting Windows computers

Install and run the Synology Assistant software on each computer. Click the **Printer Device** tab followed by **Add** and the printer(s) connected to the DiskStation should be listed. If the Printer Device tab is not present, click the **Preferences** cogwheel in the top right-hand corner and tick the **Printer Device** and **Allow compatibility with devices that do not support password encryption** boxes, followed by **OK**. Highlight the printer and click **Next**. You will be prompted to install the printer driver supplied by the printer manufacturer, which you should have downloaded previously.

The installation procedure varies, depending on the printer. Once you have successfully installed it, click **Next** within the Synology Assistant screen.

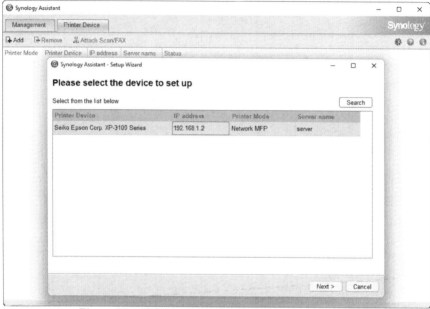

Figure 324: Select printer within Synology Assistant

On the *Completing the Add Printer Wizard* screen, click **Finish**. Within Synology Assistant, the status of the printer should change to *Attached*. The printer should now be listed under *Devices and Printers* on the computer (**Settings > Devices** on Windows 10, **Settings > Bluetooth & devices > Printers & scanners** on Windows 11). Verify that it is working correctly by printing a test page, then repeat the installation process for all the other computers.

Connecting Macs

If using macOS Ventura or later, go into **System Settings > Printers & Scanners**. Click the **Add Printer, Scanner or Fax** button. Highlight the printer on the list and click **Add**. If using earlier version of macOS, go into **System Preferences > Printers & Scanners**. Follow the standard procedure for adding a new printer i.e. click the plus sign (+) in the left-hand panel. The shared printer should be listed – simply click it. If it is not listed, click the plus sign (+), allow the list of discoverable printers to appear and choose it from there. For most popular printers, macOS will automatically install a suitable driver.

15.7 Universal Search

A typical DiskStation may have many thousands or even millions of files stored on it, and with such vast quantities of data, locating a particular file can be a difficult and time-consuming task. To help solve this challenge, DSM has a feature called *Universal Search*; this takes the form of an app that is installed automatically during the installation of DSM. Universal Search indexes files in the background, based upon their names and contents and enabling near-instantaneous searching of the file system, even when only partial search information is provided.

Figure 325: Universal Search

There are two ways to use Universal Search. The first method is by clicking its icon in the **Main Menu** to open it and display the above screen. The first time it is run, there may be a reminder in the bottom right-hand corner about the option to index the folders - this is optional but will speed-up searches. To do so, click the link to bring up the **Preferences** screen (and which can be accessed subsequently by clicking the cogwheel icon at the top of the screen). On the **File Indexing** tab, click the **Indexed Folder List** button. It is necessary to create a folder to hold the indices, so click **Create** and on the panel after that give the folder a name and select an existing one or click **Create Folder**. You can also specify the file types that will be indexed. Note: if Synology Drive is installed, Universal Search will create appropriate index files automatically.

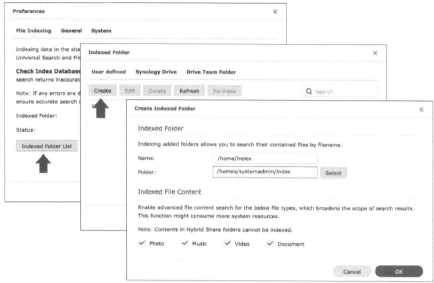

Figure 326: Create Indexed folder

Regardless of whether or not an index folder is created, the Universal Search screen can be used. Type in the query e.g. part of the filename if known or a word that might exist in a document being looked for, and Universal Search will return the results. In addition to matching files, it will also search the DSM Help System and Applications, plus Calendar and Notes Station data if these packages are installed.

Alternatively, searching can also be carried out by using the magnifying icon that appears in the top right-hand corner of the DSM screen, with an option to specify the file type (click the downward facing chevron):

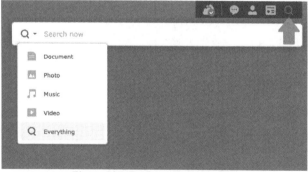

Figure 327: Desktop Search facility

Because of security and privacy implications – it might not be appropriate for every person to discover what is stored on the server – users must explicitly be given permission to use Universal Search. To do so, go into **Control Panel > User & Group** and on the **User** tab, highlight the user(s) and click **Edit**. On the *Applications* tab, place a tick in the *Allow* column against Universal Search, then click **OK**.

15.8 Task Scheduler

Many DSM tasks and applications can be scheduled to run at specified times. The mechanism which handles this behind the scenes is the *Task Scheduler*, which has its own icon in the Control Panel. From here, a summary screen of all the scheduled tasks can be viewed. Tasks can be enabled or disabled by ticking or unticking the boxes on the left-hand side of the panel. Depending on the nature of the task, it can be edited, deleted or modified from this screen.

Figure 328: Task Scheduler

New scheduled tasks can be added – an example of this was described in section **6.9 Change Port Numbers & Disable Unnecessary Services** to improve security by restricting the hours for when the VPN service was available. Users with more advanced requirements can also specify scripts than can be run on a scheduled basis, or which are triggered by key events, such as the server starting up or shutting down.

15.9 Download Station/BitTorrent

Download Station is one of the most popular applications for the DiskStation and enables you to download files from Internet-based services such as BitTorrent, FTP, eMule and others, plus subscribe to RSS feeds. Many thousands of free and public domain movies and other items are available. Downloads take place in the background on the server, with an automatic unzip service to decompress the files when the download is complete.

Download and install Download Station from the Package Center. When running it for the first time, it will prompt for a destination folder, which is where the downloads will be stored. Click **OK** and on the resultant panel select an existing folder, else click **Create folder** to make a new one. The main screen then appears.

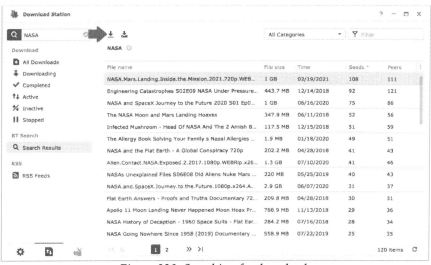

Figure 329: Searching for downloads

If you are familiar with BitTorrent, you will find that Download Station is an efficient client with all the expected features. If you are new to the topic, it has already been programmed with defaults and features to make it immediately useful and not require any additional knowledge. To search for content, type the name or subject in the search box in the top-left hand corner of the screen and hit enter. Download Station will search using several pre-defined search engines and return a list of titles.

Depending on the search criteria, this may return none, several, or many, potentially thousands of candidates, although some of these may be unsuitable due to mislabelling by posters. The results can be sorted by name and file size by clicking on the column headings. In the above example we are searching on 'NASA'.

To download a file, highlight it and click the downward-pointing arrow; multiple files can be selected whilst holding down the Control key (Windows) or Cmd key (macOS). To check progress, click **Downloading** on the left-hand panel. When complete, the file will be in your designated downloads folder. Due to the way BitTorrent operates, downloading files may take a considerable amount of time and you may prefer to download large ones overnight, for instance.

To adjust the behavior of Download Station, click the **Settings** wheel in the bottom left-hand corner of the screen. Items that can be controlled include:

Download Station:
General – eMule downloads can be enabled
Auto Extract – controls whether auto extract is used (decompression)
Notification – setup email notifications for downloads
BT/HTTP/FTP/NZB:

General – controls whether downloads take place immediately or are scheduled. As video files can be large, it can be more convenient to schedule downloads to run overnight
Location – specify/change the download location
File Hosting – specify the file sharing sites used by Download Manager. Sites can be added and deleted.
BT – technical settings for BitTorrent, including port numbers, upload/download rates, peer and seeding values
BT Search – specify the search engines used by BitTorrent
FTP/HTTP – download settings for FTP/HTTP
NZB – technical settings for NZB downloads
RSS – control over RSS Feeds update interval

15.10 Document Viewer

Document Viewer enables documents in many popular formats, including Microsoft Office, OpenOffice and PDF, to be opened and viewed. It can be used as a standalone application, but also integrates with File Station. It is an alternative to using Synology Office, Microsoft Office Online or Google Docs, but with the important proviso that documents cannot be edited. At the time of writing it is available only on x86 (Intel) based DiskStations. Document Viewer is a container-type app and uses Container Manager. If Container Manager has not already been installed, it will be added when downloading Document Viewer from the Package Center, meaning installation may take several minutes. An icon will be added to the Main Menu, plus File Station will be modified.

Documents can be viewed using two methods. The first method is to launch Document Viewer from the Main Menu, which will open it in a new browser tab. From there, click the **Open** icon in the top left-hand corner of the screen, navigate the file system to locate the document, highlight it and click **Open**. The second method is to locate the file within File Station, then right-click it and click **View > Open in Document Viewer**, which will open it in a new browser tab.

When a document is open, icons are available to search, print and rotate it. Clicking the three-dot menu gives options to download it in its native format or as a PDF. The document can also be shared, via a link or a QR can be generated. Restrictions can be placed on subsequent users downloading, printing and copying the document.

Figure 330: Methods for opening files with Document Viewer

15.11 PDF Viewer

The *PDF Viewer* adds enhanced PDF viewing support to DSM. It is downloaded and installed from the Package Center. However, if you have already installed *Document Viewer* (see **15.10 Document Viewer**) then DSM will prevent you from installing it as there would be little point in doing so, given Document Viewer supports PDF documents.

PDF Viewer can be used in two ways:

Click the PDF Viewer icon in the Main Menu, which will open it in a new browser window. Click the 'Open' icon at the top of the screen - it is the second one along from the left-hand side - navigate to the PDF file you wish to view, highlight it and click **Select**. Alternatively, locate the PDF file within File Station, right-click it and choose **View > Open in PDF Viewer** from the pop-up menu.

The standard range of PDF functionality is provided including search, navigation, different zoom levels, document rotation and printing (when a document is printed, it will be to the computer's default printer).

PDF Viewer is closed by clicking the browser window.

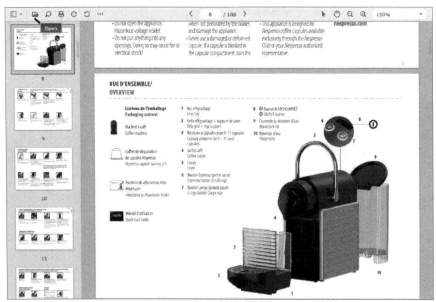

Figure 331: PDF Viewer

15.12 Text Editor

Sometimes there is a requirement to create and edit text files for the NAS. Rather than use a program on a computer e.g. WordPad on Windows or TextEdit on macOS, then have to upload the file to the DiskStation, it may be more convenient to edit files directly on the NAS using a small app that can be downloaded from the Package Center, called *Text Editor*. Having downloaded and installed it, an icon is added to the Main Menu. Click to launch the program, followed by **File > New**. Type in the document or script or code, then click **File > Save As** and navigate to the location on the server where you wish the document to be stored.

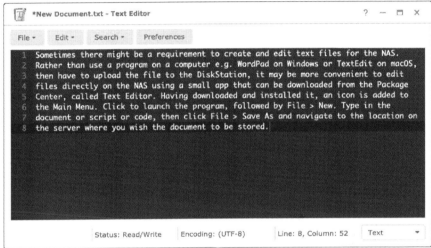

Figure 332: Text Editor

Text Editor is designed to be simple and effective for everyday tasks; it is not intended to be a word processor, although it can be used for creating short documents. There is comprehensive support for many writing systems, including non-Latin character sets (controlled with **File > Encoding**). Click **Preferences > View** to control word wrap and the display of line numbers, and **Preferences > Edit** to set font size, tab width and theme (coloring scheme).

15.13 Web Station

DSM can host websites on the internet, using the *Web Station* package. Because of security and capacity implications and, given that dedicated web hosting services are available for free or low cost elsewhere, it may not be of interest to everyone. However, it may be of use to organizations that develop websites and wish to work on them in-house i.e. not accessible from outside the organization, as well as people wanting to learn about website and applications development. New web services and portals can be created, along with support for containers (aka 'Docker'). In this brief introduction, we will assume internal use only.

Web Station is downloaded and installed from the Package Center; it can then be launched by clicking its icon in the Main Menu. The first time it is run there will be a brief overview, then the main screen will appear as follows. The default back-end package used by Synology is *Nginx*; further ones can be installed, along with Service Packages, by clicking the corresponding small icons in the Management column, which link to the Package Center.

Figure 333: Web Station

To confirm that Web Station is running correctly, use a browser to navigate to the IP address of the DiskStation. Rather than seeing the regular DSM screen, you should now be presented with the following display. Usually, DSM redirects the IP address to port 5000 (or 5001 if you are using HTTPS), but now it is displaying via the standard HTTP port 80. To view the regular DSM screens, explicitly type the address of the server followed by *:5000*, for example 192.168.1.2:5000

Figure 334: Confirmation that Web Station is running

During installation, shared folders called *web* and *web_packages* will have been automatically created. These folders will initially have Read/Write access for administrators and Read only access for all other users. If it is required to change this, go into **Control Panel > User & Group**; on the **Group** tab, highlight the *http* group and click **Edit**. Click the **Permissions** tab and change the two folders to Read/Write. Click **Save**.

The *http* group defines who has access to Web Station and the default folder, so any designated users need to be made into members. Within the main **Group** screen, highlight *http*, click **Edit > Members** and add the users to the group by placing ticks in the boxes against the names. Click **Save**. When creating new users who need access, they can be added to the *http* group at that point.

HTML files can be created using a suitable tool on a Windows PC, Linux PC or Mac, or created directly on the NAS using the *Text Editor* app, described in a previous section. Files for the website should then be placed in the *web* folder. The home page needs to be named *index.htm* or *index.html*, or *index.php* if you are using PHP.

15.14 DHCP Server

In the typical home or small business network, the router that connects it to the internet will also provide IP addresses for the computers and other devices, via a built-in DHCP server. If so, then DSM will make use of it automatically; however, if the router does not provide IP addresses, then the DiskStation itself can be configured to operate as a DHCP server. This requires a program to be downloaded from the Package Center, called *DHCP Server*.

Having installed DHCP Server, open it from the Main Menu. Highlight the network adapter and click **Edit** – if there is more than one, you need to decide which to use for the DHCP service. On the resultant panel, tick the **Enable DHCP server** box. Enter the address of your **Primary DNS** server and optionally add the **Secondary DNS** server address, as used by your ISP. If you do not know the DNS addresses, login to your router and see what it is using, contact the ISP, or go to *https://www.whatsmydns.net/dns* for the DNS details of many popular ISPs worldwide. Alternatively, there are both free and paid for services available from third parties. For instance, OpenDNS has a free, no-need-to-register, 'family friendly' service on 208.67.222.123 (primary) and 208.67.220.123 (secondary). There is no need to add a Domain name. Click the **Create** button and enter details for the Subnet list i.e. the desired range of IP addresses for the DHCP service. In this example we are using a *Start IP address* of 192.168.1.100 and an *End IP address* of 192.168.1.200. The *Netmask* is 255.255.255.0, which it commonly is in small networks and will allow for a maximum of 255 network devices. The *Gateway* (another name for the router) is on 192.168.1.1. For the *Address lease time*, specify 3600. Underneath are additional and more advanced options for those who need them. Click **Create** and upon returning to the main screen click the **Enabled** box in the *Subnet list* section, followed by **OK** to activate the settings.

The second tab is *DHCP Clients*, which lists the devices that have received leases along with the details of those leases. It can also be used for making IP reservations, which is the preferred method for handling devices such as printers and wireless access points in larger networks.

Figure 335: DHCP configuration panels

15.15 Connecting Via a Proxy Server

In most small business and home environments, a router is used to connect the server and network directly to the internet. However, in some circumstances the connection might be indirect and through a *proxy server*. Examples of where this might be the case are when managed or serviced offices are being used or in educational establishments, in which case the DiskStation needs to be configured appropriately.

Click **Control Panel > Network**. On the **General** tab, in the *Proxy* section, tick the **Connect via a proxy server** box and enter the details of the proxy server, which should be obtainable from the person or organization that controls it. Usually this consists of entering an address and port number and ticking the **Bypass proxy server for local addresses** option. If there are any additional details, they can be specified by clicking the **Advanced Settings** button, where it is possible to define separate proxy servers for HTTP and HTTPS traffic, plus any proxy authentication information. Click **Apply**.

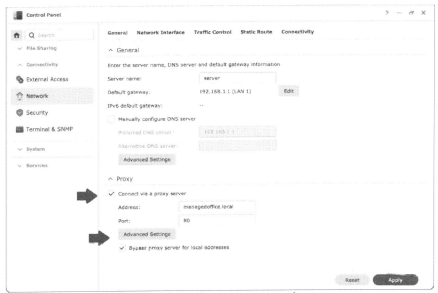

Figure 336: Proxy server example

15.16 Link Aggregation

Some DiskStations have multiple network adapters and these can be linked together in different ways in a technique referred to as *link aggregation, bonding* or *teaming*, to provide fault tolerance and/or improve performance:

Fault tolerance - There are several types of common networking failures: an adapter can fail, a port on a network switch can fail, an Ethernet cable can become unplugged. These failures can be mitigated against by bonding the network adapters together, such that if one fails then another takes over automatically.

Performance – The maximum performance of a single gigabit Ethernet adapter is 1,000 Mbits/sec, equating to around 100 Mbytes/sec of data. If there are multiple users, and especially if there are high-bandwidth activities such as video streaming or editing, this can be a bottleneck. By aggregating multiple adapters, network throughput can be increased e.g. two ports can potentially double it and four ports can quadruple it (assuming the other NAS subsystems can keep up). For instance, two gigabit adapters can provide 2,000 Mbits/sec (200 Mbytes) of data, whilst four 10 GbE adapters could potentially provide 40,000 Mbits (4 GBytes) of data per second. In this example we will assume that the DiskStation has two adapters, that both are wired to the main network switch, and that we wish to provide fault tolerance.

On the **Control Panel**, click **Network** followed by **Network Interface**. Click **Create > Create Bond**. Choose the mode: the first three options are for performance and the final one is for resilience (fault tolerance) only. We will choose the first option: click **Adaptive Load Balancing** followed by **Next**. On the subsequent screen select the network adapters (LAN 1 and LAN 2) and click **Next**. On the subsequent screen choose **Use manual configuration**, specify the IP details for the server, tick the **Set as default gateway** box, click **Done**. There will be a warning about changes to some services, which should be acknowledged by clicking **Yes**.

Note that the availability and contents of these screens may vary, depending on what adapters are in the DiskStation:

Figure 337: Choose the Link Aggregation Mode and settings

There will be a short delay whilst the change is applied, resulting in the creation of a new virtual network adapter called *BOND 1*, which will replace the real physical LAN adapters as seen from the network control panel. When dealing with any network settings, you need to specify this virtual adapter from now on. When a new bonded adaptor is created, you should test it by removing one of the network cables - the server should remain accessible.

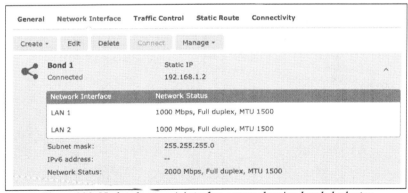

Figure 338: Updated network interface screen showing bonded adapter

Removing a Bonded Adapter

To remove a bonded adapter, highlight it within **Control Panel > Network Interface** and click the **Delete** button. Acknowledge the warning message by clicking **Delete**. After the network adapters have been unbonded, check that they have suitable IP addresses.

15.17 Resetting the Administrator Password if Lost

If the administrator password is lost or forgotten, it is relatively simple to reset it. On the DiskStation is a reset button, usually on the back of the unit. Whilst the system is running, insert a very small screwdriver or a paperclip into the reset hole and press gently for about 4 seconds until the unit makes a loud beep. This will reset the administrator password to the default value, which is blank i.e. no password at all. Log into the server immediately and assign a new password.

Whilst this feature can be useful, there is also a risk. Suppose the DiskStation is stolen, or a disgruntled employee in the organizations gains physical access to it: all they need to do is press the reset button and they can gain unrestricted access to it and the data. For this reason, you might wish to disable this feature. Go into **Control Panel > Update & Restore** and click the **System Reset** tab. In the *Reset Option* section, tick the **Keep admin password unchanged** box and click **Apply**.

15.18 Reinstalling DSM whilst Retaining Data

If the DiskStation has serious issues and behaving abnormally, you might wish to reinstall DSM but retain the existing data; this can also be done using the reset button. Before proceeding, take a full backup in case of problems and make a backup of the configuration as described in section **7.7 Backing up the Server Configuration**.

Whilst the system is running, insert a very small screwdriver or a paperclip into the reset hole and press gently for about 5 seconds until the unit makes a loud beep, then let go immediately. Straight away, do the exact same thing again. The DiskStation will beep a few more times and then reboot. After several minutes the Status light will blink orange, at which point DSM can be re-installed.

Use the Synology Assistant utility and let it search for the DiskStation, which it will show with a status of 'Configuration lost'. Double-click it and the Web Assistant will be run; click the large **Re-install** button and work through the steps described in Chapter **2 INSTALLING DSM**. Once the basic installation is complete, restore the Server Configuration file you created.

15.19 Preparing the DiskStation for Disposal

If the DiskStation is to be disposed of, make sure that backups of all your important data have been taken, using the techniques described in section **7 BACKUPS**.

From the **Control Panel** choose **Update & Restore**. Click the **System Reset** tab and on it click the **Erase All Data** button. A warning message is displayed; if you have changed your mind click **No** now, else tick the box and click the **Erase All Data** button. You will be prompted to enter the administrator password, after which the DiskStation will be restored to the initial factory state and the data on the disk(s) deleted, then it will restart.

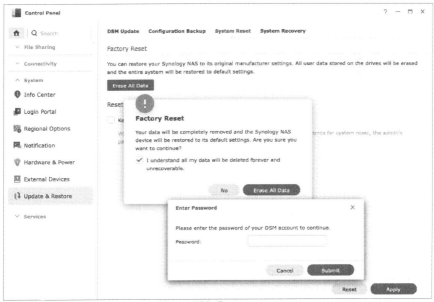

Figure 339: Factory reset

Note 1: *you cannot perform a factory reset if any folders have been configured for immutable snapshots. How to resolve this issue is described at the end of section 7.9 Snapshot Replication. Additionally, any existing snapshots associated with the folders will have to be deleted or the retention period expired.*

Note 2: *in the above screenshot, the fourth tab – System Recovery – is present only if Active Backup for Business has been installed.*

Index

2

2FA, 132, 144, 146, 149
2-factor authentication, 148

A

ACL, 86, 87
Active Backup, 72, 157, 196, 197, 198, 200, 202, 423
Active Insight, 239, 240, 241, 242, 395, 397
AFP, 57, 58, 121, 186
Android, 15, 34, 108, 122, 126, 145, 227, 242, 249, 256, 261, 263, 265, 266, 286, 293, 296, 302, 303, 368, 369
Antivirus, 139, 140, 219
Application Portals, 358, 398, 399
Audio Station, 125, 244, 258, 259, 260, 261

B

BitTorrent, 409, 410
Btrfs, 46, 51, 71, 73, 74, 78, 81, 97, 187, 190, 191, 196, 311, 341, 343, 347, 352

C

Caching, 21, 42, 331, 345
CalDAV, 299
Calendar, 14, 107, 198, 272, 294, 297, 298, 299, 300, 406
Certificates, 136, 197
Chromebook, 125
Cloning, 81
Cloud Sync, 307, 308, 309, 311
CMS, 231, 232, 234, 235, 236, 238
Compliance mode, 79, 80
Container Manager, 229, 373, 386, 388, 411

D

DDNS, 316, 317, 318, 327
Delegation, 102, 103, 199, 241
Desktop, 25, 37, 38, 39, 40, 106, 107, 111, 119, 120, 121, 282, 295, 303, 359, 363, 390, 406
DHCP, 54, 55, 401, 417, 418
DLNA, 244, 245, 246, 247, 255, 260, 261
DNS, 53, 316, 417
Docker, 373, 388, 414
Dropbox, 173, 271, 280, 306, 307
DS Finder, 34, 35, 36, 66, 108, 126, 133, 151, 204, 209, 211, 226, 227
DS Video, 265, 266

E

Encryption, 73, 74, 76, 77, 343
Ext4, 46, 71, 74, 77

F

File Station, 38, 39, 81, 93, 107, 111, 112, 125, 166, 250, 259, 263, 291, 294, 297, 300, 302, 305, 306, 411, 412
Firewall, 133, 134
FTP, 56, 59, 154, 409, 410

G

Google Drive, 14, 173, 271, 307, 310, 311
Groups, 91, 99, 102, 259, 265

H

Home Folders, 84
Hot Spare, 335, 336, 337

I

iOS, 15, 34, 108, 122, 123, 145, 227, 242, 249, 256, 261, 263, 265, 286, 293, 296, 299, 302, 303, 369
IP address, 34, 53, 54, 111, 112, 121, 122, 123, 129, 179, 200, 231, 256, 261, 266, 267, 280, 288, 295, 303, 316, 319, 354, 358, 359, 368, 369, 370, 380, 400, 401, 415, 417
iSCSI, 159, 331, 351, 352, 353, 354

K

Key Store, 76, 77

L

LUN, 167, 190, 192, 194, 219, 351, 352, 353, 354

M

MP3, 112, 244, 246, 247, 258

N

NFS, 58, 59, 124, 219
Notifications, 40, 162, 216, 222, 223, 224, 276, 283, 296

O

OneDrive, 14, 188, 271, 280, 306, 307, 310, 311

P

PDF, 241, 411, 412
Port Numbers, 153, 408
Printing, 401, 403
Proxy Server, 419

Q

QuickConnect, 13, 64, 65, 66, 112, 122, 136, 144, 173, 210, 231, 252, 256, 261, 266, 273, 280, 286, 288, 295, 303, 316, 354, 369, 370, 395, 396

R

RAID, 16, 20, 21, 42, 43, 44, 45, 46, 47, 49, 52, 187, 190, 339, 341, 344, 346, 347, 350
RAM, 16, 17, 140, 196, 199, 311, 347, 372, 377, 383, 385, 388
Resource Monitor, 212, 219, 220

S

Search, 34, 40, 116, 188, 268, 354, 405, 406, 407, 410
Secure Sign-In, 144, 145, 146, 147
Secure SignIn, 133, 144
Secure SignIn, 148
Server Configuration, 183, 422
Shared Folders, 70, 73, 83, 99, 113, 185, 215, 274
SHR, 21, 43, 45, 46, 47, 331, 338, 339, 340
SMB, 56, 57, 58, 93, 121, 124, 125, 199
SMTP, 107, 224, 225, 296, 299
Snapshot, 46, 190, 191, 192, 194, 195, 364, 423
SSD, 16, 17, 21, 42, 49, 213, 214, 281, 333, 338, 345, 346, 347, 349, 350
SSL, 136, 137, 200, 280, 288
Synology Account, 35, 64, 66, 144, 173, 183, 184, 197, 210, 224, 225, 239, 240, 242, 316, 395, 397
Synology Assistant, 116, 117, 118, 151, 403, 404, 422
Synology C2, 157, 173, 177, 365
Synology Office, 112, 273, 274, 275, 278, 291, 292, 411

T

Task Scheduler, 154, 408

Taskbar, 25, 37, 38, 114, 115, 116, 118, 188
Time Machine, 18, 56, 57, 163, 185, 186, 187

U

Updates, 205, 209, 392
UPS, 23, 62, 63

V

Video Station, 244, 247, 248, 263, 264, 265, 266, 267, 269
Virtual DSM, 199, 208, 239, 311, 373, 375, 376, 380, 382, 385
VPN, 320

W

Web Assistant, 27, 151, 422
Widgets, 40, 204, 212, 213, 240, 264
WriteOnce, 73, 78, 79, 80

Printed in France by Amazon
Brétigny-sur-Orge, FR

15085014R00239